What people are saying about ...

O F F I C E   C O M P A N I O N

" ...Delightfully written! The section on the disc operating system ranks with the best writings of the DOS guru himself, Peter Norton. "
–Newhouse News Syndicate

" A well-organized reference for the 15 million users...of all three software programs. "
–The Small Press Book Review

" Until now, each computer program brought with it an individual reference book. With his new guide, Robert Harris changes this, offering information on three popular programs for the price of one book. "
–The Office

" Written in plain English, this book teaches you what DOS is and how it relates to word processing and spreadsheet analysis. "
–The Lawyer's PC

" A new best friend! "
–The Secretary

DOS, WORDPERFECT & LOTUS

OFFICE COMPANION

THIRD EDITION

Robert W. Harris

VENTANA
PRESS

The Ventana Office Companion™ Series

DOS, WordPerfect & Lotus Office Companion, Third Edition
Copyright © 1993 by Robert W. Harris
The Ventana Office Companion ™ Series

Library of Congress Cataloging-in-Publication Data

Harris, Robert W., 1954-
    DOS, WordPerfect & Lotus office companion / Robert W. Harris. – 3rd ed.
      p.   cm.
    Includes index.
    ISBN 1-56604-048-5
    1. WordPerfect (Computer file) 2. Lotus 1-2-3 (Computer file) 3. PC-DOS (Computer file)
    4. Business-Computer programs. I. Title.
    HF5548.4.W63H37 1993
    005.36-dc20   93-13119
                                     CIP

Book design: Karen Wysocki
Cover design: Original design by Nancy Frame
Cover photography: Henderson-Muir Photography
Index services: Dianne Bertsch, Answers Plus
Technical review: Marion Laird, Pam Richardson
Editorial staff: Jean Kaplan, Marion Laird, Virginia Phelps, Pam Richardson
Production staff: Rhonda Angel, John Cotterman, Karen Wysocki

Third Edition 9 8 7 6 5 4 3
Printed in the United States of America

Ventana Press, Inc.
P.O. Box 2468
Chapel Hill, NC 27515
919/942-0220
FAX 919/942-1140

Trademarks

Trademarked names appear throughout this book. Rather than list the names and entities that own the trademarks or insert a trademark symbol with each mention of the trademarked name, the publisher states that it is using the names only for editorial purposes and to the benefit of the trademark owner with no intention of infringing upon that trademark.

About the Author

Robert W. Harris is a free-lance writer and instructional designer. He earned degrees in Visual Arts and Cognitive Psychology, and then worked at the Department of Energy's Savannah River Laboratory, where he coordinated computer training for four years. Harris is the author of a half-dozen books on personal computing and desktop publishing.

Acknowledgments

I want to thank everyone at Ventana Press who helped to improve this book and bring it to final form. Special thanks go to Elizabeth Shoemaker for her patience and perseverance in editing the ever-changing manuscript. Thanks also to Tom Droege for the use of his PCs and printers during the project. For the third edition, I want to express my appreciation once again to the entire staff at Ventana Press for their good work. Special thanks go to Karen Wysocki for enhancing the visual appeal of the book.

CONTENTS

SECTION II: WORDPERFECT

SECTION III: LOTUS

Introduction

Only fifteen years ago, most correspondence was written on typewriters, calculations were done with adding machines, and files were stored in cabinets. In just a few short years, the personal computer has introduced enormous changes in the way business professionals communicate. Today, your tasks are probably the same, but your new tools are likely to be laser printers, spreadsheets and hard disks.

Software developers have created hundreds of versatile programs that take advantage of the PC's advanced capabilities. But who buys hundreds of programs? If you're a typical PC user, you have three or four programs that meet your needs and budget.

Although many excellent application programs are available, a few outstanding ones have emerged as leaders. Among them are Microsoft DOS for the PC operating system, WordPerfect for word processing, and Lotus 1-2-3 for spreadsheet analysis. These three programs deliver high performance and flexibility—if you can get them to do what you want them to.

THE SHELF-HELP MOVEMENT

DOS, WordPerfect and 1-2-3 are sophisticated and powerful programs. Yet with greater power comes greater complexity: hundreds of commands to learn, function keys to memorize and menu items to locate. Learning the latest versions can be time-consuming and frustrating.

Most user manuals are intimidating, voluminous and poorly organized; they often take on new lives as doorstops, paper weights and plant stands. In an effort to find friendlier help, people often turn to books offering tips and instructions on DOS, WordPerfect and 1-2-3.

However, many of these books miss the mark. They assume every PC user has the time and inclination to become a "power user." But if you're like most professionals, you want practical tips and strategies that will help in your day-to-day work. You want to know which features and functions will produce the results you want from your PC. And you want to learn as much as possible in the shortest time. *DOS, WordPerfect & Lotus Office Companion* offers a concise introduction to this popular software trio.

WHO SHOULD READ THIS BOOK?

Written for beginning and intermediate PC users, *Office Companion* helps you learn more—at your own pace. In *Office Companion,* you'll find the essential features that help you get the most from your business software.

Beginners will welcome the friendly, nontechnical approach, and veterans will appreciate having the basic commands of these three important programs at their fingertips.

WHAT'S INSIDE

DOS, WordPerfect & Lotus Office Companion is designed to help you make the most of the three most popular business software programs: DOS, WordPerfect and 1-2-3. You'll find the most useful tips and techniques, the most practical ideas and strategies, without all the programmer jargon that pervades most computer books. And you'll learn time-saving features and shortcuts that even experienced PC users often overlook.

In brief, *Office Companion* isn't meant to make you an expert user but a confident and productive user. Organized into sections on DOS, WordPerfect and Lotus 1-2-3, *Office Companion* covers a wide range of topics explained in plain English. Within each chapter, the major topics are broken into manageable chunks, so you can easily digest the material.

Each technique in the book was chosen because it either solves a common problem or saves time and effort. Beyond these requirements, the main concern was that it be something most people will want to use. So be assured that the information you're getting is useful, practical and easy to learn.

HARDWARE/SOFTWARE REQUIREMENTS

Office Companion assumes that you have an IBM-compatible personal computer and that your software is up and running.

This book has been completely updated to include the following software releases:

- DOS versions through 6.0
- WordPerfect versions through 6.0
- Lotus 1-2-3 releases through 2.4

MOVING ON

As computers and related technologies force the much-heralded "information age" upon us all, business professionals must grow and change in stride. In this book, I hope to expose people to new ways of quickly gaining control of the new tools that now dominate the business community. If you occasionally find yourself saying, "I didn't know I could do that," then the book has achieved its purpose.

Robert Harris
Durham, NC

SECTION I

DOS

Getting Started
with DOS

If you flip through your DOS manual or use the new online Help feature, you'll come across commands presented like this:

keyb [*xx*[,[*yyy*][,[*drive:*][*path*]*filename*]]][/**e**][/**id**:nnn]

Although programmers love this kind of stuff, the rest of us find it a little confusing and annoying. Do we really have to memorize all of that? Why can't it be simpler?

Well, it can. The writers of your DOS User's Guide were obligated to cover every variation of every command and answer all potential questions. But they don't tell you which commands will be the most useful to you in your routine work. So in this section of *Office Companion*, you'll learn what's really important and what's not about DOS. The focus here is on practical DOS commands that give you control over your PC.

WHAT YOU'LL LEARN IN THIS SECTION

Although you'll see some familiar commands, you'll probably see many that you've never encountered before. For example, did you know that you can

- List files alphabetically or chronologically?
- Copy only files created on or after a particular date?
- Protect a file from being modified or erased?
- Recover an erased file?
- Enter a DOS command by pressing just one key?

These are just a few of the possible techniques, and they're easy to use when you know the right commands.

In the first two chapters you'll find out what DOS can do, how to tell DOS what you want it to do, and how it interacts with other software programs. Chapter 3 includes a "Quick Start" tutorial, a hands-on introduction to basic DOS functions and features. Chapters 5 through 11 explain the functions of hard disks, diskettes and disk drives, and how to create and manage files.

In Chapter 12, you'll learn how to automate commands and command sequences so that DOS will type them for you. Chapter 13 covers special commands that increase your system's flexibility and efficiency. Chapter 14 puts the "personal" back in personal computers by showing you how to customize your keyboard and video display to suit your specific needs. And finally, Chapter 15 explains how to use the DOS Shell graphical interface, which enables you to use a mouse to perform routine file management tasks.

By the time you finish this section, DOS will no longer be a mystery. You'll have the basic skills you need to be a confident DOS user.

CONVENTIONS USED IN THIS SECTION

Each chapter begins with a short discussion and outline of commands and features to be covered, followed by a hands-on exercise like the one below.

SCREEN TEST

First, the general format of the command will be shown, along with an example, like this:

Format: FORMAT target-drive *qualifiers*

Example: FORMAT A: /V Enter

Words shown in uppercase must be typed exactly as spelled (you may use uppercase or lowercase letters). Words shown in lowercase letters represent information you must supply. Finally, words in italics are optional parts of the command.

Keys that must be pressed together are shown with a hyphen, like this: Ctrl-S.

In each hands-on exercise, you'll be instructed to type a DOS command. Type only what is shown in **bold**, and be sure to include a space between parts of the command, exactly as shown. Here's an illustration:

HANDS-ON   Copy a file named JULY.RPT to Drive A.

Type: **COPY JULY.RPT A:** Enter

Each exercise will usually be followed by a screen image that shows the effect of the command.

Figure 1-1: Example of a
DOS screen.

```
1 file(s) copied
```

Keep in mind that the file names shown in these examples are taken from *my* disk. So when you try these commands on your PC, be sure to substitute file names that you have available on your own disk.

CHAPTER SUMMARY

■ DOS is the PC's Disk Operating System, the program that coordinates all activity and enables you to use programs such as WordPerfect and Lotus 1-2-3.

■ In the hands-on exercises in this section, words shown in uppercase letters must be typed exactly as spelled. Words in lowercase letters represent information that you must provide. And words shown in italic type represent optional parts of a command.

■ After typing a DOS command, you must always press Enter.

What DOS Is All About

DOS is the Disk Operating System, the manager of your PC's hardware and software. Before learning how to use DOS, it's a good idea to understand how it works and why it's important. In this chapter, you'll learn

- What DOS does.
- How DOS relates to WordPerfect and Lotus 1-2-3.
- How DOS manages your files.
- What the version number of DOS means.

THE IMPORTANCE OF DOS

You may be thinking, I do most of my work in WordPerfect and Lotus 1-2-3, so why do I need to know about DOS? Good question. Let's take a look at the connection between DOS and your other software programs.

First, take a look at the Lotus 1-2-3 screen shown in Figure 2-1:

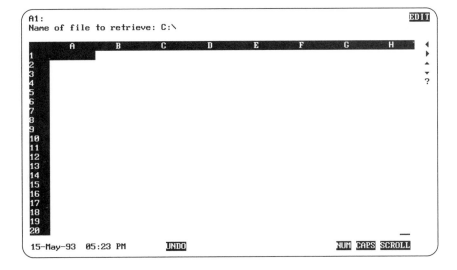

Figure 2-1: A typical Lotus 1-2-3 screen.

The 1-2-3 screen is graphic and colorful, with helpful menus and indicators, and it even prompts you for information. Very friendly. Now, a DOS screen:

Figure 2-2: A typical DOS screen.

```
C:\>
```

The DOS screen shown in Figure 2-2 looks uninviting by comparison—no frills and no assistance, just a prompt. (In DOS 4.0 and higher, you have the option of using the friendlier DOS Shell interface. The Shell is covered in Chapter 15, "Using the DOS Shell.")

The two programs seem to have nothing in common. But despite appearances, everything that goes on in your PC, no matter what software you use, is controlled by DOS.

WordPerfect and 1-2-3 do not interact directly with your hardware. They communicate with DOS, which in turn handles the job. So when you name a 1-2-3 file, you're following DOS's rules. When you erase a WordPerfect file, DOS does the real work.

There's only one operating system on your PC, and every program plays by that system's rules. That's why it's important for you to become comfortable with DOS.

USING COMMANDS WITHIN PROGRAMS

You don't have to be at the DOS prompt to use DOS commands. WordPerfect and 1-2-3 incorporate some common file management capabilities such as copying and erasing files. You'll probably want to take advantage of these "in-software" commands because of their convenience. Although they don't show you the DOS prompt, those programs are actually using standard DOS commands to accomplish the work.

WHAT DOS DOES

Without DOS, your PC would be useless. (Well, it could still accumulate Post-It notes.) The operating system brings the hardware to life and enables it to function.

THE ROLE OF DOS

DOS performs several major functions that enable your PC to work:

- DOS controls and coordinates all the hardware, including disk drives, printers and monitors.
- DOS keeps your files organized and accessible.
- DOS enables you to manage your files and do productive work via WordPerfect, 1-2-3 and other programs.

The first two activities take place behind the scenes. DOS efficiently manages the flow of information throughout your system. The third activity is the one part of DOS you can control to manipulate files and organize your disks. So in this section, you'll learn how to exercise control over DOS's activities by using the right commands.

DOS VERSIONS

Since its introduction in 1981, DOS has been continually improved. Each time the improvement is significant, the version number increases. For example, there's a big difference between Versions 2 and 3. When the changes are modest, the number increases only fractionally. For example, the differences between Versions 3.1 and 3.3 are small.

DOS is now up to Version 6. But if you're not using the most up-to-date version, don't worry.

> **TIP** If you're using Version 3.1 or higher, all but a few commands in this book will be available to you. (The ones that aren't will be noted in the text.) If you have Version 6, you'll be able to use all the commands presented here.

As DOS becomes more sophisticated, software programs are being designed to take advantage of its capabilities. Software user manuals always specify what version of DOS is needed to run particular programs. For example, WordPerfect 5.0 requires that you have DOS Version 2.1 or higher.

FINDING YOUR VERSION

Do you know what version of DOS you have? To find out, you can use the VERSION command, abbreviated VER.

HANDS-ON   Check the version of DOS currently in use.

> Type: **VER** [Enter]

```
MS-DOS Version 6.00

C:\
```

Figure 2-3: Result of the
VER command.

As you can see in Figure 2-3, the system indicates that it's running MS-DOS Version 6.

If you tried this command and got an error message, it probably means that DOS needs directions to the location of that command file. Review "Locating DOS Commands" in Chapter 3, "DOS Quick Start," to find out how to help DOS find its own command files.

CHAPTER SUMMARY

- All your PC's software works within the DOS environment and follows DOS's rules.
- Programs like WordPerfect and 1-2-3 let you perform routine file management activities without being at the DOS prompt.
- DOS's main functions are to control your hardware, keep files organized and accessible and enable you to manage your work.
- DOS 6 is the most recent version of the disk operating system.
- The VER command displays the version of DOS in use.

DOS Quick Start

I f you're like most people, you want to get your hands on the key-board *now*. So here's a quick hands-on tour to give you imme-diate experience in using the most important DOS commands. The commands are explained in depth later on; but for now, just follow the instructions and you'll get a feel for what DOS does and how you can control it.

When you turn on your PC, it *boots up* (loads the DOS program) and displays the DOS prompt. The prompt is probably C> or C:\>, but since it can be changed, yours might look different. The "C" indicates that Drive C (your hard disk) is the drive you booted up on. The drive shown in the prompt is the *current drive*. When you type a command, DOS uses only the files on the current drive–unless you tell it to use files on another drive.

It's possible that your PC is set up to go directly into a specific program, such as WordPerfect. If you were automatically taken into a program when you booted, exit the program now to return to the DOS prompt.

DIRECTORIES & SUBDIRECTORIES

When you file a letter, you don't just throw it into a drawer. You put it in a specific place so that you can easily find it later when you need it. In the drawer, the first level of organization consists of hanging folders. Then, within each hanging folder, you add file folders to create a second level of organization. In each file folder, you put one or more related items such as letters, reports or memos. When you organize your hard disk, think of a file drawer as a model.

YOUR HARD DISK

On the hard disk, the *Root* directory is like a file drawer. Within the Root, other directories are like hanging folders, and subdirectories are like individual file folders within them. So, the directories and subdirectories serve as the filing system for your hard disk. Figure 3-1 illustrates how a hard disk can be organized.

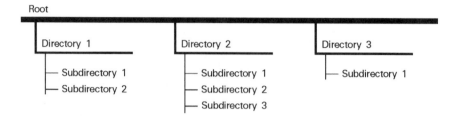

Figure 3-1: Hard-disk organization under DOS.

So you've got the picture. The Root is the main directory, within which you can create other directories. And within directories, you can create subdirectories in which you can keep related files together and separate them from other files.

The names of directories always start with a backward slash. For example, \WP could be the directory containing your WordPerfect program. The Root directory has no name, so it's always represented with just a backward slash.

CHANGING DIRECTORIES

Just as you have a current drive, you also have a current directory. When you type a command, DOS applies that command to the files in the current directory—unless you specify another directory.

> **TIP** Changing the current directory is like placing one hanging folder back in the drawer, then taking out another one. Now let's make sure we all start at the same place.

HANDS-ON Change to the Root directory. (Remember to include a space between the parts of a command, exactly as shown, and to press Enter after the command.)

Type: **CD** \ Enter

The CD (Change Directory) command tells DOS to change the current directory; the backslash tells it to change to the Root directory. If you were changing to a directory other than the Root, you'd include its name. (For example, to change from the \123 directory to the \WP directory, you'd type CD \WP.)

LISTING FILES

Now that you're in the Root directory, let's see what it contains.

HANDS-ON Check the contents of the current directory.

Type: **DIR** [Enter]

```
Volume in drive C is OFFICE
Directory of  C:\

.                <DIR>      01-17-93   12:20p
..               <DIR>      01-17-93   12:20p
123              <DIR>      01-17-93   12:21p
WP               <DIR>      01-17-93   12:21p
DOS              <DIR>      01-17-93   12:22p
AUTOEXEC BAT         53     01-17-93   12:06a
CONFIG   SYS         46     01-17-93    3:24p
         7 file(s)              99 bytes
                          8704990 bytes free
```

Figure 3-2: Contents of the current directory.

Figure 3-2 shows that the DIR (Directory) command lists all files in the current directory (in this case, the Root). The message "Volume in Drive C has no label" will appear unless you've used the LABEL command to name your disk (see "Adding a Label to a Formatted Diskette" in Chapter 5).

If there are a lot of files in the Root, those at the top of the list may have scrolled off the screen. If that happened, you can list the files in the current directory one screen at a time by typing DIR /P.

/P is called a *qualifier* because it changes the way the command is carried out. Many commands have qualifiers you'll find useful. Here, /P causes the screen to pause each time it fills. To see the next screen, press the Space bar or Enter.

The DIR command provides a number of other useful qualifiers that will be introduced later in this section of the book.

WHAT'S IN A NAME?

Notice in the DIR listing that each file has five fields of information. The first field is the file name. The second, the file name *extension*, identifies the type of file. In the listing, there's a space between file name and extension. But when you use a file name in a command, you'll use a period instead of a space: ERASE AUTOEXEC.BAT.

The other three fields list the file size and the date and time the file was created (or last modified). If you have any directories on your disk, they're indicated in the listing with <DIR>.

THE DOS PROMPT

Unless you (or someone) changed the DOS prompt, it looks like this: C>. It tells you the current drive is C, but nothing else.

Since you're going to be changing from one directory to another as you manage your files, you need to know your current directory as well as your current drive. Before proceeding, change from the Root to the \DOS directory now by typing CD DOS [Enter].

HANDS-ON Make the prompt display the current directory.

Type: **PROMPT $P** [Enter]

Figure 3-3: Prompt indicating the current drive and directory.

```
C:\DOS
```

As you can see in Figure 3-3, the $P qualifier tells DOS to show the current directory in the prompt. Now the prompt looks like this: C:\DOS. The backward slash \ followed by "DOS" indicates that the \DOS directory is current.

Other qualifiers will change the appearance of the prompt or make it more informative.

HANDS-ON Use the $P and $G qualifiers in the PROMPT command.

Type: **PROMPT PG** [Enter]

Figure 3-4: A commonly used DOS prompt.

```
C:\DOS>
```

The $G qualifier adds the > symbol to the prompt (see Figure 3-4). The symbol has no special meaning; it simply separates the prompt from the commands you type. You could also type some spaces or a tab after the $P qualifier to add a little room between the prompt and the commands you type.

> **TIP** If you're using DOS 4 or higher, you may interact with DOS either at the prompt or in the Shell, a graphical interface. The Shell will be discussed in Chapter 15, "Using the DOS Shell."

PATHS

Unless you tell it otherwise, DOS will work only in the current drive and current directory (indicated in the DOS prompt). So, if you want DOS to perform an operation somewhere besides the current directory, you have to clearly tell it where.

The way to direct DOS to another location is to include a *path* in a command. A path simply tells DOS how to get to a location following the directory structure of your hard disk. It's like finding a memo in a file drawer: first you have to find the right hanging folder, and then you have to find the right file folder inside it. When you're giving a command, you must direct DOS to the correct *directory* and then, if necessary, to the correct *subdirectory* that contains the file.

Let's say that the current directory is now \123, and you want to copy a file called SAMPLE from it to the \WP directory. Since the \WP directory isn't the current directory, you have to show DOS the way, like this: COPY SAMPLE \WP.

If you need to go to a deeper level, the path becomes longer. So if you want to copy the file to the \LETTERS subdirectory within the \WP directory, the command would look like this: COPY SAMPLE \WP\LETTERS.

But let's say the file named SAMPLE isn't in the current directory, but in the \DRAW directory. Just include a path that tells DOS where to find it, like this: COPY \DRAW\SAMPLE \WP\LETTERS.

That's all there is to it. Any time a file or location is outside of the current directory, you have to specify the complete path so that DOS can find the way.

> **TIP** If the action takes place within the current directory, no path is necessary in the command.

LOCATING DOS COMMANDS

You know now that DOS cannot locate files outside the current directory unless you tell it where to look. But what about DOS's own command files? Let's say your current directory is \123, and you want to copy a file. Well, the COPY command is a DOS file, and all of your DOS files are in either the Root or the \DOS directory. Neither of these is the current directory. So what's the solution?

The solution is simple. Just enter a PATH command that tells DOS to look in the Root and \DOS directories if it can't find the files it needs in the current directory. Your PC is probably set up to enter a PATH command automatically when it boots. To find out if a PATH command is in effect, type PATH [Enter] at the DOS prompt. If no PATH command is displayed, you can enter one by following the instructions below.

HANDS-ON Write a PATH command that includes paths to the Root and \DOS directories. If your DOS directory has a different name, use it on the command.

Type: **PATH \;\DOS** [Enter]

The PATH command tells DOS to search other directories if necessary to carry out your commands. The command you just typed tells DOS to look in the Root directory (\) and then, if necessary, in the \DOS directory. So now, no matter which directory is current, you can use your DOS commands. These alternate search paths set up by the PATH command will remain in effect until you turn off your PC.

Many DOS files are *executable* files. This type of file has the extension .COM, .BAT or .EXE. Files that start programs are also executable files. For example, when you type the command 123, you're really executing the file 123.EXE. So if you want to be able to start the Lotus 1-2-3 program from any directory, you'll need to include the path name for your Lotus directory in your PATH command (for example, PATH \;\DOS;\123).

LOOKING AT THE DISK STRUCTURE

Now that you have a feel for directories, let's look at how your hard disk is organized. First, change to the Root directory by typing CD \ [Enter].

HANDS-ON Display the structure of your hard disk.

Type: **TREE** [Enter]

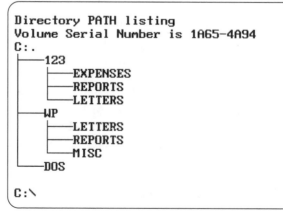

```
Directory PATH listing
Volume Serial Number is 1A65-4A94
C:.
├───123
│       ├───EXPENSES
│       ├───REPORTS
│       └───LETTERS
├───WP
│       ├───LETTERS
│       ├───REPORTS
│       └───MISC
└───DOS

C:\
```

Figure 3-5: The hard disk directory structure.

In Figure 3-5, you see that the TREE command lists all directories and their subdirectories.

Did some of the information scroll off the screen? If so, try the command again and this time freeze the screen by pressing Ctrl-S. Then, to release it, press the Space bar.

A better solution is to add the |MORE qualifier to stop the screen each time it fills. The command is TREE |MORE.

To see the disk structure plus the files within each directory, add the /F (Files) qualifier, like this: TREE /F |MORE.

MAKING DIRECTORIES

Now that you understand disk organization a little better, you're ready to create your own directories and subdirectories. The way you set up your disk depends on the type of work you do. For example, if you write a lot of letters, you might want to create a subdirectory just for your business letters.

To make new directories and subdirectories, use the MD (Make Directory) command. When you make a directory, you're making it *inside* of some other directory (remember the file folders inside the hanging folders inside the drawer). In official DOS terminology, the Root directory is the *parent* of the other directories, and each directory can in turn be the parent of subdirectories.

TIP To make things easy, always change to the parent (using the Change Directory command) before creating a directory.

Here's an example. Suppose you want to create a subdirectory for your interoffice memos. If you use WordPerfect to write the memos, you can put a \MEMOS subdirectory within the \WP directory.

HANDS-ON Make a subdirectory called \MEMOS within the \WP directory. (If your WordPerfect directory has a different name—for example, WP60— use that name instead of WP.)

Type: **CD WP** [Enter]

Type: **MD MEMOS** [Enter]

That's all there is to it. Although DOS doesn't confirm it, you now have a subdirectory just for your memos. Its complete path is \WP\MEMOS. (*Note:* If you try to use an existing directory name, DOS will tell you that the directory already exists.)

WORKING WITH DISKETTES

You won't always be working on the hard disk. Sometimes, you'll need to copy information to or from a floppy diskette. The same DOS commands apply here, so there aren't any new ones to learn.

The first thing to know is that a new diskette fresh out of the box is probably not ready to use. To be usable, it must first be *formatted*. If a diskette contains any files, formatting will erase them. So make sure you check the diskette for files by typing DIR A: Enter before formatting it.

HANDS-ON Format a blank diskette in Drive A. First, insert a blank diskette into Drive A and close the door.

Type: **FORMAT A:** Enter

Figure 3-6: Prompt to insert a diskette for formatting.

```
Insert new diskette for drive A:
and strike ENTER when ready
```

DOS will ask you to insert a diskette (see Figure 3-6). You've already done that, so press Enter. When it finishes, DOS will ask if you want to format another. Type N (no) or Y (yes) and press Enter.

WHAT'S NEXT?

You've just worked through some of the basic commands you need to use your PC effectively. In the next chapters, you'll get a more complete understanding of these commands. And, of course, there will be many hands-on examples for you to try. Just go at your own pace and remember that confident PC users were all beginners once.

CHAPTER SUMMARY

▐ In this section of the book, DOS commands are written like this: FORMAT target-drive *qualifiers*. The uppercase words must be typed exactly as spelled. The lowercase words represent information you must provide. And words in italics are optional parts of the command.

▐ The current drive and current directory are the ones in which you are working, identified in the DOS prompt.

▐ To specify action outside the current drive or directory, you must include a path in the command to indicate the location.

Telling DOS What You Want

I f you've ever had trouble getting DOS to do what you want, you may have felt like you were entering DOS *suggestions* instead of DOS commands. Since DOS has definite rules about what's acceptable "language," it's important to learn how to communicate effectively with it. So in this chapter, you'll learn

- The correct way to write DOS commands.
- Three categories of DOS commands.
- How to fine-tune a command with qualifiers to get the results you want.
- How to understand DOS error messages and spot errors in your commands.

TAKING CONTROL OF DOS

To accomplish these objectives, you'll need to do three things:

- Focus on the most useful and helpful commands, and put the others aside.
- Learn the correct way to write a command, including how to add qualifiers to modify the standard commands.
- Learn what to do when DOS gives you an error message and how to identify problems in your commands.

NARROWING DOWN THE FIELD

The latest DOS manual defines more than 100 commands. If you count all the commands plus all their variations, you come up with several hundred valid DOS expressions.

But there are only about a dozen commands you need to know well, and another dozen or so you'll use occasionally. So relax—it's not as overwhelming as you thought.

HOW TO WRITE DOS COMMANDS

For most DOS commands, you must enter not only the command name, but also include *qualifiers* that determine how the command will be executed. Here are a few examples of how qualifiers affect commands; notice that the command name always comes first in a DOS command.

ERASE REPORT.FEB	The qualifier REPORT.FEB specifies the file to be erased.
FORMAT A:	The qualifier A: indicates which drive contains the disk to format.
DIR /P	The qualifier /P causes the screen to pause each time it fills with information.

As you can see, qualifiers can be many things: a file name, a location or a special function.

COMMAND LANGUAGE

DOS is very particular about the way you enter commands. If it doesn't like what you've typed, it will respond with a blunt but clear error message. On the other hand, DOS is easygoing in some respects. For example, you may use either uppercase or lowercase letters in commands. You may abbreviate some command names. And you may even rename some commands if you like.

TIP If you're using DOS 4.0 or higher, you have the option of entering commands through the DOS Shell program. DOS Shell is a utility that simplifies interaction with your files and programs. It lets you select commands from menus, thereby saving keystrokes and minimizing errors. (For details on the DOS Shell, see Chapter 15.)

TYPES OF DOS COMMANDS

There are three types of DOS commands: those that require qualifiers, those that allow them and those that don't allow them.

QUALIFIERS REQUIRED

Most commands *must* have qualifiers. For example, with the ERASE command, you indicate which file is to be erased, such as ERASE REPORT. The COPY command requires you to indicate the file to be copied and the destination of the copy, such as COPY REPORT A:.

QUALIFIERS ALLOWED

Most commands, whether they require qualifiers or not, *may* contain optional qualifiers. For example, DIR will list your files, but DIR /P will cause the screen to pause each time it fills. This type of optional qualifier is called a *switch*; adding it to the command turns on a feature that's unique to that command.

QUALIFIERS NOT ALLOWED

A few commands stand alone and allow no qualifiers. The two covered in this book are Clear Screen (CLS) and Version (VER). The CLS command clears the screen of everything but the DOS prompt. The VER command displays the version of DOS your system is using.

ERROR MESSAGES

Everything seems so straightforward. But even experienced users can sometimes make mistakes. When you err, DOS wastes no time in telling you about it. Here are some common error messages you're likely to run into when using DOS commands.

SPELLING ERRORS

Spelling errors are the most common problem. If you enter a command incorrectly, DOS will not be able to figure out what you intended. Try the exercises below.

HANDS-ON Misspell the ERASE command.

Type: **ERASW AUGUST.RPT** Enter

TIP Maybe in DOS Version 10, the message will be "Excuse me, but did you mean to type ERASE?" For now, we must all live with DOS's less-than-friendly error messages like the one shown in Figure 4-1.

Figure 4-1: Response to a misspelled command.

```
Bad command or file name
```

SLASHES

Another common error is using the wrong slash. The forward slash (/) indicates a switch on a command. The backward slash (\) indicates a directory location.

HANDS-ON Use a switch in a DIR command, but use the wrong slash. (The correct way to type it would be DIR /W [Enter].)

Type: **DIR \W** [Enter]

```
Volume in drive C is OFFICE
Directory of  C:\

File not found
```

Figure 4-2: Response to using the wrong slash with a switch.

Figure 4-2 shows that DOS interpreted \W as a directory location, not as a switch.

DRIVE NAMES

When you enter a drive name, you must follow it with a colon.

HANDS-ON Omit the colon when specifying Drive A in a FORMAT command. (The correct way to type it is FORMAT A: [Enter].)

Type: **FORMAT A** [Enter]

Figure 4-3: Response to an invalid drive name.

```
Parameter format not correct - a
```

Figure 4-3 shows that DOS doesn't recognize A as being a drive name.

MISSING QUALIFIERS

If you leave off a required qualifier in a command, DOS will let you know.

HANDS-ON Leave off the new name for a file using the RENAME (abbreviated REN) command. (The correct way to type it is to include the new name following the old one.)

Type: **REN AUGUST.RPT** [Enter]

Figure 4-4: Response to a command with missing parameters.

```
Required parameter missing
```

As you can see in Figure 4-4, DOS tells you that a parameter is missing—but it doesn't tell you which one.

MY PERSONAL FAVORITE

Most DOS error messages are helpful and understandable, but there's one message that can be confusing. It's sometimes given when the PC is having trouble writing onto a diskette.

HANDS-ON   Leave the door of Drive A open and try to list the files contained on the diskette.

Type: **DIR A:** [Enter]

Figure 4-5: Response to a command when the drive is not ready.

```
Not ready error reading drive A
Abort, Retry, Fail?
```

Figure 4-5 shows that you have three choices. The choice here is obvious: close the drive door and type R for Retry. When the problem isn't so simple, it's usually best to type A for Abort and try another diskette.

GETTING HELP

If you're using DOS 5 or higher, you can get help with any command by typing HELP followed by the command name.

HANDS-ON   Display information on using the TREE command.

Type: **HELP TREE** [Enter]

Figure 4-6: Help screen for the TREE command.

```
 File  Search                                                    Help
                            MS-DOS Help: TREE
 <Note>  <Examples>
─────────────────────────────────────────────────────────────────────
                                  TREE

Graphically displays the structure of a directory.

Syntax

     TREE [drive:][path] [/F] [/A]

Parameters

drive:
     Specifies the drive that contains the disk for which you want to display
     the directory structure.

path
     Specifies the directory for which you want to display the directory
     structure.

Switches
 <Alt+C=Contents> <Alt+N=Next> <Alt+B=Back>                      00001:002
```

If you want more complete information, just type HELP. This command displays a list of commands and topics for which help is available. When you select a topic, you get detailed help that includes notes and examples.

CHAPTER SUMMARY

■ Of the several hundred valid DOS expressions, only about two dozen are useful to most people.

■ Most DOS commands require or allow qualifiers that specify exactly how the command will be executed.

■ A switch is a qualifier that turns on a feature that is unique to the command. It is always preceded by a forward slash (/).

■ You may type DOS commands in uppercase or lowercase letters.

■ Common mistakes in typing DOS commands include misspelling, using the wrong slash, omitting the colon in a drive name, and leaving off a required qualifier.

■ In DOS 5 and higher, you can get assistance by using the HELP command.

Understanding Disks & Drives

Since all your work is saved on disks, it's important to understand how to use them effectively and how to protect them from damage. So in this chapter, you'll learn

- About different types of disks.
- How to care for disks and diskettes.
- How to prepare a diskette to accept your files.
- How to name a diskette.
- How to "unformat" a diskette.

DISKS & DISKETTES

Although your PC can juggle lots of numbers and words as you work, it retains absolutely nothing in RAM (Random Access Memory) when you turn the machine off. If you intend to keep a file that you've worked on, you must transfer it to a more permanent storage medium— a disk.

COMING TO TERMS

Magnetic disks come in two basic varieties: fixed and removable. I'll use the term *hard disk* to refer to a fixed, internal, high-capacity disk; and *diskette* for a removable, external "floppy" disk. Diskettes are also known as disks, floppies and floppettes. There are removable hard disks, but these are less common. The latest innovation in disk technology is the CD ROM. These read-only disks provide high capacity and quick access to data by using optical laser technology. As prices drop, CD ROMs will become commonplace.

DIFFERENCES

The other main difference between hard disks and diskettes is their storage capacity. A diskette can hold from 200 to 800 pages, while a typical hard disk can hold 30 times that much information. Another difference is speed: hard disks can be read and written to faster than diskettes.

But hard disks and diskettes are also similar in several ways. First, most DOS commands can be used for both hard disk and diskette files (the exceptions will be noted in this section). Second, DOS lets you organize your files in the same manner on both.

CARING FOR DISKETTES

In a nutshell, to protect and prolong the life of your diskettes,

- Don't bend, staple or mutilate them.
- Don't expose them to extreme heat.
- Don't expose them to magnetic fields.

If your diskette got cold, let it return to room temperature before using it. The diskette will shrink a bit when it gets very cold, and may not be read properly by your drive.

Since your hard disk is inside your PC, it requires minimal care: don't expose your PC to excessive moisture, heat or dust, and don't drop it.

> **TIP** Mini-Diskettes: The newer PCs use the high-capacity, 3.5-inch diskettes, which have the advantage of a protective hard plastic shell. Even though they're more rugged than the 5.25-inch diskettes, the same care guidelines apply.

FORMATTING DISKETTES

Before you can copy information onto a diskette, it must be *formatted*. Formatting allows DOS to set up a "table of contents" to keep track of your files. Your hard disk was formatted for you, so no further preparation is needed to copy files onto it.

When you format a diskette, you must specify the drive that contains the diskette.

Format: FORMAT target-drive *qualifiers*

Example: FORMAT A:

> **TIP** If any files are present on a diskette, the formatting process will erase them, so always check each diskette with the DIR A: command.

HANDS-ON From Drive C, format a diskette in Drive A. First, insert a blank diskette into Drive A and close the door.

Type: **FORMAT A:** [Enter]

Figure 5-1: Prompt to insert a diskette to be formatted.

```
Insert new diskette for drive A:
and strike ENTER when ready
```

Figure 5-1 shows that DOS will wait for you to press Enter before executing the FORMAT command. Press Enter now to continue.

Before formatting the disk, DOS will indicate that it is "saving UNFORMAT information." UNFORMAT, explained later in this chapter, is a technique that enables you to remove the formatting from a diskette. As it formats, DOS will give a running count of the percentage complete.

When it finishes, DOS will prompt you to enter a volume label, which is an identifying name for the disk (see Figure 5-2). A volume label may have up to 11 characters (including spaces). After you enter the volume label, DOS will ask if you want to format another diskette.

Figure 5-2: Indication of a successful FORMAT command.

```
Checking existing disk format.
Saving UNFORMAT information.
Verifying 1.2M
Format complete.

Volume label (11 characters, ENTER for none)?

    1213952 bytes total disk space
    1213952 bytes available on disk

       512 bytes in each allocation unit.
    2371 allocation units available on disk.

Volume Serial Number is 143A-14CA

Format another (Y/N)?
```

Type N for no and then press [Enter]. The diskette is now ready for your use.

FORMATTING WITH SWITCHES

Three qualifiers you'll find useful with the FORMAT command are the *Volume label switch*, the *System switch* and the *Quick switch*.

The Volume Label Switch

If you're using an older version of DOS, you'll have to add the /V (Volume) switch in the FORMAT command if you want to label a diskette.

HANDS-ON   Format a diskette in Drive A using the /V switch, and name the diskette WP FILES.

Type: **FORMAT A: /V:WP FILES** [Enter]

If you use the /V switch without including a label, DOS will prompt you to enter the label after the formatting is complete.

Now, each time files on this diskette are listed with the DIR A: command, the volume label will appear at the top of the screen, as shown in Figure 5-3.

Figure 5-3: The volume label of a formatted diskette.

```
Volume in drive A is WP FILES
Directory of   A:\
```

The System Switch

If you need a diskette that can boot a PC, the /S (System) switch copies the necessary system files to the diskette during the formatting.

HANDS-ON   Format the same diskette in Drive A so that it can boot the PC.

Type: **FORMAT A: /S** [Enter]

This time, DOS shows you how much room the system files are taking (see Figure 5-4).

```
Checking existing disk format.
Saving UNFORMAT information.
Verifying 1.2M
Format complete.
System transferred

Volume label (11 characters, ENTER for none)?

    1213952 bytes total disk space
     183296 bytes used by system
    1030656 bytes available on disk

        512 bytes in each allocation unit.
       2013 allocation units available on disk.

Volume Serial Number is 350B-14CC

Format another (Y/N)?
```

Figure 5-4: Indication that the System files were copied during formatting.

The Quick Switch

If you want to reformat a diskette that's already been formatted, you can save time by using the /Q (Quick) switch (available in DOS 5 and higher). The command is FORMAT A: /Q.

USING MULTIPLE SWITCHES

As long as switches don't conflict with one another, you may use more than one in a command. So FORMAT A: /V/S would be acceptable. This command would format the diskette, allow you to name the diskette, and add the system files.

ADDING A LABEL TO A FORMATTED DISKETTE

If you didn't add a volume label when you formatted a diskette, you can add a label with the LABEL command (available in DOS version 3.0 and higher).

Format: LABEL drive label

Example: LABEL A: MY REPORTS

If you omit the label in the command, DOS will prompt you to enter the label.

TIP Checking the Volume Label: If you don't know whether a diskette has a label, use the VOLUME (VOL) command. For example, VOL A: would check the volume label of the diskette in Drive A.

UNFORMATTING DISKETTES

In DOS 5 and higher, it's possible to restore a newly formatted diskette to its former condition using the UNFORMAT command. So if you accidentally format a diskette containing important files, you can most likely recover them.

Format: UNFORMAT drive *qualifiers*

Example: UNFORMAT A:

You can save yourself this trouble, however, simply by checking the contents of each diskette before formatting.

DISK DRIVES

Information is read from and written to disks by *disk drives*. When you tell DOS where to look for a file, you must first specify which drive contains the disk on which the file is located.

DRIVE NAMES

A typical PC has an internal hard drive and one external diskette drive. The hard disk drive is Drive C. The diskette drive is usually called Drive A. The interesting feature of the external drive is that it can serve as either Drive A or B. For example, the commands FORMAT A: and FORMAT B: would both format the diskette in the external drive. However, those commands would refer to different drives if you had an additional external drive connected to your system.

CHAPTER SUMMARY

- Most DOS commands work on hard disk and diskette files.
- The primary precautions with diskettes are to avoid exposing them to magnetic fields and extreme heat.
- Diskettes must be formatted before they can be used.
- The FORMAT command has three important switches: /V lets you add a volume label to the diskette; /S copies the system files to the diskette so it can boot the system; and /Q reformats a formatted diskette quickly.
- The LABEL command lets you add a volume label to a diskette that has already been formatted.
- Your diskette drive can function as two distinct drives (A and B).
- The UNFORMAT command can restore a newly formatted diskette to its original condition (DOS 5 and higher).

Understanding Directories

In order to use DOS effectively, you need to know where your files are located and how to get to them. So in this chapter, you'll learn how

- Your disk is structured.
- To know your location on a disk at all times.
- To tell DOS where to find your files.
- To get from one location to another—by conventional means and shortcuts.

When you file a letter in a drawer, you put it where you can easily find it later. The typical approach used in most offices is to use hanging folders to organize the drawer, and then to add file folders within them. This way, you can keep related items together and separate them from other items. When you organize your hard disk, you can use this same sort of structure to arrange your files.

ORGANIZING A HARD DISK

A hard disk comes with only one storage area, called the *Root directory*. It is like a file drawer with no organization. To find an individual file, you have to look through the entire drawer.

In the Root directory, you can add other *directories* that act like hanging folders. So you may have one directory for spreadsheets, another for documents and another for graphs and illustrations.

If there were only a few files in each directory, finding a file would be no problem. But in real life, things aren't always so simple. The next logical step is to create *subdirectories* within directories, which is like adding file folders within the hanging folders. Now, finding an individual file is a snap. First you go to the right directory, and then to the right subdirectory.

> **TIP** You can, of course, create additional levels of subdirectories, just as you can put folders within folders. But at some point, your organization will turn into inconvenience, so it's best not to go too deep. Besides, there are other ways to add organization to your disk (for example, by using carefully chosen file names).

Now that you've got the picture, let's take a closer look at the structure of a disk.

THE DISK STRUCTURE

Figure 6-1 shows the structure of a hard disk. It illustrates the hierarchical arrangement that DOS lets you use to organize your files.

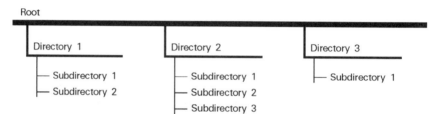

Figure 6-1: The DOS hierarchical file structure.

Notice that each directory exists within the Root, and that each subdirectory exists within a directory. It's just like the file drawer: hanging folders are placed within the drawer, and file folders are placed within hanging folders. The Root is said to be the *parent* of each directory, and each directory can, in turn, be a parent of subdirectories.

Going Out on a Limb

To see the structure of a disk, you can use the TREE command. This command is most commonly used to show how the directories and subdirectories are organized on a hard disk. First, change to the Root directory by typing CD \ [Enter]

Format: TREE *path qualifiers*

Example: TREE A: /F

HANDS-ON Examine the directory structure of your hard disk (Drive C). If C is the current drive, you don't have to include it in the command.

Type: **TREE** [Enter]

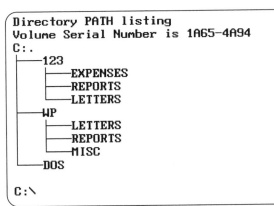

```
Directory PATH listing
Volume Serial Number is 1A65-4A94
C:.
├─────123
│         ├─────EXPENSES
│         ├─────REPORTS
│         └─────LETTERS
├─────WP
│         ├─────LETTERS
│         ├─────REPORTS
│         └─────MISC
└─────DOS

C:\
```

Figure 6-2: The directory structure for Drive C (hard disk).

Figure 6-2 shows three subdirectories within \123, three within \WP and none within \DOS.

> **TIP** If you want to print the directory structure, type TREE >PRN at the prompt.

Using the |MORE Qualifier

If you have more than a few directories, the TREE information will scroll quickly off the screen. To display it one screen at a time, add the |MORE qualifier (TREE |MORE). (Be sure to press Enter each time the screen fills.)

Using the Files Switch

If you also want to see the files contained in each directory, you can add the Files (/F) switch.

HANDS-ON List the files contained within each directory and subdirectory.

Type: **TREE /F |MORE** Enter

```
Directory PATH listing
Volume Serial Number is 1A65-4A94
C:.
    │   AUTOEXEC.BAT
    │   CONFIG.SYS
    │   ANAFAADK
    │   ANAFAAFA
    │
    ├──123
    │   │   EXP#1.DAT
    │   │   EXP#2.DAT
    │   │   EXP#3.DAT
    │   │   RESUME.LET
    │   │   COVER.LET
    │   │   COVER2.LET
    │   │   FORMAT.MEM
    │   │   DRAFT1.MS
    │   │   OUTLINE.LET
    │   │   FORMAT.LET
    │   │
    │   ├──EXPENSES
    │   │   DEC93.EXP
    │   │   SUMMARY.EXP
    │   │   AUG93.EXP
```

Figure 6-3: Result of using the /F switch with the TREE command.

Only part of the listing is shown in Figure 6-3.

CHANGING THE DOS PROMPT

The drive and directory you're working in are the *current drive* and *current directory.* When you type a command, DOS applies the command only to the files in the current drive and directory (unless you specify otherwise). So how do you know what's current?

THE PROMPT COMMAND

The default DOS prompt shows the current drive. So right now, C> indicates that C is the current drive. But what about the directory? Can we make DOS tell us the current directory?

Yes. The PROMPT command lets you make the DOS prompt say just about anything you want it to say.

Format: PROMPT *qualifiers*

Example: PROMPT $P $T

Let's look at some of the more informative prompts.

Showing the Current Directory

The $P qualifier causes DOS to show both the current drive and the current directory. This prompt is the most useful because it lets you know exactly where you are.

HANDS-ON   Make the prompt display the current drive and directory.

> Type: **PROMPT $P** Enter

Figure 6-4: This prompt indicates the current drive and the current directory.

```
C:\
```

The prompt shown in Figure 6-4 looks almost the same as before. The subtle but important difference is the backward slash (\ ) character, which always indicates a directory location. By itself, it indicates the Root directory. For any other directory, it will be followed by the directory name (for example, \123).

Showing the Time

The $T qualifier causes DOS to include the time in the prompt. This feature isn't a "ticking" clock. It shows the current time only at the moment you press Enter (see Figure 6-5).

HANDS-ON   Fix the prompt so that it shows both the current directory and the time.

Figure 6-5: When you use the $T qualifier in the PROMPT command, the prompt includes the current time.

> Type: **PROMPT PT** Enter

```
C:\ 15:07:46.42
```

Including the > Character

The $G qualifier adds the > (greater than) character to the prompt. This character has no special function—it just separates the prompt from the commands you type.

HANDS-ON   Have the prompt display both the current directory and the > symbol.

> Type: **PROMPT PG** Enter

Figure 6-6: A prompt including the > character.

```
C:\>
```

The prompt shown in Figure 6-6 is one that's commonly used.

Being Clever

If you're feeling down, you can always change the prompt to give yourself a little boost.

HANDS-ON Make the prompt uninformative but uplifting.

Type: **PROMPT Command me, all knowing One $G** ⏎

Figure 6-7: A respectful DOS prompt.

```
Command me, all knowing One>
```

The prompt shown in Figure 6-7 makes it clear who's in charge. But in the spirit of humility, change the prompt back to "normal," using the command PROMPT PG.

> **TIP** Making DOS Do the Typing: Any command that you have to type each time you boot up—like the PROMPT command—can be automated. By including such commands in a special file called AUTOEXEC.BAT, you're telling DOS to type them for you when you turn on your PC. The AUTOEXEC.BAT file is discussed in Chapter 13, "Increasing the Power of Your PC."

USING PATHS IN COMMANDS

As you've learned, DOS executes your commands within the current drive and directory. Now let's say your current drive is C. If you enter ERASE REPORT.FEB, but the file REPORT.FEB is on Drive A, DOS will need more information to do what you've asked. By specifying a *path* in the command, you can direct DOS to look on another drive or directory for the REPORT.FEB file.

To indicate a path in a command, start at the highest level of organization—the disk drive—and then work down through the directory structure. Here's the format:

Format: drive\directory\subdirectory\filename

Example: C:\123\REPORTS\EXPENSES.APR

It's like finding a report in a cabinet: you open the correct drawer, choose a hanging file, then a file folder and finally the report.

When you write a path, you never have to indicate the *current* drive or directory. (The BACKUP command is an exception.)

HANDS-ON   From Drive C, list all files in the Root directory of Drive A.

Type: **DIR A:** ⏎

```
Volume in drive A is WP FILES
Volume Serial Number is 350B-14CC
Directory of  A:\

LETTERS         <DIR>      03-13-93    5:33p
ORDER1    PUR       9767   03-22-93    2:47p
CHECKLST           7406    04-12-93    3:07p
ORDER2    PUR      14429   04-02-93    1:06p
NOTICE    DOC       5316   05-08-93    3:55p
PROPOSAL  DOC      17123   04-18-93   12:19p
JULIE     MEM       3334   05-01-93    3:09p
        7 File(s)          57375 bytes
                         1125857 bytes free
```

Figure 6-8: The contents of the diskette in Drive A.

Here, the path directs DOS to carry out the command on Drive A, not on the current drive. So the files listed are the ones located on Drive A (see Figure 6-8).

Now try a command that includes a path to another directory on the current drive.

HANDS-ON   Erase a file that's not in the current directory. Here, the \WP directory is current. The file named 1992.EXP is being erased from the \123 directory.

Type: **ERASE \123\1992.EXP** ⏎

Here, the path tells DOS to locate the file in the C:\123 directory. Since Drive C is the current drive, it wasn't necessary to include it in the path.

LOCATING DOS COMMANDS

Files with the extensions .COM, .BAT and .EXE are called *executable* files. They include DOS commands (like FORMAT.COM) and files that start programs (like 123.EXE). To use your PC without frustration, you need to be able to use DOS commands and other executable files while working in any directory.

As you've already learned, DOS can't find anything outside the current directory unless you tell it where to look. So with executable files, the solution involves a special command called PATH.

Format: PATH directory-paths

Example: PATH \;\DOS;\WP

In the PATH command, you specify each directory path that you want DOS to search for executable files (such as DOS commands if they aren't in the current directory). When you include more than one directory path, use a semicolon to separate the paths.

To see if a PATH command is currently in effect, type PATH `Enter` at the DOS prompt. If no PATH command is displayed, follow the instructions below.

HANDS-ON Instruct DOS to search, if necessary, the Root directory and then, if necessary, the \DOS directory.

Type: **PATH \;\DOS** `Enter`

Now, you can use your DOS commands (like COPY, RENAME, ERASE and others) from any directory. And if you also include the directories containing your WordPerfect and 1-2-3 programs in the PATH command, you'll be able to start WordPerfect and 1-2-3 from any directory.

You need to enter a PATH command only once per work session. From that point on, DOS will check the specified directories automatically as needed.

> **TIP** Like the PROMPT command, the PATH command can be typed for you if you include it in your AUTOEXEC.BAT file (explained in Chapter 13).

CHANGING THE CURRENT DRIVE & DIRECTORY

Now you know how a disk is organized and how to determine your location. Let's learn how to change the current drive and directory.

To change the current *drive*, enter the drive letter name followed by a colon. For example, entering A: would make Drive A the current drive.

To change the current *directory*, use the CD (Change Directory) command.

Format: CD directory-name

Example: CD 123

No path is needed if you're changing from the Root to one of its directories, or from a directory to one of its subdirectories (in other words, the backslash is not needed).

HANDS-ON Change the current directory from the Root to the \123 directory.

Type: **CD 123** `Enter`

Figure 6-9: Prompt showing
that the current directory is
now \123.

```
C:\123>
```

Figure 6-9 shows that the current directory is now \123. So how
do you change back to the Root? Since it doesn't have a name, use the
backward slash by itself to indicate the Root directory.

HANDS-ON From the \123 directory, change back to the Root.

Type: **CD ** [Enter]

Figure 6-10: Prompt showing
that the current directory is
now the Root.

```
C:\>
```

The Root is once again the current directory (see Figure 6-10).

Using Complete Paths

To make a *subdirectory* current, you must include its parent directory.
It's like finding a particular file folder: first you find the hanging folder
and then the file folder within it.

HANDS-ON From the Root directory, change to the \LETTERS subdirectory
within the \WP directory.

Type: **CD WP\LETTERS** [Enter]

Figure 6-11: Prompt
indicating the new
current directory.

```
C:\WP\LETTERS>
```

You can see in Figure 6-11 that \WP\LETTERS is now the current
directory.

The Road Less Traveled

When you list your files with the DIR command, you always see two
directories at the top of the list, as shown in Figure 6-12.

```
Volume in drive C is OFFICE
Directory of  C:\WP\LETTERS

.           <DIR>       01-17-93   12:21p
..          <DIR>       01-17-93   12:21p
```

Figure 6-12: Part of the
directory listing.

The (.) directory represents the current directory itself, while the (..) directory represents the parent directory. So, to go up one level to the parent, you can simply change to the (..) directory and save a few keystrokes.

HANDS-ON Change from a subdirectory to its parent directory. Here, the change is from the \WP\LETTERS subdirectory to \WP.

Type: **CD ..** [Enter]

Figure 6-13: Prompt
indicating that \WP is the
current directory.

```
C:\WP>
```

CHAPTER SUMMARY

■ Directories and subdirectories let you group related files and keep them separate from other files.

■ The Root directory is the parent of each directory, and each directory can be a parent of subdirectories.

■ The TREE command shows the directory structure of a disk. Adding the /F switch instructs DOS to list all files as well.

■ The most useful PROMPT command includes the $P qualifier because it causes the current drive and directory to be displayed in the prompt.

■ The PATH command enables DOS to locate executable files (such as DOS commands and program-starting commands) from any directory.

■ A file can be manipulated from any directory simply by using a path to tell DOS where the file is located.

■ The CD command changes the current directory.

Organizing Your
Hard Disk

If you're not already using directories and subdirectories, you should start now—the sooner the better. The longer you wait to organize your files, the longer it will take. So, this chapter focuses on creating and using directories and subdirectories. You'll learn

- The reasons for creating directories.
- How to make directories and subdirectories.
- How to remove a directory.
- How to rename a directory.

Before going ahead, let's review some terminology. The Root directory is the main directory. Within the Root, you may create directories. Within directories, you may create subdirectories.

WHAT GOES WHERE?

To start, you'll want to make a separate directory for each large group of related files, such as software programs. If you followed the directions that came with your software, you probably have directories for WordPerfect, Lotus 1-2-3 and other software programs. (The actual names of your directories probably reflect the versions of the software you're using—for example, \WP60 for WordPerfect 6.0. Because I don't know which versions you're using, I'll use the generic names \WP and \123 in this book.) It's also a good idea to put your DOS command files in a directory called \DOS.

Subdirectories allow you to carry your organization a step further. Here's a practical illustration: if you have WordPerfect, you should have its program files in a directory called \WP. To keep your files separate from the program files, you could create several subdirectories within \WP: one for letters, one for reports and one for miscellaneous files. So it would be like having three file folders within a hanging folder.

DRAWBACKS

One disadvantage in using subdirectories is that a DIR listing doesn't give any clue about what they contain. So, you have to enter a separate DIR command for each subdirectory to see what files it contains. DOS 5 introduced the /S (Subdirectory) switch to overcome this problem (explained in Chapter 9, "Listing Files").

Another drawback is that as the disk structure becomes more complex, you have to write longer paths to help DOS find your files; the more levels of subdirectories, the more steps required to get to a particular file.

MAKING DIRECTORIES

To make a new directory, first change to the Root. Then use the MD (Make Directory) command.

Format: MD directory-name

Example: MD MEMOS

If you're making a directory that's one level below the current directory, no path is required. If it belongs deeper in the structure, you would need to indicate the path, like this: MD MEMOS\PERSONAL.

HANDS-ON Make a directory on the hard disk. Here, the directory is called \SAMPLE. Start in the Root directory.

Type: **MD SAMPLE** [Enter]

Figure 7-1: DOS prompt following the MD command: the prompt doesn't change.

```
C:\>
```

Although DOS doesn't confirm it (Figure 7-1), you now have a directory called \SAMPLE.

> **TIP** The Current Directory: Making a directory doesn't change the current directory. In other words, making a directory does not take you there. To make \SAMPLE the current directory, you would have to enter the command CD SAMPLE.

MAKING SUBDIRECTORIES

Making a subdirectory is similar to making a directory. But here, instead of starting in the Root, you first go to the directory that will contain the subdirectory.

HANDS-ON Make a subdirectory. Here, a subdirectory called \ARTICLES is being made within the \WP directory.

Type: **CD WP** Enter

Type: **MD ARTICLES** Enter

Again, you get no confirmation from DOS.

WHERE'S MY SUBDIRECTORY?

If you list the contents of the current directory using DIR, you'll see the subdirectory you just created. (Figure 7-2 shows a portion of the directory listing.)

```
Volume in drive C is OFFICE
Volume Serial Number is 1A65-4A94
Directory of  C:\WP

.               <DIR>        01-17-93   12:21p
..              <DIR>        01-17-93   12:21p
WP       EXE    215040       01-17-93   12:21p
KEYS     MRS      4800       01-17-93   12:21p

LETTERS         <DIR>        01-17-93   12:21p
REPORTS         <DIR>        01-17-93   12:21p
MISC            <DIR>        01-17-93   12:21p
RESUME   LET      5316       02-08-93    3:55p
COVER    LET      4972       02-13-93    3:30p
COVER2   LET      4972       03-13-93    3:30p
FORMAT   MEM      3556       05-01-93    1:41p
ARTICLES        <DIR>        01-30-93    3:20p
DRAFT1   MS      10923       05-09-93   10:04a
OUTLINE  LET      5374       05-30-93   11:08a
FORMAT   LET      3482       04-29-93    3:47p
        120 file(s)      3839368 bytes
                         8665401 bytes free
```

Figure 7-2: Contents of the current directory.

If the \WP\ARTICLES subdirectory is the most recently created item, why isn't it at the bottom of the list? It's because DOS uses the first available space it finds on a diskette. In this case, DOS found an empty space where a file was erased earlier.

REMOVING DIRECTORIES

The RD (Remove Directory) command lets you remove directories and subdirectories from a disk.

Format: RD directory-name

Example: RD REPORTS

If the directory is one level down from the current directory, no path is required. If it is deeper in the structure, you would need to indicate the path, like this: RD REPORTS\WEEKLY.

HANDS-ON Remove a directory. Here, the \SAMPLE directory is being removed. First, change to its parent directory (the Root in this case).

Type: **RD SAMPLE** Enter

DOS gives no confirmation when it removes a directory.

This command has a built-in safety feature: if there are files in the directory you're trying to remove, DOS will give you the message shown in Figure 7-3.

Figure 7-3: Message indicating that a directory can't be removed.

```
Invalid path, not directory,
or directory not empty
```

The DELTREE Command

If you do want to remove a directory that contains files, use the DELTREE command (available in DOS 6).

Format: DELTREE *qualifier* path

Example: DELTREE /Y ACCOUNTS\WIDGET

DELTREE removes all files and subdirectories within the specified directory. The only available qualifier, /Y, causes DOS to delete the specified directories and files without checking with you first. If you omit /Y, DOS will ask you to type Y (Yes) to continue or N (No) to abort the operation.

> **TIP** Renaming a Directory: Unfortunately, DOS doesn't provide a command for renaming directories. So, if you want to change a directory name, you have to go through four steps: create a new directory, copy the files from the original to the new one, erase the files from the original and then remove the original. You can, however, easily rename a directory in the DOS Shell.

CHAPTER SUMMARY

- To make a directory or subdirectory, use the MD command.
- The most recently created directory (or file) might not appear at the bottom of the DIR listing.
- Making a directory doesn't change the current directory.
- To remove a directory, use the RD command. A directory must be empty of files before it can be removed.
- The DELTREE command can be used to remove a directory and all of the files and subdirectories it contains.
- You can't rename a directory at the command prompt, but you can in the DOS Shell.

Creating & Erasing Files

DOS 8

The whole point of using a PC is to have quick and easy access to your work. One key is to use appropriate file names. Another is to keep your disk clear of unwanted files. So in this chapter, you'll learn

- The difference between good and bad file names.
- How to rename a file.
- How to erase a file.
- How to recover an erased file.
- How to manipulate several files with one command.

FILE NAMES

After creating a file in WordPerfect or any other program, you have to name the file in order to save it. DOS limits a file name to eight characters (the name) plus an optional three (the extension). The extension can be used to identify the file type. A period must separate the name from the extension. (See Figure 8-1.)

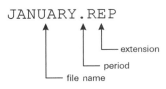

Figure 8-1: Parts of a file name: you can use numbers as well as letters within the 11-character limit.

Sometimes this limitation is no problem. For example, it's clear that REPORT.TUE is Tuesday's report. But things get confusing when you start abbreviating longer names. For example, at the time you create it, 1QTREXP.LOC may seem logical for a file that contains first quarter expenses for local trips. But a few months later, that name may not make much sense. So naming files is a matter that deserves thought and creativity.

SUGGESTIONS

Choose descriptive file names. For example, MEMO.4 is a poor name for a memo about the office picnic. A more descriptive name that will make sense later is PICNIC.MEM.

> **TIP** For related files, use either the same name or the same extension. Then you'll be able to manipulate the entire group with single commands. For example, if all your business correspondence files have a .BUS extension, you can list, copy or erase them all with one command.

RULES FOR FILE NAMES

DOS has some definite rules about what you can use as a file name. If you break a rule, DOS may let you know with an error message like the one shown in Figure 8-2.

Figure 8-2: This error message indicates there's a problem with a file name you've given.

```
File creation error
        0 file(s) copied
```

Here are DOS's rules for file names:

Use no more than eight characters in the name and three in the extension. Separate the name and extension with a period.

Don't include spaces. However, you can use an underscore (_) to simulate a space.

Don't use these characters: ' " / \ | <> + = : ; . , ^

SECOND-HAND NAMES

In a given directory, you can use a name-plus-extension only once. If you try to use it again in the current directory, DOS, WordPerfect and Lotus 1-2-3 will warn you by asking if you want to replace the existing file. If you answer "yes," the original file will be lost as the new version takes its place.

RENAMING FILES

Sometimes you may forget to plan ahead. If you expect to make only one sales report, you might name your file SALES.RPT. But if you later find you have to create three different versions of that report, you must rethink the name choice.

Fortunately, DOS lets you change your mind and rename a file with the RENAME command.

Format: REN old-name new-name

Example: REN LETTER.4 APRIL.LET

TIP If the file is not in the current directory, you must include the file's path in the command.

HANDS-ON Rename a file in the current directory. Here in the \123\REPORTS subdirectory, the file SALES.RPT is given the new name SALES1.RPT.

Type: **REN SALES.RPT SALES1.RPT** Enter

Figure 8-3: The prompt does not change following a RENAME command.

```
C:\123\REPORTS>
```

Although DOS doesn't confirm it, the file name SALES.RPT is now history, and SALES1.RPT has taken its place. (However, you can check by using the DIR command; see Chapter 9, "Listing Files," for details.) You can now create the other versions of the sales report and name them SALES2.RPT and SALES3.RPT.

ERASING FILES

The ERASE command erases a file and removes it from the directory listing. The DEL (Delete) command achieves the same effect.

Format: ERASE filename

Example: ERASE FISCAL.91

TIP If the file is not in the current directory, you must include the file's path in the command.

HANDS-ON Erase a file in the current directory. Here, the file called DRAFT1.MS is being erased from the current subdirectory (\WP\MISC).

Type: **ERASE DRAFT1.MS** Enter

DOS doesn't confirm a successful erasure; but you can by using the DIR command (explained in Chapter 9, "Listing Files").

> **TIP** Notice that DOS doesn't give you a chance to change your mind, so always be careful. It may take weeks to create a file, but it takes only a second to accidentally erase it.

WHAT HAPPENS TO ERASED FILES?

If a file is gone, it's gone, right? Well, not exactly. When you erase a file, DOS simply makes that space on the disk available. The file actually remains intact until new information is written over it.

So it's possible to recover an erased file if no new work is written over it. Before DOS 5, you couldn't do it with DOS commands. You needed a utility program that provided a file recovery command.

But DOS 5 introduced the UNDELETE command that makes it possible to recover erased files.

Format: UNDELETE *filename qualifiers*

Example: UNDELETE REPORT.AUG

DOS will show the file name as ?EPORT.AUG and ask if you want to undelete it. If you type Y (Yes), you will be prompted to type the first character of the file name–R, in this example.

Using UNDELETE without a filename tells DOS to try to recover all erased files in the current directory. You will be prompted to type either Y (Yes) or N (No) for each file to indicate whether you want to recover it.

> **TIP** Be aware that UNDELETE might not be successful if you've created or modified other files since erasing the original file.

WORKING WITH SEVERAL FILES AT ONCE

There will be many times when you want to work with groups of files. You might want to copy all your weekly report files or erase all your out-of-date expense sheets. If you choose your file names carefully, you can manipulate a group of files with a single command.

WILDCARD CHARACTERS

Wildcard characters can be used in file names to represent other characters: the ? character represents a single character, while the * character (usually called "star") represents any number of characters. These wildcard characters allow you to manipulate a group of files that have something in common by using just one file name. The * wild-card is the more useful of the two, so here are a few examples of how to use it.

MANIPULATING FILES WITH A COMMON EXTENSION

To work with files that have a common extension, use * as the file name.

HANDS-ON Rename a group of files that have the same extension. Here, all files with the extension .REP are being renamed to have the extension .RPT.

> Type: **REN *.REP *.RPT** Enter

After a successful Rename operation, DOS displays the prompt without confirmation.

MANIPULATING FILES WITH A COMMON NAME

To work with files that have a common name, use * as the extension.

HANDS-ON Erase a group of files that have the same name. Here, all files with the name EXP1991 are being erased from the current subdirectory (\123\EXPENSES).

> Type: **ERASE EXP1991.*** Enter

Since the Erase operation was successful, DOS doesn't display an error message.

Obviously, you should be very careful when erasing groups of files. One way to be careful is to add the /P switch (for example, ERASE EXP1991.* /P). It causes DOS to pause before erasing each file, continuing only if you type Y (Yes) at the prompt. This switch is available in DOS 4.0 and higher.

MANIPULATING ALL FILES

By using the file name *.*, you can manipulate all files in a directory. For example, you could erase all files in the current directory using the command ERASE *.* (this is not an exercise!).

HOUSEKEEPING

Files accumulate quickly. Before you know it, your disk will be clut-tered, so it's important to clear your disk of old and unneeded files on a regular basis.

THE TYPE COMMAND

When you clean out your hard disk, you might run across a Word-Perfect file that you want to check before erasing. One way to check it is to go into WordPerfect, retrieve the file and examine it, and then exit to DOS. The quicker way is to use the TYPE command. It lets you look at a text file without leaving DOS.

Format: TYPE filename

Example: TYPE TRAVEL.EXP

TIP If the file name is not in the current directory, you must include the file's path in the command.

HANDS-ON Look at a file using the TYPE command. Here, the file TOM.MEM is being viewed.

Type: **TYPE TOM.MEM** Enter

```
15 February 1993

Tom,

I'd like to meet with you this week to discuss the new Acme Widget account.
Let's plan on Wednesday after lunch for a meeting in my office.  If another
time would be better, give me a call.

Robert
```

Figure 8-4: Result of the command TYPE TOM.MEM: the contents of the TOM.MEM text file.

Although the screen won't show the formatting (like boldface and underlining), the words are all there.

STOPPING THE SCREEN

When you use the TYPE command on a long file, you may want to freeze the screen at some point. To stop a scrolling screen, press Ctrl-S; to resume scrolling, press the Space bar. Many instruction books say you may press "any key," but this is vague and not entirely correct. A few keys won't work (for example, the Num Lock key).

CHAPTER SUMMARY

■ DOS limits a file name to eight characters for the name itself, plus an optional three for the extension. A period must separate the name from the extension.

■ If related files have a common name or extension, you can copy, erase or list them with single commands using the * wildcard character.

■ In file names, don't use spaces or any of these characters:
' " / \ | <> + = : ; . , ^

■ To rename a file, use the REN command.

■ To erase a file, use the ERASE or DEL command.

■ In DOS 5 and higher, the UNDELETE command can restore recently erased files.

■ The TYPE command displays the contents of a text file.

■ Pressing Ctrl-S will freeze a scrolling screen. Pressing the Space bar will unfreeze the screen.

Listing Files

Using your PC efficiently depends on knowing what files you have and where they're located. So in this chapter, you'll learn how to

■ List all files or a selected group of files.

■ Freeze a long listing each time the screen fills.

■ Sort a list of files alphabetically and chronologically.

■ Send a file listing directly to the printer or save it in a file.

As you continue to work on your PC—creating new files, renaming files and moving files around—your disk begins to fill up, and file management becomes complicated. What files do you have? What are their names? And where are they located? It can be confusing.

DIRECTORY ASSISTANCE

To answer the who, what and where questions about your files, you can use the DIR (Directory) command, which instructs DOS to list the files contained in a directory.

If you use the "standard" DIR command, you get a listing that's not organized in any useful way. But the command can be modified in a number of ways to make it more useful. For example, the list can be sorted alphabetically by file name or extension. You can also sort by date or file size.

Although these reorganizations are temporary, DOS provides two ways to preserve them. You can save the list in a file, so that it's always available. Or you can immediately print out the list so you have a hard copy of it. Both of these techniques are examples of *redirecting* output that normally would appear on the screen.

LISTING ALL FILES

The DIR command lists all files in the current directory or in the directory you specify. If you don't include a path, DOS will list the files in the current directory.

Format: DIR path *qualifiers*

Example: DIR \123

> **TIP** If you're looking at files outside the current directory, you must include the directory's path.

HANDS-ON List all files contained in the current directory (here, it's \123).

Type: **DIR** [Enter]

```
Volume in drive C has no label
Volume Serial Number is 1A65-4A94
Directory of C:\123

.            <DIR>          01-17-93    12:46p
..           <DIR>          01-17-93    12:46p
INSTALL  EXE     105137     01-17-92     1:23a
INSDSK24 RI        3110     01-17-92     1:23a
INSTXT24 RI       30459     01-17-92     1:23a
PKUNZIP  EXE      23528     01-17-92     1:23a
123      EXE      18368     01-17-93     2:26p

RESUME   LET       5316     02-08-93     3:55p
COVER    LET       4972     02-13-93     3:30p
COVER2   LET       4972     02-13-93     3:30p
FORMAT   MEM       3556     04-01-93     1:41p
DRAFT1   MS       10923     05-09-93    10:04a
OUTLINE  LET       5374     05-30-93    11:08a
FORMAT   LET       3482     04-29-93     3:47p
EXPENSES     <DIR>          03-05-93    12:51p
REPORTS      <DIR>          03-05-93    12:51p
LETTERS      <DIR>          03-05-93    12:52p
      65 file(s)       2473816 bytes
                       9316791 bytes free
```

Figure 9-1: Typing DIR gives you a listing of the contents of the current directory (in this case, \123).

WHAT THE LIST TELLS YOU

As you can see in Figure 9-1, the DIR listing gives you five pieces of information about your files:

■ The file name.

■ The file-name extension (useful for identifying the file type).

■ The size of the file, in bytes. (Usually, one double-spaced page of text will take up about 2,000 bytes.)

■ The date the file was created or last modified.

■ The time the file was created or last modified.

Notice that some items in the list aren't individual files but directories (indicated with <DIR>). What files are in these directories? You won't know until you list their files.

> **TIP** In DOS 5 and higher, you can add the /S (Subdirectory) switch to the DIR command to display the contents of subdirectories as well.

USING THE /W & /P SWITCHES

With each file taking up an entire row, there will be times when you have too many files to fit on one screen. One solution is to press Ctrl-S when you want to stop the screen, and then press the Space bar to let it continue. But if your PC is fast, you may need to use either the Wide switch or the Pause switch.

THE WIDE SWITCH

The Wide switch (/W) lists files across the screen, allowing more file names to fit on the screen.

HANDS-ON Use the Wide switch to list the contents of the current directory (\123\REPORTS).

Type: **DIR /W** [Enter]

Figure 9-2: When you add the /W switch to the DIR command, you lose the size, date and time information as well as the <DIR> indicators.

```
Volume in drive C is OFFICE
Volume Serial Number is 1A65-4A94
Directory of  C:\123\REPORTS

.            ..             EMPLOYEE SIC    EMPLOYEE VAC    PURCHASE AUG
EMPLOYEE REV    PROGRESS 1      EMPLOYEE CMP
     8 file(s)       13972 bytes
                  8692629 bytes free
```

THE PAUSE SWITCH

If the DIR list is long, the Pause switch (/P) will cause the screen to pause when it fills. When you're ready to see the next screen, press the Space bar. The command is DIR /P.

LISTING FILES ALPHABETICALLY

One of the most useful ways to list files is to show them in alphabetical order. This sorting occurs only on the screen, and doesn't alter the actual sequence on the disk. But later in this chapter, you'll learn how to preserve a sorted list in a file and in a printout.

THE ALPHABETICAL SORT (before DOS 5)

To create an alphabetical listing, add the |SORT qualifier to the DIR command.

HANDS-ON List all files in a subdirectory in alphabetical order. Here, in Figure 9-3, files in the \WP\LETTERS subdirectory are being sorted.

Type: **DIR |SORT** [Enter]

```
Volume in drive C is OFFICE
Volume Serial Number is 1A65-4A94
Directory of  C:\WP\LETTERS
.                 <DIR>        01-17-93   12:21p
..                <DIR>        01-17-93   12:21p
0F34193A                  0    07-19-93    3:52p
0F34193F                  0    07-19-93    3:52p
ACME1    LET           1174    05-26-93   10:32a
ACME2    LET           5316    03-08-93    3:55p
DR_SMITH JUN          9028    06-09-93    2:41p
DR_SMITH MAR          1190    03-30-93   12:14p
DR_SMITH MAY          1898    05-26-93   10:52a
EASTERLY LET           3556    05-01-93    1:41p
JUDY     MEM            450    04-07-93    9:53a
OFFICE1  MEM           1898    05-26-93   10:52a
PICNIC   MEM           1174    05-26-93   10:32a
PURCHASE LET           7301    03-14-93    4:39p
REEVES   LET           3216    05-24-93   10:47a
SURVEY   LET           4972    05-13-93    3:30p
TOM      MEM            886    05-25-93    2:36p
      17 file(s)        42059 bytes
                      8692629 bytes free
```

Figure 9-3: In the directory listing, the two files with zero size are created by DOS during the alphabetical sort, then automatically erased.

Reversing the Sort

To reverse the alphabetical sort, add the Reverse (/R) switch; for example, DIR |SORT /R.

Pausing After Each Screen

If you have too many files to fit on one screen, you'll want to make the listing pause after each screen. Unfortunately, the Pause switch (/P) doesn't work with SORT. Instead, you have to use the |MORE qualifier; for example, DIR |SORT |MORE.

THE ALPHABETICAL SORT (DOS 5 & higher)

Sorting the DIR listing alphabetically in DOS 5 and higher is easy.
All you need to do is add the /O: (Order) switch and the letter N.
So to get an alphabetical listing, one screen at a time, you would enter
DIR /O:N /P.

   If you want to see the list in reverse order, use –N instead of N in
the command, like this: DIR /O:-N /P.

LISTING FILES CHRONOLOGICALLY

Another useful way to list files is in the order you created or modified
them. This type of sort requires a different method.

THE CHRONOLOGICAL SORT (before DOS 5)

In the standard directory listing, you see the file name and extension,
size, date and time. Each field starts in a particular column. For
example, the file-name extension begins in column 10. To sort on any
field other than File Name, you have to add a switch that tells DOS the
column on which you want the sort to begin.

   To sort files by date, you need to tell DOS that the Date field
begins in column 24.

HANDS-ON   Sort the files in a directory by date. In Figure 9-4, the files in the
\WP\LETTERS subdirectory are being sorted.

   Type: **DIR |SORT /+24** [Enter]

```
     .              <DIR>       01-17-93    12:21p
     . .            <DIR>       01-17-93    12:21p
    ACME2     LET     5316      03-08-93     3:55p
    DR_SMITH  MAR     1190      03-30-93    12:14p
    JUDY      MEM      450      04-07-93     9:53a
    EASTERLY  LET     3556      05-01-93     1:41p
    SURVEY    LET     4972      05-13-93     3:30p
    PURCHASE  LET     7301      05-14-93     4:39p
    REEVES    LET     3216      05-24-93    10:47a
    TOM       MEM      886      05-25-93     2:36p
    ACME1     LET     1174      05-26-93    10:32a
    PICNIC    MEM     1174      05-26-93    10:32a
    DR_SMITH  MAY     1898      05-26-93    10:52a
    OFFICE1   MEM     1898      05-26-93    10:52a
    DR_SMITH  JUN     9028      06-09-93     2:41p
    13122427            0       07-19-93     7:18p
    1312242D            0       07-19-93     7:18p
         17 file(s)         42059 bytes
                          8692629 bytes free
      Volume in drive C is OFFICE
      Volume Serial Number is 1A65-4A94
      Directory of  C:\WP\LETTERS
```

Figure 9-4: In this listing,
files are sorted chronologically
by date.

If you have lots of files, add the |MORE qualifier to make the screen pause each time it fills; for example, DIR |SORT /+24 |MORE.

Feeling Out of Sorts?

There's more. You can also sort by file-name extension and file size. The file-name extension begins in column 10 and the file size in column 13 (using column 13 allows for very large file sizes).

Unfortunately, sorting on the Time field (column 34) doesn't work; for example, it places 2:00p (PM) before 10:00a (AM).

THE CHRONOLOGICAL SORT (DOS 5 & higher)

In DOS 5 and higher, you can sort a DIR listing by date and time by adding the /O: (Order) switch and the letter D. So to get a chronological listing, one screen at a time, you would enter DIR /O:D /P.

If you want to list the files in reverse chronological order, use –D instead of D in the command, like this: DIR /O:-D /P.

OTHER DIR OPTIONS

DOS 5 and higher versions provide other ways of sorting a DIR listing using the /A: (Attribute) switch. The most useful version causes DIR to list either files only or subdirectories only.

To list only the subdirectories contained within the current directory, use D as the attribute, like this: DIR /A:D. To list only files, use –D instead of D in the command.

LISTING SELECTED FILES

Occasionally, you'll want to list a particular subset of files, such as your weekly report files or your monthly expense sheets. If you chose your file names carefully, you can list groups of files using wildcard characters. The asterisk (*) represents any number of characters, while the question mark (?) represents only one character.

LISTING FILES WITH A COMMON EXTENSION

To list all files with a common extension, use the * character as the file name.

HANDS-ON List a group of files that have the same extension. In Figure 9-5, all files in the \WP\LETTERS subdirectory that have the .MEM extension are being listed.

Type: **DIR *.MEM** ⏎Enter

```
Volume in drive C is OFFICE
Volume Serial Number is 1A65-4A94
Directory of  C:\WP\LETTERS

OFFICE1  MEM      1898  05-26-93  10:52a
PICNIC   MEM      1174  05-26-93  10:32a
JUDY     MEM       450  04-07-93   9:53a
TOM      MEM       886  05-25-93   2:36p
        4 file(s)        4408 bytes
                      8692629 bytes free
```

Figure 9-5: Directory listing of files having a common extension–in this case, .MEM.

LISTING FILES WITH A COMMON NAME

To list all files that have a common name, use the * character as the file extension.

HANDS-ON List a group of files that have the same name. Here, in Figure 9-6, all files in the \WP\LETTERS subdirectory that have the name DR_SMITH are being listed.

Type: **DIR DR_SMITH.*** ⏎Enter

```
Volume in drive C is OFFICE
Volume Serial Number is 1A65-4A94
Directory of  C:\WP\LETTERS

DR_SMITH MAR      1190  03-30-93  12:14p
DR_SMITH MAY      1898  05-26-93  10:52a
DR_SMITH JUN      9028  06-09-93   2:41p
        3 file(s)       12116 bytes
                      8692629 bytes free
```

Figure 9-6: Directory listing of all files with the name DR_SMITH.

TIP Also, you can use wildcards to list specific subgroups of files. For example, DIR F* will list all files that start with the letter F. And DIR *.? will list all files that have extensions of, at most, one character.

SAVING A LISTING IN A FILE

The screen isn't the only possible destination for a DIR listing. By sending the listing to a file, you'll have a permanent record of the contents of your disk at a particular time.

To save a DIR list, use the > character to redirect the output to a file.

HANDS-ON Save a directory listing in a file. Here, the DIR listing of the \WP\LETTERS subdirectory is being saved in a file called DEC93LET.DIR.

Type: **DIR > DEC93LET.DIR** [Enter]

Although DOS doesn't confirm it, this file is now a permanent record of the directory contents on the day it was saved.

Next month, you might create another file called JAN94LET.DIR. To further organize things, you could put all the monthly listings in a separate directory called \LISTS. Then, of course, you would need to include the full path, like this: DIR > \LISTS\JAN94LET.DIR.

Once the listing is saved in a file, you can even retrieve it into WordPerfect and add notes and comments. This feature will be covered in the section titled "Working With Non-WordPerfect Files" in Chapter 18 of *Office Companion.*

PRINTING A DIRECTORY LISTING

Sometimes you might want a printed copy of a particular directory listing. Instead of sending the listing to the screen or a file, you can send it to the printer.

To print a DIR listing, use the > character to redirect the output to the printer (abbreviated PRN).

HANDS-ON Send the listing of Drive A's Root directory to the printer.

Type: **DIR A: > PRN** [Enter]

The printed contents of the directory can be kept in the diskette jacket or taped to the diskette.

CHAPTER SUMMARY

■ The DIR command lists files in a specified directory.

■ Adding the /W switch creates a wide display that allows more file names per screen, and adding /P causes a long listing to pause each time it fills the screen.

■ With the DIR command, you can sort files by file name, extension, date or size.

■ Using the DIR command in DOS 5 and higher, you can list just directories (with the /A:D qualifier) or just files (with the /A: D qualifier).

■ To make a sorted listing pause after filling the screen, add the |MORE qualifier (in DOS 5 and higher, you can use /P).

■ To redirect a listing to a file, use the greater-than character (for example, DIR > LETTERS.DIR).

■ To redirect a listing to the printer, use the abbreviation PRN (for example, DIR > PRN).

Copying & Moving Files

Now that you're organizing your disk with directories and sub-directories, you'll want to know how to transfer files from one location to another. So in this chapter, you'll learn how to

- Copy single files and groups of files.
- Speed up the copying process.
- Copy files from a directory and all its subdirectories with one command.
- Copy entire diskettes.
- Move a file from one directory to another.

There are many reasons for making a copy of a file. You might want to make extensive changes to a file but retain the original version to refer to later. You might want to share your data with another person. Or you might want to make a backup copy "just in case."

Making copies is a fundamental skill you need to make effective use of your PC. For your convenience, DOS provides several commands, each for a different type of copying.

COPYING COMMANDS

The three commands for copying files discussed in this chapter are COPY, XCOPY and DISKCOPY.

COPY, the copying command with which most people are familiar, is good for copying single files or groups of files.

XCOPY (available in DOS 3.1 and higher) does what COPY does, but it's faster when copying groups of files. It also has some options that COPY doesn't have.

DISKCOPY is useful for copying all files from one diskette to another.

COPY and XCOPY can be used on both diskette and hard disk files, while DISKCOPY is for diskette files only. Two other copying commands, BACKUP and MSBACKUP, are for hard disk files only. These two commands will be discussed in Chapter 11, "Protecting Your Files."

THE COPY COMMAND

The COPY command allows you to copy one or more files either within a directory or to another directory.

Format: COPY filename *copy-filename*

Example: COPY PICNIC.MEM A:\PICNIC.COP

TIP If the original file or the copied file is not located in the current directory, you must specify the file's path.

Copying Within a Directory

When copying a file within a directory, you must give the copy a name that's different from the original name. And there's no need to specify the destination since it's the current directory.

HANDS-ON Make a copy of a file in the current directory. In Figure 10-1, the file AUG92.RPT is being copied and given the name (Just In Case).

Type: **COPY AUG92.RPT AUG92.JIC** [Enter]

Figure 10-1: A successful COPY command will always be followed by this message.

```
        1 file(s) copied
```

Copying to Another Directory

When you copy a file to another directory, you must specify a path telling DOS where to put the copy. If you don't give the copy a new name, DOS will give it the same name as the original.

HANDS-ON Copy a file to another drive. Here in Figure 10-2, the AUG92.RPT file is being copied to the Root directory of Drive A, and the copy will have the same name as the original.

Figure 10-2: Again, this message indicates that the COPY command was executed successfully.

Type: **COPY AUG92.RPT A:** [Enter]

```
        1 file(s) copied
```

HANDS-ON Copy a file to another directory on the current drive. In Figure 10-3, the file AUG92.RPT is being copied to the \123 directory, and the copy is named AUG_1992.RPT.

Type: **COPY AUG92.RPT \123\AUG_1992.RPT** [Enter]

Figure 10-3: The file has been successfully copied to another directory.

```
    1 file(s) copied
```

Copying More Than One File

Wildcard characters can be used to copy a group of files with one command. The files need to have something in common—for instance, the file name extension.

Copying Files With a Common Extension

HANDS-ON Copy a group of files that have the same extension. Here in Figure 10-4, all files that have the .RPT extension are being copied to Drive A.

Type: **COPY *.RPT A:** Enter

```
AUG93.RPT
3Q.RPT
2Q.RPT
1Q.RPT
MODEL.RPT
        5 file(s) copied
```

Figure 10-4: When you copy a group of files, DOS lists them as shown here.

Copying Files With a Common Name

HANDS-ON Copy a group of files that have the same name. In Figure 10-5, all files named DR_SMITH are being copied to Drive A.

Type: **COPY DR_SMITH.* A:** Enter

```
DR_SMITH.MAR
DR_SMITH.MAY
DR_SMITH.JUN
        3 file(s) copied
```

Figure 10-5: Copying files with a common name: again, DOS lists these files as it copies them.

Copying All Files

You can use *.* to indicate any file with any extension (in other words, all files in the current directory) when you want to copy all files from a directory.

THE XCOPY COMMAND

Instead of reading each file and then writing it, XCOPY reads as many files as it can hold in memory and then writes them all. So it's faster when copying groups of files. XCOPY is available in DOS 3.1 and higher.

Format: XCOPY filename *target copy-filename qualifiers*

Example: XCOPY EXPENSES.* A:

> **TIP** If the original file or the copied file is not located in the current directory, you must specify the file's path.

HANDS-ON Copy a group of files to another drive, using XCOPY. In Figure 10-6, all .LET files are being copied to Drive A.

Type: **XCOPY *.LET A:** Enter

```
Reading source file(s)...
ACME2.LET
SURVEY.LET
EASTERLY.LET
PURCHASE.LET
ACME1.LET
REEVES.LET
        6 file(s) copied
```

Figure 10-6: DOS lists files involved in an XCOPY command.

Using the Subdirectory Switch

The Subdirectory (/S) switch copies specified files from the current directory and its subdirectories.

HANDS-ON Copy files from a directory and its subdirectories, using XCOPY. Here, in Figure 10-7, all .MEM files from the current directory and its subdirectories are being copied to Drive A.

Type: **XCOPY *.MEM A: /S** Enter

```
Reading source file(s)...
FORMAT.MEM
LETTERS\OFFICE1.MEM
LETTERS\PICNIC.MEM
LETTERS\JUDY.MEM
LETTERS\TOM.MEM
        5 file(s) copied
```

Figure 10-7: DOS response to an XCOPY command with /S switch: again the affected files are listed.

Here it found one .MEM file in the current directory and four in the \WP\LETTERS subdirectory.

Using the Date Switch

The Date (/D:date) switch copies only the files that were created or modified on or after a specified date.

HANDS-ON Copy files that were created or modified after a particular date, using XCOPY. Here, all files in \WP\REPORTS that were created or modified after May 15, 1993, are being copied to the Root directory of Drive A.

Type: **XCOPY *.* A: /D:05-15-93** [Enter]

Figure 10-8: DOS response to an XCOPY command that includes the /D switch.

```
Reading source file(s)...
REVIEW.DOC
3Q.RPT
PURCHASE.93
        3 file(s) copied
```

Figure 10-8 shows that three files in the current directory were created or modified after May 15, 1993.

THE DISKCOPY COMMAND

The DISKCOPY command is used only for copying the contents of one diskette to another.

Format: DISKCOPY source-drive target-drive

Example: DISKCOPY A: B:

> **TIP** Unlike the other copying commands, **DISKCOPY** doesn't require that the target diskette be formatted.

Copying a Diskette

With the DISKCOPY command, you can read the "source" diskette and write on the "target" diskette using the same disk drive (see Figures 10-9 and 10-10).

HANDS-ON Using Drive A, diskcopy a diskette to a blank diskette. DOS will prompt you to switch diskettes at the appropriate times.

Type: **DISKCOPY A: A:** [Enter]

Figure 10-9: When you enter the DISKCOPY command, you'll be prompted to insert the "source" diskette.

```
Insert SOURCE diskette in drive A:

Press any key when ready  .  .  .
```

Figure 10-10: When DOS has read as much information as it can, you'll be prompted to insert the target diskette.

```
Insert TARGET diskette in drive A:

Press any key when ready . . .
```

Depending on your PC's memory, you may have to switch diskettes several times, so read the prompts carefully.

MOVING FILES

At long last, DOS (Version 6) includes a MOVE command. Twelve years in the making, this simple command moves one or more files from one directory to another. Optionally, you may rename a file when you move it.

Format: MOVE filename *new-filename* target

Example: MOVE REPORT.MAY \123\REPORTS

> **TIP** If the file is in the current directory, you don't need to specify its path. If you specify a new filename, the file will be renamed as it is moved to the target directory.

If you're using an older version of DOS, you can create your own MOVE command. The technique for this is explained in Chapter 14, "Personalizing Your PC."

CHAPTER SUMMARY

- The COPY command can be used to copy single files or groups of files.
- XCOPY does what COPY does, but it's faster when copying groups of files.
- XCOPY has two useful switches: /S copies the specified files from a directory and all of its subdirectories; /D:date copies files created on or after a particular date.
- When copying a file within a directory, you must give the copy a different name.
- The wildcard characters * and ? can be used to copy groups of related files.
- The DISKCOPY command will copy the contents of one diskette to another.
- The MOVE command (DOS 6) moves files from one directory to another.

Protecting Your Files

Because of the time and effort you spend creating files, it's crucial that you take steps to safeguard your work. In this chapter, you'll learn how to

- Protect files from accidental erasure.
- Avoid overwriting diskette files by formatting.
- Protect your PC hardware.
- Protect a file from being modified or erased.
- Use the BACKUP command to make copies of your hard disk files.
- Protect your data from computer viruses.

CHAPTER OVERVIEW

Files or portions of files can be lost through carelessness, poor planning or circumstances beyond your control, such as co-worker error or power interruption. In most cases, you can protect your files and thereby avoid the frustration of redoing hours or days of work.

Many people take the attitude, "It hasn't happened to me yet." But it will. Everyone loses work from time to time. It might be a little or a lot, depending on your work habits and your tolerance for pain.

ERASING A FILE

If you're using DOS 5 or higher, it's possible to recover an erased file using the UNDELETE command. But with earlier versions, if you erase a file, DOS won't let you retrieve it. If you need it at a later date, you'll experience a condition known as SOL (sorry, outta luck).

One solution is to buy a utility program that includes a file recovery command. This protection isn't foolproof, however, because an erased file is recoverable only if it hasn't been overwritten on the disk with new information. (The same is true of the UNDELETE command.)

REPLACING A FILE

When you create a file, you give it a name. Then when you update the file, you normally replace the old version with the new, keeping the same name. But what happens if you want the old version back? SOL. It's not that you weren't warned.

> **TIP** When you try to use a filename already in use, most programs ask if you're sure you want to replace the existing version of a file. So if there's a possibility you might want the original file again, save the updated version under a different name.

LOSING YOUR LATEST WORK

Occasionally, the power goes off. On a good day, it happens while you're having coffee. On a bad day, it happens when you're updating an important file. When the power goes off, you'll lose everything you typed since you last saved the file.

Here are three ways to limit the amount of data you lose:

- Save often while you're working—it takes only a few seconds.
- Use the automatic save feature when it's available in a program. (WordPerfect has this feature.)
- Buy a battery backup power supply to keep your PC running during a power outage.

TAMPERING BY UNAUTHORIZED USERS

If other people share your PC, unfortunate things can happen. If you think someone may have altered one of your files, do a DIR listing. If the date and time fields are more recent than they should be, your file may have been modified. The best protection against such an occurrence is to have a backup copy of each important file just in case.

The next best thing is to put a *password* on your file. Both Word-Perfect and 1-2-3 offer this feature. Of course, if you forget your password, there's absolutely no way to gain access to the file. Another problem is that even though the file cannot be opened without the password, it can be erased (by anyone) at the DOS prompt.

MAKING A FILE READ-ONLY

The ATTRIB command (DOS 3.0 and higher) allows you to change various attributes of a file. The most practical use of the command is to designate a file as "read-only," thereby preventing it from being modified or erased.

Format: ATTRIB qualifier filename

Example: ATTRIB +R REPORT.93

To change a file to read-only, use the +R qualifier. To return the file to normal, use the –R qualifier.

PROTECTING YOUR DISKETTES

You already know how to physically take care of a diskette. But what about taking care of the files on the diskette? If you're not careful, you can wipe out the contents through carelessness.

FORMATTING A DISKETTE THAT HAS FILES

When you format a diskette, any files on it will be erased. To protect against overwriting files in this way, you can do three things:

1. Always use the DIR A: command to check the diskette first.

2. Write-protect your diskettes. The small cutout on 5.25-inch diskettes is called the write-protect notch. To prevent DOS from writing anything on a diskette, cover the write-protect notch with one of the tabs that came with the diskette. When the notch is covered, you cannot add any new information to the diskette. If you need to add other files, you can remove the tab temporarily. This may be a little inconvenient, but at least it will prevent formatting an important diskette. Three-and-a-half-inch diskettes have a small switch instead of a cutout. To write-protect a diskette, slide the switch to the open position.

3. Label your diskettes. Without labels, formatted diskettes look just like unformatted ones.

PROTECTING YOUR PC

If your PC isn't working, your files aren't going to do you much good. So a few precautions are in order to keep your PC operational.

POWER SURGES

Your PC contains delicate circuitry that could be damaged if an intense electrical surge comes in through the power supply. To protect yourself against this disaster, plug all your components into a *surge protector*. This device cuts off the power when a potentially damaging electrical surge occurs. The higher-quality models have a convenient reset switch, while others have replaceable fuses.

> **TIP** Don't confuse a surge protector with a surge suppressor. A suppressor offers some protection, but cannot handle powerful surges. So, be sure you know what you're buying.

DIRTY HEADS

No, that's not the name of a new rock group. Dirty disk-drive heads can sometimes interfere with reading and writing to a diskette. So, buy a head cleaning kit and use it regularly.

HEAD CRASH

A head crash is the nightmare that every PC user fears. You try to boot up, but nothing happens. The files on your hard disk are no longer accessible. The only way to protect yourself from this disaster is to have backup copies of your files.

CREATING BACKUPS

Backup copies are your best protection against losing work. Earlier, you learned how to copy files using COPY, XCOPY and DISKCOPY. In this section, you'll learn about a command that copies hard disk files only. The way you back up hard-disk files depends on the version of DOS you're using.

BACKUPS BEFORE DOS 6

If you're using a version of DOS earlier than 6, you can use the BACKUP command to make backup copies of your files.

Format: BACKUP source-drive\directory target-drive *qualifiers*

Example: BACKUP C:\WP A:

Contrary to the usual custom, you must specify the source drive and directory even if they are the current ones.

The main advantages of BACKUP are

1. When DOS fills up one diskette, it asks you to insert another. It numbers the diskettes sequentially.

2. It stores files more compactly, thereby requiring fewer diskettes to store your files.

3. It has a number of useful switches that can save you time when backing up.

4. It can format each diskette if necessary.

Using the BACKUP Command

HANDS-ON   Back up all files from a subdirectory to Drive A. Here, all files in the C:\WP\LETTERS subdirectory are being backed up to a formatted diskette in Drive A. You'll get a warning message that any files on the diskette will be erased, as shown in Figure 11-1. So check the diskette for files before you do the backup.

Type: **BACKUP C:\WP\LETTERS A:** Enter

```
Insert backup diskette 01 in drive A:

Warning! Files in the target drive
A:\ root directory will be erased
Strike any key when ready


*** Backing up files to drive A: ***
Diskette Number: 01

\WP\LETTERS\ACME2.LET
\WP\LETTERS\SURVEY.LET
\WP\LETTERS\EASTERLY.LET
\WP\LETTERS\PURCHASE.LET
\WP\LETTERS\DR_SMITH.MAR
\WP\LETTERS\DR_SMITH.MAY
\WP\LETTERS\OFFICE1.MEM
\WP\LETTERS\ACME1.LET
\WP\LETTERS\REEVES.LET
\WP\LETTERS\DR_SMITH.JUN
\WP\LETTERS\PICNIC.MEM
\WP\LETTERS\JUDY.MEM
\WP\LETTERS\TOM.MEM
```

Figure 11-1: DOS's response to the BACKUP command.

What's on a Backup Diskette?

HANDS-ON   Look at the contents of the backup diskette.

Type: **DIR A:** Enter

```
Volume in drive A is BACKUP   001
Directory of   A:\

BACKUP   001     61339  12-17-93   4:33p
CONTROL  001       753  12-17-93   4:33p
         2 file(s)       62092 bytes
                       1121140 bytes free
```

Figure 11-2: Contents of the BACKUP diskette.

Now compare this listing with the DIR listing of the subdirectory you backed up (see Figure 11-3).

Type: **DIR \WP\LETTERS** [Enter]

```
Volume in drive C is OFFICE
Volume Serial Number is 1A65-4A94
Directory of   C:\WP\LETTERS
.              <DIR>       01-17-93   12:21p
..             <DIR>       01-17-93   12:21p
ACME1    LET    1174       05-26-93   10:32a
ACME2    LET    5316       03-08-93    3:55p
DR_SMITH JUN    9028       06-09-93    2:41p
DR_SMITH MAR    1190       03-30-93   12:14p
DR_SMITH MAY    1898       05-26-93   10:52a
EASTERLY LET    3556       05-01-93    1:41p
JUDY     MEM     450       04-07-93    9:53a
OFFICE1  MEM    1898       05-26-93   10:52a
PICNIC   MEM    1174       05-26-93   10:32a
PURCHASE LET    7301       03-14-93    4:39p
REEVES   LET    3216       05-24-93   10:47a
SURVEY   LET    4972       05-13-93    3:30p
TOM      MEM     886       05-25-93    2:36p
        17 file(s)        42059 bytes
                        8692629 bytes free
```

Figure 11-3: Contents of a non-BACKUP diskette.

On the backup diskette, DOS packs all files into a single file called BACKUP. Other information, such as file sizes and dates, is kept in another file called CONTROL. The extension .001 indicates that this is the first backup diskette.

TIP If you're using a DOS version earlier than 3.3, the backup files will be stored a little differently. But you write the command the same way.

Important Switches

The BACKUP command has several time-saving switches you'll find extremely useful.

/A Adds new files to a backup diskette without affecting the files already on the diskette.

/M Backs up only the files you've modified since your last backup.

/D:date Backs up only the files created on or after a specified date. For example: BACKUP C:\WP A:/D:12-15-92.

/F Formats each diskette before it starts copying (available in DOS 3.3 or higher). In DOS 4 and higher, formatting will be done automatically if necessary.

/S Backs up the specified files from the specified directory and its subdirectories.

/T:time Backs up only the files created on or after a specified time. For example: BACKUP C:\WP A:/T:12:30:00.

BACKUPS WITH DOS 6

The MSBACKUP command, available in DOS 6, replaces the BACKUP command. The new command combines improved backup capability with ease of use.

Format: MSBACKUP *setup-file qualifiers*

Example: MSBACKUP WEEKLY

Setup Files

With MSBACKUP, a *setup file* is a file that contains the settings for a particular backup routine—the names of the directories and files to be backed up, as well as the type of backup. To create a setup file, type MSBACKUP and the name you want for the setup file (for example, MSBACKUP WEEKLY). (DOS will add the extension .SET to the setup file name.) Then follow the onscreen prompts to select the backup type and the directories and files to include in that setup file.

Making Backups With MSBACKUP

To make backups in DOS 6 using the default setup file, just type MSBACKUP at the DOS prompt. To use one of your own setup files, type MSBACKUP, followed by your setup file name (for example, MSBACKUP WEEKLY). You will then see a menu of options. Then select Backup.

Then you will see a "dialog" screen that allows you to enter the following items:

1. The backup type. MSBACKUP lets you make three types of backups: a) Full: backs up all files or selected files; b) Incremental: backs up only those files that have been modified since your last Full or Incremental backup; c) Differential: backs up only those files that have been modified since your last Full backup.

2. The "From" location; that is, the location of the files to be backed up (for example, C:\).

3. The "To" location; that is, the location of the diskettes to which the hard disk files will be backed up (for example, drive A:).

After entering the specifications, select OK to perform the backup. For more about making backups, type HELP MSBACKUP at the DOS prompt.

RESTORING BACKED-UP FILES

Files on a BACKUP diskette aren't accessible with the RENAME, ERASE and DIR commands. To use files copied with BACKUP, you must first restore them on the hard disk.

BEFORE DOS 6

To restore files backed up with the BACKUP command (in versions before DOS 6), use the RESTORE command.

Format: RESTORE backup-drive target drive\directory

Example: RESTORE A: C:\WP\LETTERS

When you use RESTORE, DOS will prompt you to insert the first backup diskette and strike a key to continue. It then tells you the date on which the files were backed up. (See Figure 11-4.)

```
Insert backup diskette 01 in drive A:
Strike any key when ready


*** Files were backed up 06-30-1993 ***

*** Restoring files from drive A: ***
Diskette: 01
```

Figure 11-4: DOS prompts you to insert the first BACKUP diskette for restoration.

> **TIP** Note that files cannot be restored if the original files are still on the hard disk.

DOS 6

If you backed up files using the MSBACKUP command (DOS 6), you can easily restore the files if necessary. Simply enter the command MSBACKUP to display the Backup screen, and then select the Restore option. You will then see a screen on which you need to specify the backup set you want to restore, the "Restore From" location and the "Restore To" location.

OFF-SITE BACKUPS

Let's say you're a careful user who keeps current backups in the file cabinet in your office. Then let's say there's a fire, flood or other calamity—it doesn't happen often, but it does happen. If it does, can you afford to lose all your work? If not, it's a good idea to keep backups of very important files both in your office and at another location.

PROTECTING DATA FROM VIRUSES

Computer viruses are programs that are intentionally designed to disrupt other programs and destroy data. The effect of viruses can range from mildly annoying (for example, a message that appears periodically on the screen) to devastating (for example, an inaccessible hard disk). Because of the amount of work at risk, you owe it to yourself to protect your data from viruses.

> **TIP** DOS 6 introduced two data protection features: Anti-Virus and VSafe.

ANTI-VIRUS

The Anti-Virus program scans your PC's memory and disk drives for viruses. The program can detect more than 1,000 different viruses that can infect your PC.

Format: MSAV *drive qualifiers*

Example: MSAV /C

If you don't specify a drive, Anti-Virus will scan the current drive. Some of the more useful qualifiers that you can use with MSAV are:

/C Scans for and removes viruses.

/S Scans for, but does not remove, viruses.

/R Creates a report showing the number of files checked, viruses found, and viruses removed. The report is named MSAV.RPT and is placed in the root directory. (You can view it by typing TYPE MSAV.RPT.)

/A Scans all drives except A and B.

/P Displays the Anti-Virus screen using a command-line interface instead of a graphical interface.

> **TIP** To have your disk scanned automatically when you boot your PC, add the MSAV command to your AUTOEXEC.BAT file (explained in Chapter 13, "Increasing the Power of Your PC").

VSAFE

VSafe is a program that scans *continuously* for viruses. Unlike Anti-Virus, VSafe is always active. As with any memory-resident program, it requires a portion of your RAM to operate (44 kilobytes, to be exact).

If VSafe detects a potential virus threat, it will display a warning message.

Format: VSAFE *qualifiers*

Example: VSAFE

If you enter the command VSAFE without qualifiers, the program's default settings will be used. To see which VSafe features are active, press Alt-V.

> **TIP** If you need to remove VSafe from memory, press Alt-V to display the VSafe screen, and then press Alt-U. Alternatively, you may type VSAFE /U at the DOS prompt.

To save yourself some typing, you can include the VSAFE command in your AUTOEXEC.BAT file (explained in Chapter 13, "Increasing the Power of Your PC").

CHAPTER SUMMARY

■ When a diskette's write-protect notch is covered, data cannot be written onto the diskette. This precaution can prevent accidental formatting of a diskette that has important files.

■ Surge protectors can minimize the possibility of damage to your PC in the event of an intense electrical surge.

■ The BACKUP command stores hard disk files on diskettes using a space-saving format. In DOS 6, the command is MSBACKUP.

■ Several useful switches are available with BACKUP. /A adds new files to an existing backup diskette; /M backs up only files that have been modified since the last backup; /D:date and /T:time back up only files that were created on or after a specified date or time; /F formats each diskette before the files are copied (no switch is needed in DOS 4 or higher); and /S backs up files from all subdirectories within the specified directory.

■ The RESTORE command restores files that were backed up using the BACKUP command.

■ The MSAV command activates Anti-Virus, a program that scans your PC's memory for viruses.

■ The VSAFE command activates VSafe, a memory-resident program that scans continuously for virus threats.

Letting DOS
Do the Typing

DOS
12

Taking control of your PC means letting DOS do the work for you. So in this chapter, you'll learn how to

■ Repeat commands using function keys.
■ Specify a long path by typing a short name.
■ Automate commands you use often.
■ Store sequences of commands that DOS will type for you.

You can communicate with a PC in a number of ways. Depending on your system, you may be able to select menu items with a mouse, draw with a digitizing tablet, or enter commands by touching the screen. But, by far, the most common means of communicating with your PC is through the keyboard.

JUST YOUR TYPE

You type letters and memos. You type spreadsheet data. You type DOS commands. Type, type, type. If only there were a way to avoid some of this typing.

Well, you'll be glad to know there are several ways to make DOS do some of the typing for you, and we'll focus on four of them in this chapter. Later in the book, you'll learn how to do the same in Word-Perfect and Lotus 1-2-3. With a little planning, you can not only save yourself time and effort, but also minimize errors.

FOUR WAYS TO AVOID TYPING

DOS provides four ways to save you time and effort at the keyboard:

Function keys F1, F2 and F3: These keys can be used to retype all or some of the last command you entered.

SUBSTITUTE command: It lets you call any path by a drive letter name. For example, \123\EXPENSES could be called E:.

Doskey feature: In DOS 5 and higher, it allows you to "type" recently executed commands just by pressing a single key.

Batch files: These are the most useful ways to automate typing in DOS. You store often-used commands in them; then when you type the name of the batch file, DOS executes all the commands listed in that file.

USING FUNCTION KEYS

It's common to make typing errors when entering DOS commands. Instead of typing the entire command again, you can use the F1, F2 and F3 keys to make DOS do most of the work for you.

THE F2 KEY

The F2 key repeats the last command up to a character you specify. So let's say you entered COPY 2Q.RPT A: to copy a file to Drive A. If you then wanted to copy the same file to the \123 directory on Drive C, you could press F2 and type the letter A. DOS would display COPY 2Q.RPT. Then you could complete the command by typing \123.

THE F3 KEY

The F3 key repeats the entire last command you entered.

HANDS-ON Try to copy a file to Drive A, but don't specify the destination for the copy. Here, in Figure 12-1, the file 2Q.RPT is being copied.

Type: **COPY 2Q.RPT** Enter

Figure 12-1: You'll get this error message following the incorrect command.

```
File cannot be copied onto itself
        0 file(s) copied
```

Figure 12-2: Pressing the F3 key causes DOS to retype the last command that was entered.

Now, instead of retyping, press F3. (See Figure 12-2.)

```
C:\WP\REPORTS>COPY 2Q.RPT
```

Now you have a chance to add a space and then A: Enter to complete the command.

THE F1 KEY

The F1 key repeats the last command one letter at a time. So, if you mistakenly entered COPU 2Q.RPT A:, you could press F1 three times, type Y and then press F3 to complete the command.

THE SUBSTITUTE COMMAND

Writing long paths in commands can be tedious if you do it often. With the SUBSTITUTE command, you can "name" a path (in DOS 3.1 and higher). The name must be like a drive name, for example, E:.

Format: SUBST drive-name path

Example: SUBST D: \WP\LETTERS

You probably can't go beyond Drive E right now; but in Chapter 13, you'll learn how to make other drive names available.

USING SUBST

HANDS-ON   Substitute the name E: for a subdirectory path. Here, E: is being substituted for the path \123\EXPENSES.

Type: **SUBST E: \123\EXPENSES** `Enter`

Now when you need to use the \123\EXPENSES path, you can substitute E:. For example, DIR E: would list all files in that subdirectory. Keep in mind that when you turn off your PC, the substitution won't be saved.

THE DOSKEY FEATURE

In DOS 5 and higher, a utility program called Doskey stores the commands you type in a list. If you need to use a command that you used earlier, you can simply page through the list until the command is displayed, and then press Enter.

Format: DOSKEY *qualifiers*

Example: DOSKEY

Once you load the Doskey program (by typing DOSKEY at the prompt), you can use the following keys to display commands you've already typed:

Up/Down arrow	Displays the previous/next command.
Page Up/Down	Displays the first/last command.
Esc	Clears a command shown at the prompt.
Alt F7	Erases the existing command list and begins a new one.

To save yourself some trouble, you can add the command DOSKEY to your AUTOEXEC.BAT file (see Chapter 13, "Increasing the Power of Your PC").

BATCH FILES

Let's say that for the next few weeks or so, you'll be working mostly in WordPerfect on a large document called 4Q_FIN.RPT. Since the file is in the \WP\REPORTS subdirectory, each time you want to work on it you'll have to type WP \WP\REPORTS\4Q_FIN.RPT to start the program and go directly to that file.

Every day, you'll have to retype this lengthy command. Or will you?

LET DOS DO IT

For any command or sequence of commands, DOS will do the typing for you. You need to type the commands only once, then save them as a file. When you're ready for DOS to type the commands, you just enter the name of the file.

This type of file is called a *batch file*. When you name it, you must give it a .BAT extension to tell DOS that the file contains commands that are to be executed in sequence.

> **TIP** A batch file takes only a minute to create. But once you've done it, it will pay off every time you use your PC.

USES FOR BATCH FILES

Batch files can be created for any command or sequence of commands. Following are three of the most useful applications of batch files.

Starting a Program

The previous illustration showed how to go directly into a Word-Perfect file that's located in a subdirectory. To save some typing, you can put the command in a simple batch file called WP1.BAT. Then, to execute the command, just type WP1, and DOS will start WordPerfect and retrieve the file.

Time-Savers

If you use certain commands frequently, you can automate them with batch files. For example, if you routinely copy all of your correspondence files to a diskette in Drive A, you can put the command COPY C:\WP\LETTERS*.* A: in a batch file called CL.BAT. Whenever you want to copy those files, you simply type CL.

Initial Settings

When you boot your PC, it doesn't remember anything from your last work session. So, if you want your prompt, path and other settings to be the way they were yesterday, you have to enter them all over again. But by putting these commands in a special batch file that's called AUTOEXEC.BAT, DOS will automatically enter these commands for you during boot-up. The AUTOEXEC.BAT file will be discussed further in Chapter 13, "Increasing the Power of Your PC."

PUTTING BATCH FILES IN THEIR PLACE

To get really organized, you can put all your batch files (except the AUTOEXEC.BAT file, discussed in the next chapter) into a separate directory called \BATCH. If you do, you need to give DOS access to that directory. So enter a new PATH command that includes the \BATCH directory, like this: PATH \;\DOS;\BATCH (or include the command in your AUTOEXEC.BAT file). See Chapter 6 for more information on the PATH command.

CREATING SIMPLE BATCH FILES

The quick way to create a batch file is to use a variation of the COPY command. Here, you tell DOS to copy the keystrokes you type on the console (the keyboard) into a file. To create a batch file, you must give the file a .BAT extension.

Format: COPY CON filename

Example: COPY CON TEST.BAT

The two following examples illustrate how to create batch files.

A BATCH FILE FOR STARTING A PROGRAM

HANDS-ON Create a batch file that starts WordPerfect and brings up a particular file. Here, the file will be 4Q_FIN.RPT (located in the \WP\REPORTS subdirectory). Start in the Root directory.

Type: **COPY CON WP1.BAT** [Enter]

The DOS prompt disappears. You can now enter the command needed to start WordPerfect and load the file. When you're finished, press F6 to indicate the end of the file, and then Enter to bring back the DOS prompt.

Type: **WP \WP\REPORTS\4Q_FIN.RPT** [Enter]

Press: **F6**

Press: [Enter]

The batch file is now complete. You can test it by going to any directory and typing WP1 [Enter]. Keep in mind that you created this executable file in the Root directory. So DOS can find it only if you have entered a PATH command that includes the Root. If you haven't entered such a PATH command, type PATH \;\DOS. For a refresher on the PATH command, you might want to review Chapter 6.

BATCH FILES FOR FREQUENTLY USED COMMANDS

HANDS-ON Put a commonly used DOS command in a batch file. Here, the command COPY \WP\LETTERS*.* A: is being saved in a batch file called CL.BAT.

Type: **COPY CON CL.BAT** [Enter]

Again, the DOS prompt disappears. Now enter the command.

Type: **COPY \WP\LETTERS*.* A:** [Enter]

Press: **F6**

Press: [Enter]

Now to copy all the files in the \WP\LETTERS subdirectory to Drive A, you just have to type CL.

> **TIP** A disadvantage of COPY CON: The COPY CON command doesn't warn you if you're about to use a file name that already exists. So always use the DIR command to check for a particular file name before using it in a COPY CON command. Also, you can't edit the file using COPY CON.

OTHER WAYS TO CREATE BATCH FILES

For more flexibility in creating your batch files, you might want to try any of the following three methods:

- Create the file in WordPerfect (or other word processing program) and save it as a "nondocument"; that is, as an ASCII file.
- Create the file using EDLIN, the DOS Line Editor. EDLIN is like a very crude word processor.
- Create the file using the DOS Editor (available in DOS 5 and higher). Editor is a full-screen, easy-to-use text editor.

USING WORDPERFECT

To create a new batch file in WordPerfect 6.0, open a new document, then

1. Type one command per line.

2. Press F10 (Save As), and specify ASCII as the file format, to save the batch file.

If you're using an earlier version of WordPerfect:

1. Type one command per line.

2. Press Ctrl-F5 (Text In), then select 1 (DOS Text), then 1 (Save) to save the file.

To edit an existing batch file in WordPerfect 6.0, simply retrieve it using Shift-F10 (Retrieve). If you're using an earlier version of the program, press Ctrl-F5 (Text In), then select 1 (DOS Text), then 2 (Retrieve (CR/LF to [HRt])) to retrieve the file.

USING DOS EDITOR

To create a new batch file in the DOS Editor (available in DOS 5 and higher), type EDIT followed by the name you want to give the new file (or the name of an existing file). For example, EDIT AUTOEXEC.BAT. You'll see the Editor screen. To create a batch file, simply type one command per line, then

1. Press Alt to activate the menu.

2. Press F to select the FILE command.

3. Press S to select the SAVE command. Then type the file name and press Enter.

4. When you're finished, open the File menu and press X to exit the Editor.

Note: Editor will not work unless DOS can find the file QBASIC.EXE.

USING EDLIN

Since the WordPerfect and Editor methods are so easy, you'll probably want to use them to create and edit batch files. But for those who want to use EDLIN, here's how to do it.

At the prompt, type EDLIN followed by the file name (for example, EDLIN AUTOEXEC.BAT). If the file exists, you will see the message "End of input file" and the EDLIN prompt (*). If the file is new, you will see "New file" and the prompt.

EDLIN Commands

At the EDLIN prompt (*), you can use any of the following commands to edit your file.

To list the file, enter L.

To insert a new line at the bottom of the file, enter I. Then enter your new line. EDLIN will then automatically give you another new line. If you don't want to add another line, press Ctrl-C to return to the * prompt.

To insert a line within the file, enter the line number followed by I, such as 3I.

To delete a line, enter the line number followed by D, such as 7D.

To modify a line, enter the line number, such as 6. You'll see the current line and below it a space for you to type the new version of the line.

To exit EDLIN and save the file, enter E.

CHAPTER SUMMARY

- The F1 key repeats the last command one character at a time. The F2 key repeats the last command up to a character you specify. The F3 key repeats the entire last command you entered.
- The SUBST command lets you substitute a drive name (such as E:) for a path.
- A batch file consists of one or more commands that DOS will execute, in sequence, when you enter the name of the file.
- A batch file must have a .BAT extension.
- You can create a batch file using the COPY CON method; Editor (in DOS 5 and higher); the EDLIN line editor; or WordPerfect (or most other word processors).
- You can't edit an existing file using COPY CON.

Increasing the Power of Your PC

There's more to DOS than just file manipulation commands such as ERASE and COPY. DOS also provides several ways to enhance the speed and efficiency of your PC. So in this chapter, you'll learn how to

■ Have DOS set up your system the way you want it each time you boot up.

■ Modify the characteristics of your screen and keyboard.

■ Speed up DOS's access to your files.

PERFORMANCE ENHANCERS

You can expand your PC's capabilities with some special DOS files and commands that increase speed, efficiency and convenience.

The AUTOEXEC.BAT file is a special batch file that's read during boot-up. In it, you can put any commands you want DOS to execute, thereby saving the trouble of typing them yourself. For example, you can include a PROMPT command, a PATH command and other useful setup instructions.

The CONFIG.SYS file, another special file that's read during boot-up, can include commands that determine how efficiently your PC handles the flow of information through the system.

The ANSI (American National Standards Institute) system extends your control over your PC. You make it available to DOS by including a special command in the CONFIG.SYS file. Once the ANSI system is activated, you'll be able to customize your video screen and your keyboard to suit your taste.

THE AUTOEXEC.BAT FILE

The most important batch file you can have is the AUTOEXEC.BAT file. Located in the Root directory, this batch file is read automatically when you boot your PC. So, any commands you type each day (for example, the PROMPT command) can be entered automatically by DOS.

If you don't have an AUTOEXEC.BAT file, you can create it using any of the methods explained in the previous chapter. If you already have one, you can edit it using EDLIN, DOS Editor or WordPerfect.

> **TIP** When you create or modify the AUTOEXEC.BAT file, keep in mind that the commands won't be executed until you type AUTOEXEC and press Enter, or until you reboot.

A TYPICAL AUTOEXEC.BAT FILE

A typical AUTOEXEC.BAT file, as shown in Figure 13-1, might include these commands:

Figure 13-1: The AUTOEXEC.BAT is your most important file.

```
PATH C:\;\DOS;\BATCH;\WP;\123;\MOUSE
PROMPT $P$G
GRAPHICS LASERJETII
DOSKEY
FASTOPEN C:
CLS
```

PATH: Directs DOS to search other directories if it can't find the executable files it needs in the current directory. Executable files have the extensions .COM, .EXE or .BAT. These files include the DOS commands (like FORMAT.COM) and commands that start programs (like 123.EXE and WP.EXE). Use a semicolon (;) after each path.

Example: PATH C:\;\DOS;\BATCH;\WP;\123;\MOUSE

This example makes it possible to use DOS commands and your own batch files from any directory. It also lets you start WordPerfect and Lotus 1-2-3 from any directory.

PROMPT: Determines the DOS prompt.

Example: PROMPT PG

This example causes DOS to display the current directory and the greater than (>) symbol.

GRAPHICS: Enables you to print graphics screens by pressing Shift-PrtSc. Without this command, Shift-PrtSc will effectively print only text screens.

Example: GRAPHICS LASERJETII

This example specifies a Hewlett Packard LaserJet II printer. Other widely used printer types include GRAPHICS (for the IBM Personal Graphics Printer, Proprinter and Quietwriter printer) and LASERJET (for the Hewlett Packard LaserJet).

DOSKEY: In DOS 5 and higher, this command tells DOS to load the Doskey program, a utility that remembers the commands you type (explained in Chapter 12, "Letting DOS Do the Typing").

Example: DOSKEY

This example loads the Doskey program.

FASTOPEN: This command instructs DOS to keep track of the directories and files you have recently accessed. For a directory or file that you access repeatedly, DOS will be able to locate it more quickly.

Example: FASTOPEN C:

This example improves the performance of the hard drive (Drive C). If your PC uses extended memory, use the command SMARTDRV instead of FASTOPEN C:. SMARTDRV activates a program called SMARTDrive (available in DOS 6).

CLS: Clears the screen of all text except the DOS prompt.

THE CONFIG.SYS FILE

The way your PC is set up to operate is called the system configuration. To modify the standard configuration, you need to modify a file called CONFIG.SYS. In it, you may include commands that will enhance your PC's performance. In this section, you'll learn four of these commands.

> **TIP** To see your CONFIG.SYS file, go to your Root directory and type TYPE CONFIG.SYS. It will probably look similar to the one shown in Figure 13-2. If you want to modify the file, use any of the methods explained in the previous chapter--the COPY CON method, EDLIN, DOS Editor or WordPerfect. Just remember to reboot your PC after making changes to the CONFIG.SYS file.

A TYPICAL CONFIG.SYS FILE

The CONFIG.SYS file must be located in the Root directory. Since it's read only at start-up, be sure to reboot your system after you edit the file. A typical file might include the commands shown in Figure 13-2.

```
DEVICE=C:\DOS\SETVER.EXE
DEVICE=C:\DOS\ANSI.SYS
FILES=20
SHELL=C:\DOS\COMMAND.COM C:\DOS /P
LASTDRIVE=H
```

Figure 13-2: A typical CONFIG.SYS file.

The DEVICE Command

The DEVICE command loads special programs called *drivers* that extend the command range of DOS.

The ANSI.SYS driver enables your PC to make use of the ANSI system described at the beginning of this chapter. By having it in your CONFIG.SYS file, you'll be able to modify the characteristics of your monitor and keyboard. (These techniques are discussed in Chapter 14, "Personalizing Your PC.")

You must tell DOS where to find the ANSI.SYS file. If it's in \DOS, the command is DEVICE=C:\DOS\ANSI.SYS. If it's in the Root directory, the command is DEVICE=C:\ANSI.SYS.

The FILES Command

Sophisticated software programs often need to work with a number of files simultaneously. To accommodate them, you can use the FILES command to tell DOS how many files it should allow open at any given time. While the optimum setting is different for different programs, a value of 20 is generally accepted as a good setting. The command is FILES=20.

The SHELL Command

The SHELL command specifies the name and location of the DOS Command Interpreter (COMMAND.COM). The command is needed if COMMAND.COM is not in the Root directory.

The LASTDRIVE Command

This command extends the number of drive names you can use in SUBSTITUTE commands (available in DOS 3 and higher). The SUBSTITUTE command is discussed in Chapter 12.

Format: LASTDRIVE=drive

Example: LASTDRIVE=H

Contrary to the usual rule, you must not include a colon after the drive name. And don't use more drive names than you need–they take up memory.

BYPASSING THE CONFIG.SYS FILE

If you experience problems when you boot your PC, the source might be one of the commands in your CONFIG.SYS file. In DOS 6, you can bypass the CONFIG.SYS file at startup. When the message "Starting MS-DOS..." appears on the screen, either hold down the Shift key or press and release the F5 key. This technique also causes DOS to bypass the AUTOEXEC.BAT file.

CHAPTER SUMMARY

- The AUTOEXEC.BAT file is read when you boot your PC; any commands it contains will be executed automatically.

- AUTOEXEC.BAT must be located in the Root directory.

- The FASTOPEN command enables DOS to get to recently accessed directories and files more quickly. If your PC has extended memory, use the SMARTDRV command instead.

- The CONFIG.SYS file allows you to modify your system's configuration to improve performance.

- After making changes to either the AUTOEXEC.BAT or CONFIG.SYS file, you must reboot to make those changes effective.

- The ANSI system, activated in the CONFIG.SYS file, extends your control over your video display and your keyboard.

Personalizing
Your PC

There are many ways to make your personal computer more personal. These techniques allow you to customize your PC so that it "fits" you a little better. So in this chapter, you will learn how to

- Create a useful "new" DOS command that moves files.
- Customize your DIR command.
- Adjust your video display to suit your preferences.
- Make function keys perform commands.

> **TIP** All the techniques discussed here are optional. You can certainly be a productive PC user without them. But they're fun, and they may add to your enjoyment while you're working on your PC.

USING THE ANSI SYSTEM

In Chapter 13, you learned how to access the ANSI system by having the command DEVICE=C:\DOS\ANSI.SYS in your CONFIG.SYS file. Because it's there, you can now do some clever things with your monitor and keyboard. Specifically, the ANSI system enables you to

- Control various attributes of your video display, including color, boldface, reverse video and others.
- Redefine the functions of particular keys so that they execute DOS commands.

These techniques require a special version of the PROMPT command that works only if the ANSI system is available.

USING BATCH FILES

Now that you know how to create batch files, you can use them for some interesting applications, such as

■ Creating a useful MOVE command.
■ Automating frequently used commands.

CREATING A NEW DOS COMMAND

DOS has lots of useful commands, but it doesn't do everything you'd like. By using batch files, you can create commands that the writers of DOS left out.

MAKING A MOVE.BAT COMMAND

DOS 6 lets you move a file from one directory to another at the DOS prompt. But earlier versions of DOS don't. That's OK—you can fake it. What you can do is write a batch file called MOVE.BAT that will do four things:

1. Copy the files from the current directory to a directory that you specify.

2. List the files in the target directory so you can verify that the files were copied without problem.

3. Give you the choice of continuing or ending the operation before the original files are erased.

4. Erase the files from the original directory.

HANDS-ON   If you're using a DOS version earlier than 6, create a MOVE command.

Type: **COPY CON MOVE.BAT** Enter

The prompt disappears. Now type these commands, one per line:

COPY %1 %2 Enter

DIR %2\%1 /P Enter

PAUSE Press Enter to continue, Ctrl-C to interrupt. Enter

ERASE %1 Enter

Then press F6 and Enter to complete the file.

The percent characters are replaceable names. In their places, DOS will use the names you give it in the MOVE command. So, if you enter MOVE *.RPT \123, DOS will use *.RPT as item 1 (%1), and the directory \123 as item 2 (%2). The PAUSE command gives you a chance to change your mind.

AUTOMATING MISCELLANEOUS COMMANDS

If you often list your files alphabetically, which would you rather type: DIR /O:N /P or DIRA?

By putting long commands in batch files with short names, you can save yourself some typing. Here are a few good candidates for this technique (using commands available in DOS 5 and higher).

Batch File	Command	Function Name
FORV.BAT	FORMAT A: /V	Formats the diskette in Drive A and lets you add a volume label.
DIRA.BAT	DIR /O:N /P	Lists all files in the current directory alphabetically.
DIRD.BAT	DIR /O:D /P	Lists files in chronological order.

TIP To keep things organized, you can put these batch files in the \BATCH directory you created earlier.

CUSTOMIZING YOUR DIR COMMAND

DOS 5 introduced the option of customizing the DIR (Directory) command. Let's say you usually want to see files listed alphabetically, one screen at a time. So you have to type DIR /O:N /P each time. But you can tell DOS to use that command each time you type just DIR.

In your AUTOEXEC.BAT file, add this line (be sure to reboot after making this change):

SET DIRCMD=/O:N /P

Now, each time you type DIR, DOS will execute DIR /O:N /P. To reset the DIR command back to normal for the rest of a work session, just type SET DIRCMD= at the prompt and press Enter.

REDEFINING KEYS

If you like the idea of having DOS do the typing for you, you can assign DOS commands to the function keys. The command DEVICE=C:\DOS\ANSI.SYS in your CONFIG.SYS file makes this possible. (See Chapter 13 for an explanation of ANSI.SYS.)

To redefine a key's function, you use a special version of the PROMPT command. The command must begin with *PROMPT $e[0;* and end with *;13p.* In between, you must specify the key's ANSI code (a two-digit number, described below) and the DOS command you're assigning to the key.

Format: PROMPT $e[0;code; "command";13p

Example: PROMPT $e[0;93; "FORMAT A:";13p

Use a zero, not a capital O; and use lowercase letters for e and p. Because of the Shift, Ctrl and Alt key combinations, you have access to a total of 40 function keys. The ANSI redefinition codes for those keys are

59-68 for F1 through F10.

84-93 for Shift-F1 through Shift-F10.

94-103 for Ctrl-F1 through Ctrl-F10.

104-113 for Alt-F1 through Alt-F10.

HANDS-ON Assign a DOS command to a function key. Here, the command DIR /P is being assigned to the F7 (code 65) key.

Type: **PROMPT $e[0;65;"DIR /P";13p** `Enter`

If you entered the command correctly, DOS will return the prompt without any confirmation.

Now test it by pressing F7. *Voila*—isn't that wonderful! Just keep in mind that some programs reset the function keys, so you may have to enter the PROMPT command again after exiting a program.

TIP You must enter a separate command for each key you want to redefine. To make things easy, you can put the redefinition commands in your AUTOEXEC.BAT file.

CONTROLLING YOUR VIDEO DISPLAY

The ANSI system gives you extended control over your monitor as well as your keyboard. Although a complete discussion of these techniques is beyond the scope of this book, we can try a few of them. To modify your video display, you must enter a special version of the PROMPT command similar to the one used to redefine keys. Here, the command begins with *PROMPT $e[* and ends with *m.* In between, you put a code number (explained below) that determines the screen attribute.

Format: PROMPT $e[codem

Example: PROMPT $e[7m

Note that the letters e and m must be lowercase.

The *code* is the ANSI code number for screen attributes. Some of the codes that you can use are

0 All attributes off

1 Bold

5 Blinking

7 Reverse video

HANDS-ON Cause the DOS prompt to appear in bold letters (note that "0" in the command is a *zero*).

Type: **PROMPT $e[1m$p$g $e[0m** [Enter]

Figure 14-1: A special version of the PROMPT command tells DOS to display your standard prompt in boldface.

```
C:\>
```

This command turns on the boldface ($e[1m), displays the standard prompt (pg) and then turns off the boldface ($e[0m) as shown in Figure 14-1. You may need to adjust the brightness of your monitor to see the effect.

HANDS-ON Display directory listings in reverse video.

To automate this technique, write a simple batch file called DIRX.BAT that will turn on the reverse video, execute the DIR command, and then turn off the reverse video. Include these commands in the batch file:

PROMPT $e[7m

DIR/P

PROMPT $e[0m pg

Now when you type DIRX [Enter], you'll see the directory listing shown in Figure 14-2.

```
C:\>prompt $e[ 7m

dir

Volume in drive C has no label
Volume Serial Number is 1A65-4A94
Directory of C:\OFFICE

.                <DIR>       01-17-93   12:46p
..               <DIR>       01-17-93   12:46p
123              <DIR>       01-17-93   12:46p
WP               <DIR>       01-17-93   12:47p
DOS              <DIR>       01-17-93   12:47p
AUTOEXEC BAT        63       01-17-93    9:33a
CONFIG   SYS        46       01-17-93   12:50p
        7 file(s)              99 bytes
                          4818944 bytes free

prompt $e[ 1m$p$g $e[ 0m

C:\>
C:\>
```

Figure 14-2: This is how the directory listing looks in reverse video.

If you like this effect, you can put this command in your AUTOEXEC.BAT file. If you do, put it *after* any key redefinition commands that you have.

Keep in mind that a video feature will remain in effect until you enter a different PROMPT command that turns off the feature.

CHANGING COLORS

If you have a color monitor, you can also control the screen's colors. Refer to your DOS *User's Guide* for more information.

CHAPTER SUMMARY

■ Using replaceable names in batch files enables you to create "new" commands.

■ To save keystrokes, you can put long commands in batch files with short names.

■ The SET DIRCMD= command lets you customize the DIR command (DOS 5 and higher).

■ Activating the ANSI system in your CONFIG.SYS file allows you to customize your monitor and keyboard.

■ Special versions of the PROMPT command are needed to modify the characteristics of your video display and to assign DOS commands to individual function keys.

Using the DOS Shell

With earlier versions of DOS, you could manage your programs and files in only one way—by typing commands at the prompt. The DOS Shell, introduced in version 4, gives you another way: it allows you to select commands and files from organized lists. Using the Shell might save you some time and effort. So in this chapter, you'll learn how to

- Load the DOS Shell program.
- Perform routine DOS operations with or without a mouse.
- Load WordPerfect and Lotus 1-2-3 from the Shell.
- Get help with Shell functions.

UNDERSTANDING THE SHELL PROGRAM

Let's load the Shell and see what it's all about. (See Figure 15-1.)

HANDS-ON Load the Shell program.

Type: **DOSSHELL** Enter

> **TIP** If you want to load the Shell each time you boot up, you can put the DOSSHELL command in your AUTOEXEC.BAT file.

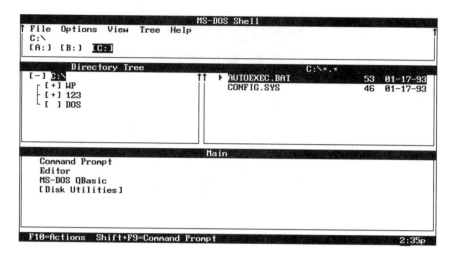

Figure 15-1: The DOS Shell.

HOW THE SHELL IS ORGANIZED

The Shell is initially divided into a Menu Bar and four areas (which I'll call windows):

The *Menu Bar* is shown at the top of the screen. It gives you access to DOS commands and Shell options. To activate the Menu Bar, press F10; to leave it, press Esc.

The top window has no name, so let's call it the *Top window*. Here, you see the current drive and directory as well as the drive icons (A:, B: and C:).

The *Directory Tree window* shows how your directories and subdirectories are organized on the current drive. Directories marked with + contain one or more subdirectories.

The *Files window* (presently labelled C:*.*) lists all files in the current directory.

The *Main window* lists the Command Prompt option (for exiting the Shell temporarily) and several utility programs.

In each window, a highlight bar is used to identify the command or file you want to use.

BASIC SKILLS

Moving the Cursor

If you're using a mouse, you move the cursor (the small arrow) in the Shell by dragging the mouse. If you're not using a mouse, you move the cursor from one window to another with the Tab key, and within a window with the arrow keys (Up, Down, Left and Right).

Selecting an Item

In the Shell, you'll be selecting files, commands, disk drives and other items. If you're using a mouse, you select an item by pointing to it and clicking or double-clicking the left mouse button. If you're using the keyboard, you select an item by moving the cursor or highlight bar to the item and pressing Enter.

Opening a Menu

To open a menu, point to a menu name and click the left mouse button. If you're not using a mouse, first press F10 to activate the Menu Bar. Then move the highlight bar to the desired menu name and press Enter. You can also select a menu by typing its highlighted letter (displayed in a contrasting shade or color).

Once a menu is open, you may select a command. Commands that are not available will be dimmed or invisible.

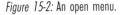 Open the HELP menu.

Press: **F10**

Type: **H**

Figure 15-2 shows the open Help menu. When you're ready to close the menu, press Esc.

```
                          MS-DOS Shell
↑ File   Options   View   Tree  Help                                    ↑
  C:\
  [A:]  [B:]  [C:]            ┌──────────────┐
                             │ Index        │
  ┌────Directory Tree────    │ Keyboard     │         C:\*.*
  [-] C:\                     │ Shell Basics │────────────────────────
   ┌ [+] WP                   │ Commands     │ UTOEXEC.BAT    53  01-17-91
   │ [+] 123                  │ Procedures   │ ONFIG.SYS      46  01-17-91
   └ [ ] DOS                  │ Using Help   │
                             │              │
                             │ About Shell  │
                             └──────────────┘
                                  ↑↑
  ───────────────────────────────Main───────────────────────────────
    Command Prompt
    Editor
    MS-DOS QBasic
    [Disk Utilities]


  ──────────────────────────────────────────────────────────────────
   F10=Actions   Shift+F9=Command Prompt                        2:35p
```

Figure 15-2: An open menu.

Activating a Window

You can work in only one window at a time. To make a window active, move the cursor (the small arrow) inside it (and then click if you're using a mouse). The title bar of the active window is highlighted.

Changing the Current Drive & Directory

To change the current drive, activate the Top window and then select the desired drive name.

> **TIP** To change the current directory, activate the Directory Tree window and then select the desired directory. When you change the current directory, the Files window changes to show the files in that directory.

Scrolling

If a window contains more items than can be shown, it will have a scroll bar on the right side. You use the scroll bar to scroll up or down through a list of items. The scroll bar arrows indicate the direction. Using a mouse, point to an arrow and hold down the mouse button to scroll line by line. Using the keyboard, press either the Up arrow or Down arrow key to scroll.

Manipulating a File

Before you can manipulate a file, you must activate the Files window and move the highlight bar to the file. Then the RENAME and COPY commands become available. To use them, press F10 to activate the Menu Bar and then select the File menu.

You may select more than one file for an operation. For example, you may want to copy several files to Drive A. With a mouse, just hold down the Ctrl key and click on each file name. With the keyboard, move the highlight bar to one of the files you want to select, and then press Shift-F8. To select other files, move the highlight bar to each and press the Space bar. When you've selected the files you want, press Shift-F8. Then press F10 to activate the Menu Bar.

Completing a Dialog Box

A "dialog box" will be displayed whenever DOS needs additional information to execute a command. Such commands are displayed with ellipsis dots (...). Let's take a look at a dialog box.

HANDS-ON Open the FILE menu and then select the RENAME... command. First, move the highlight bar to any file in the Files window.

Press: **F10**

Select: **File**

Select: **RENAME...**

```
┌──────────────────┤ Rename File ├──────────────────┐
│                                                     │
│                                                     │
│   Current name:    WEEKLY.RPT            1 of    1  │
│                                                     │
│   New name . . [. . . . . . . . . . .]              │
│                                                     │
│                                                     │
│                                                     │
│       ▓▓ OK ▓▓        ▓▓ Cancel ▓▓       ▓▓ Help ▓▓ │
│                                                     │
└─────────────────────────────────────────────────────┘
```

Figure 15-3: Dialog box for the RENAME... command.

Because you selected the RENAME... command, DOS needs to know what name you're giving the file. Type the name at the "New Name" prompt (see Figure 15-3).

> **TIP** Notice the Command buttons at the bottom of the box. "OK" means you want to proceed with the operation. "Cancel" means you want to stop (pressing the Esc key achieves the same effect). And "Help" means you want help completing the box.

If there's more than one text line in the box, move from one to another by pointing the mouse and clicking (or on the keyboard, by using the Tab key).

Expanding and Collapsing Directories

In the Directory Tree window, a + (plus sign) beside a directory name means that it contains one or more subdirectories. To see that directory's structure, activate the Tree window. Then click on the + (or move the highlight bar to the directory name and press the [+] key). The directory tree will expand to show its structure.

An expanded directory is indicated with a – (minus sign) beside the name. To collapse an expanded directory, click on the – (or move the highlight bar to the directory name and press the [–] key).

STARTING PROGRAMS FROM THE SHELL

The Shell provides several ways to start a program such as Word-Perfect or Lotus 1-2-3. The two easiest ways are:

▌ In the Tree window, select the appropriate directory (for example, \WP). Then activate the Files window and select the program's executable file name (for example, WP.EXE).

▌ Press F10 to activate the Menu Bar. Then open the FILE menu and select the RUN... command. Then in the Run dialog box, type the program's executable file name, including its full path (for example, C:\WP\WP.EXE). Click on OK or press Enter.

To return to the Shell from a program, press Ctrl-Esc. When you do, the Active Task List window will appear in the lower right quadrant of the screen. Here, you will see the currently active program. To return to the program, select its name from the Active Task List. To exit an active program, use the program's quit or exit command.

RUNNING MORE THAN ONE PROGRAM

The Shell's Task Swapper feature makes it possible to have two or more programs running at the same time and to switch between them. This technique can save time and make your work a little easier.

To enable the Task Swapper, press F10 to activate the Menu Bar. Then open the Options menu and select Enable Task Swapper. The Active Task List window will then appear.

Now, start a program, then press Ctrl-Esc to return to the Shell. That program will be listed in the Active Task List window. In the Shell, start another program, press Ctrl-Esc, and you'll find this program also listed as an active task. (See Figure 15-4.)

```
                              MS-DOS Shell
↑ File   Options   View   Tree   Help                              ↑
  C:\
  [A:]  [B:]  [C:]

         Directory Tree                         C:\*.*
  [-] C:\                       ↑↑   ▶ AUTOEXEC.BAT        53  01-17-93
      ┌ [+] WP                           CONFIG.SYS        46  01-17-93
      ├ [+] 123
      └ [ ] DOS



              Main                           Active Task List
  Command Prompt                ↑↑    WordPerfect
  Editor                              Lotus 1-2-3
  MS-DOS QBasic
  [Disk Utilities]



  F10=Actions   Shift+F9=Command Prompt                          2:35p
```

Figure 15-4: The DOS Shell, including an Active Task List.

To go back to an active program, select it from the Active Task List. To exit a program shown in the Active Task List, go into the program and use its quit or exit command.

EXITING THE SHELL

To exit the Shell temporarily, press Shift-F9. Or activate the Main window and select "Command Prompt." Then to return to the Shell, type EXIT at the prompt.

To exit the Shell, make sure you've exited all programs listed in the Active Task List. Then press F10 to activate the Menu Bar, open the FILE menu, and select Exit. Or you can just press F3.

CHAPTER SUMMARY

- To activate a Shell window, point inside it and click the mouse. Using the keyboard, press the Tab key to move the cursor from one window to another.

- To select a menu or command, point to it and click (on the keyboard, use the arrow keys to position the highlight bar, and then press Enter). An alternative is to type the option's highlighted or underscored letter.

- To run two or more programs at the same time, open the OPTIONS menu and select Enable Task Swapper.

- To return to the Shell from a program, press Ctrl-Esc.

- To exit the Shell temporarily, press Shift-F9. Then to return to the Shell, type EXIT at the DOS prompt.

- To exit the Shell, open the FILE menu and then select the EXIT command.

SECTION II

WordPerfect

Getting Started With WordPerfect

Like most software manuals, your WordPerfect manual is a comprehensive reference book that presents topics in alphabetical order. Unfortunately, this arrangement offers no clues about what's important and what's not. If you know the name of a particular feature, the manual works just fine. But if you're trying to learn the basics, it can be quite a challenge.

So in this section, you'll learn the WordPerfect features you'll need most in your day-to-day work. The following chapters focus on developing your skill and confidence in using WordPerfect.

WHAT WORDPERFECT CAN DO

WordPerfect is a sophisticated word processor with desktop publishing features that help you produce attractive and readable printed materials. The program gives you total control over formatting and graphics features, such as

- Typefaces, type styles and type sizes.
- Placement, alignment and hyphenation of text.
- Margins, headers and footers, and page numbers.
- Drawing lines, and inserting and manipulating images.

For almost any project, WordPerfect provides the power and flexibility you need to produce a well-designed, effective document.

WORDPERFECT VERSIONS

This section of *Office Companion* is based on WordPerfect 6.0, the most recent version of the program. If you still have Version 5.1 on your PC, all but a few of the features covered here will be available to you. (Features available exclusively to 6.0 users are noted in the text.) If you're using 5.1, you should be aware that most of the menus have changed. For each exercise, the Version 5.1 command sequence is also given, but you'll probably need to refer to your WordPerfect user manual occasionally to get information specific to your version of the program.

WHAT YOU'LL LEARN

In this section, you'll read about the "standard" word processing features, with which many of you are already familiar. But you'll also learn a number of new tricks and techniques. For example, you can

- Look at one page of a document while editing another page.
- Have WordPerfect automatically print the current date on a document.
- Bring back the last three text blocks you deleted.
- Enter a series of commands by pressing only two keys.
- Insert graphic images into a document and then rotate, invert and distort them.
- Use a mouse to select commands and work with text.

These are just a few specific examples of practical features that can make your work a lot easier and more productive.

Chapters 17 and 18 explain how WordPerfect operates and how its features are organized; and you'll be introduced to moving the cursor, saving and retrieving files, and getting help.

Chapters 19, 20 and 21 cover formatting text, lines, paragraphs and pages. You'll learn how to

- Select size, style and appearance of type.
- Create special characters that aren't on your keyboard.
- Shape the layout of text with line spacing, margins, alignment and hyphenation.
- Handle automatically repeating features such as headers, footers and page numbers.

Chapter 22 shows you how to delete and undelete text, replace words, move and copy text, and use the spelling checker and thesaurus. Chapter 23 discusses different ways to print your document, how to change print settings and how to use a special technique to reduce printing time. In Chapter 24 you'll learn how to perform file management operations such as copying, deleting and renaming files.

Chapter 25, "Using Columns," teaches you how to arrange information in parallel columns and continuous newspaper-style columns. Chapter 26 explains helpful techniques for opening two documents at once and for constructing one document from several smaller ones. Chapter 27, "Creating Access Aids," covers setting up a table of contents, an index, a list of figures or tables, and page references.

Chapter 28 focuses on how to draw lines, insert graphics into a document and modify graphic images. Chapter 29 shows you how to merge documents automatically and extract information. And the final chapter explains how to use two simple yet powerful techniques—styles and macros—that automate typing to save time and effort.

> **TIP** When you reach the end of this section, you'll be familiar with the most important and useful features of WordPerfect, and you'll have the skills you need to get things done quickly and confidently.

CONVENTIONS USED IN THIS SECTION

The information presented in this section follows a format similar to the one used in the DOS section. In each chapter, a brief discussion of the topics to be covered is followed by an overview and a hands-on exercise for each function or feature.

Here's an illustration:

HANDS-ON   Change the line spacing to double-spaced.

Press: **Shift-F8** (Format) or select *Layout*

Select: **1** (Line), **3** (Line Spacing)

Type: **2** Enter

Select: **OK**

(In WordPerfect 5.1, the sequence is Shift-F8, 1, 6.)

The exercises will usually involve several steps. Here, you're instructed to press Shift-F8 (Format) if you're using the keyboard (or select *Layout* from the Menu Bar if you're using a mouse). Then you would select 1 (Line) from the next menu, and 3 (Line Spacing) from the next. (You'll learn more about menus in the next chapter.) Notice that each key or option is followed by its description.

> **TIP** If the WordPerfect 5.1 command sequence is different from the WordPerfect 6.0 sequence, it will be shown in parentheses.

Remember that you must always press the Enter key (or click the right mouse button) after typing text. This step is shown with the "Enter" icon after the "Type" instructions. Also remember that you can always return to the editing screen by pressing F7 (Exit) one or more times (or by clicking the right mouse button). Another method is to select the OK or Close command shown at the bottom of the menu. This step—exiting a menu—will not be mentioned in the instructions.

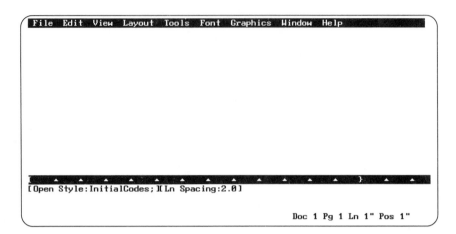

File   Edit   View   Layout   Tools   Font   Graphics   Window   Help

[Open Style:InitialCodes;][Ln Spacing:2.0]

Doc 1 Pg 1 Ln 1" Pos 1"

Figure 16-1: Example of a WordPerfect screen.

> **TIP** The screen image shown in the figure that follows each exercise (as in Figure 16-1) will make clear the results of the action taken in the hands-on instructions. Following some of the screens you'll find comments pointing out important features.

The figures show how the WordPerfect screens look when the program runs in *text mode,* where each character takes the same amount of space onscreen. In version 6.0, the alternative is *graphics mode,* where text fonts, sizes and styles are portrayed more accurately. Graphics and text modes are explained more fully in Chapter 17, "How WordPerfect Works."

CHAPTER SUMMARY

■ The latest DOS version of WordPerfect is 6.0; but 5.1 contains most of the features of the new version.

■ Performing an operation in WordPerfect usually involves selecting commands from a series of menus.

■ After typing a response to a prompt, you must press Enter or click the right mouse button.

■ To exit a menu after making a selection, select F7 (Exit) or select OK or Close. With a mouse, click the right button.

How WordPerfect Works

WordPerfect is one of the most powerful word processors available. Because the program's complexity can be overwhelming, it's important to have a clear understanding of how it works and how its features are organized. So in this chapter, you'll learn

- How WordPerfect uses function keys for frequently used operations.
- How to select operations from menus.
- What WordPerfect's codes are all about.
- The difference between paired and open codes.
- How to change some of WordPerfect's default settings so that the program looks and acts the way you want it to.

USING FUNCTION KEYS

Unless you're using a mouse, the way to get things done in WordPerfect is with the function keys. These keys enable you to format text, check spelling, manage files and much more.

Each of the keys F1 through F10 (and F12 on some keyboards) has an assigned function. But if you hold down the Shift key while pressing a function key, the function changes. And it changes again if you hold down either the Alt or Ctrl key while pressing the function key. So, there are really 40 or more function keys—a lot of convenience at your fingertips, but also a lot to remember.

THE TEMPLATE

To help you with the function keys, WordPerfect provides a plastic template to place on your keyboard. It uses this color-coding scheme:

Black   Function key alone

Green   Shift + function key

Blue   Alt + function key

Red   Ctrl + function key

TIP Notice that related operations often share the same function key. For example, Retrieve and Save both use the F10 key.

You'll want to become familiar with the function-key layout—a few keys at a time. But for now, make sure you know two special keys: the Esc (Escape) key terminates an operation (in Version 5.1, it's F1); and F7 (Exit) lets you exit a menu after completing an operation. It also lets you exit WordPerfect.

TWO TYPES OF FUNCTION KEYS

Some function keys perform complete operations. For example, F8 (Underline) underlines text. Other keys take you to *menus* that give you a variety of choices. For example, Shift-F8 (Format) gives you more than 20 options for formatting text, lines and pages.

USING MENUS

WordPerfect displays a menu when it needs to present a number of options for carrying out an operation. As you work through Word-Perfect, you'll encounter many menus. But for routine work, much of the action will take place at two menus:

The Format menu (displayed by pressing Shift-F8 or by selecting *Layout*) allows you to format lines, paragraphs and pages.

The Font menu (displayed by pressing Ctrl-F8 or by selecting *Font/Font*) allows you to change the size and appearance of text.

The operations available in these menus will be covered in detail later in this section.

SELECTING A MENU OPTION

Menu options are paired with numbers or letters, like the one illustrated in Figure 17-1:

Figure 17-1: A typical WordPerfect menu.

TIP You select an option by typing its number. Each menu option also has a highlighted letter, usually its initial letter. As an alternative, you can select a menu option by typing that letter.

In WordPerfect 6.0, other options are presented in the "button bar" at the bottom of the menu. In Figure 17-1, you see the Close button, which closes the menu. Other commonly used buttons include OK (to confirm your choices) and Cancel (to cancel the operation). To move the cursor from one button to another, you can press the Tab key, or simply point to the button with the mouse.

LEVELS OF MENUS

Sometimes, you have to go through several levels of menus to find the operation you want. For example, to turn on the italic text format, you'd select Ctrl-F8 (Font), then select 3 (Appearance) and 4 (Italics). In version 5.1, you'd press Shift-F8 (Format), then select 2 (Appearance), and 4 (Italc).

PULL-DOWN MENUS (VERSION 5.1 & HIGHER)

An alternative way to use commands is to select them from pull-down menus (available in WordPerfect 5.1 and higher). In Version 5.1, you have to click the right mouse button to display the first-level menu; in Version 6.0, it's displayed when you enter the program, as shown in Figure 17-2.

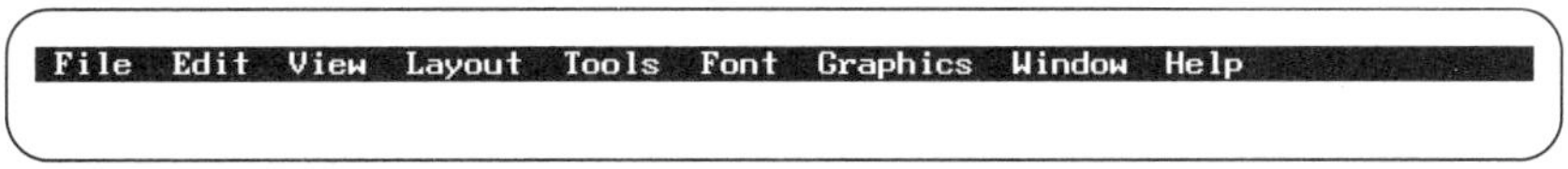

Figure 17-2: The main pull-down menu selections in WordPerfect 6.0.

    File   Edit   View   Layout   Tools   Font   Graphics   Window   Help

TIP To select a command, point to it and click the left mouse button. You will then see another pull-down menu or a more conventional menu. For example, if you select Font and then Size/Position, you'll see a menu of size and position options for text (see Figure 17-3).

```
┌──────────────────────────────────────────────────────────┐
│ File  Edit  View  Layout  Tools  Font  Graphics  Window  Help │
│                              Font...           Ctrl+F8          │
│                                                                 │
│                              *Normal           Ctrl+N           │
│                              Size/Position     Ctrl+F8  ┌───────────────────┐
│                              Bold              F6       │*Normal Size       │
│                              Underline         F8       │ Fine              │
│                              Double Underline           │ Small             │
│                              Italics           Ctrl+I   │ Large             │
│                              Outline                    │ Very Large        │
│                              Shadow                     │ Extra Large       │
│                              Small Caps                 │                   │
│                              Redline                    │*Normal Position   │
│                              Strikeout                  │ Superscript       │
│                                                         │ Subscript         │
│                              Print Color...    Ctrl+F8  └───────────────────┘
│                                                                 │
│                              WP Characters... Ctrl+W            │
│                              Hidden Text...                     │
└──────────────────────────────────────────────────────────┘
```

Figure 17-3: A second-level pull-down menu.

You can also use pull-down menus without a mouse. Just press Alt and the equals key (=) together to display the first-level menu. Then move the highlight bar to the option you want (using the arrow keys) and press Enter. Alternatively, you can type the highlighted letter of the option.

EXITING A MENU

After most operations, you'll need to exit the menu by selecting either the OK or Close button, or by pressing F7 (Exit). In some cases, you'll need to back out through several levels of menus. You can just press F7 (Exit) one or more times to return to the editing screen. With a mouse, click the right button to exit.

UNDERSTANDING CODES

WordPerfect keeps up with every change you make to your document with codes. If you underline a word, indent a paragraph or change the font, WordPerfect inserts the appropriate code into your document. These codes are kept hidden until you want to see them.

TWO TYPES OF CODES

One type of code is the *paired* code, which identifies formatting applied to a specific section of text. "On" and "off" codes show where a format begins and ends. For example, in the sentence "This is a **test**," the code for the boldfaced word would look like this:

This is a **[Bold On]**test**[Bold Off]**.

In WordPerfect 5.1, the "on" code is shown in uppercase letters, and the "off" code is shown in lowercase letters.

The other type, called an *open* code, has no end mark. Open codes are used to change features such as fonts, tabs and margins; they remain in effect through the entire document or until you enter another code of the same type.

WHERE'S THE CURSOR?

On your text screen, you don't see the formatting codes. WordPerfect keeps them out of the way so that the screen will be less cluttered. And because the codes are hidden, it's relatively easy to become confused and make errors. For example, if the cursor is still inside the [Bold On] and [Bold Off] codes, whatever you type will be boldface.

But isn't it obvious where the cursor is? Unfortunately, no. If you use the Left or Right arrow key to move through your text, each press of the key moves the cursor to the next item. If that item is a code, the cursor will appear not to move in your text. For example, let's say you have both bold and underline formatting codes around a word, like this:

This is a **[Und On][Bold On]**test**[Bold Off][Und Off]**.

If the cursor were on the [Bold Off] code, you would have to press the Right arrow key *three times* before you'd see the cursor move in your text.

LOOKING AT THE CODES

To get a clearer idea of what's going on here, you can look at the hidden codes by pressing Alt-F3 (Reveal Codes) or selecting *View/ Reveal Codes* (in Version 5.1, it's *Edit/Reveal Codes*).

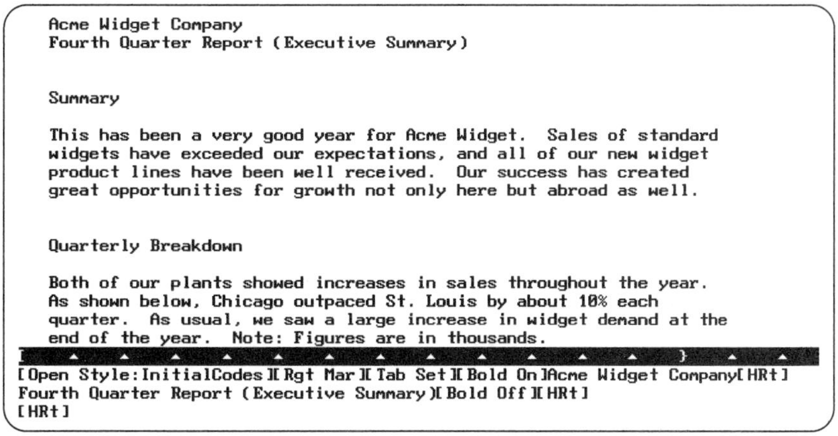

Figure 17-4: You can see all your formatting and appearance codes in the Codes window.

At first (or second) sight, the codes can be a little disorienting, but you'll get used to it (Figure 17-4). The horizontal bar across the screen shows the current tab settings. The top of the screen shows your text; the bottom, the text plus the formatting codes.

> **TIP** Codes are shown in bold letters to help you distinguish them from your text. Also notice that the cursor is shown in both windows.

If you want to change the size of the Codes window, you would

Press: **Ctrl-F3** (Screen) or select *View/Screen Setup*

Press: **Shift-F1** (Setup)

Select: **5** (Reveal Codes), **2** (Window Percentage)

Then type the percentage of the screen you want the Codes window to use. (In WordPerfect 5.1, the sequence is Shift-F1, 2, 6, 6.)

DELETING CODES

With the codes revealed, you can delete a code by positioning the cursor on it and pressing Del. If it's a paired code, both codes in the pair will be deleted at once, and the code formatting will no longer be in effect. You can also delete a code without displaying the codes, but seeing them makes it a lot easier.

HIDING CODES

To hide the codes again after revealing them, you'd press Alt-F3 (Reveal Codes) or select *View/Reveal Codes* (in 5.1, it's *Edit/Reveal Codes*).

CHANGING DEFAULT SETTINGS

WordPerfect is set up to produce "typical" documents. For example, "standard" settings include

- Tabs—every $1/2$ inch
- Paper size—8 $1/2$ by 11 inches
- Margins—1 inch

While some changes you make apply only to the current document, others will affect all new documents you create. These settings are found on the Shift-F1 (Setup) or *File/Setup* screen, as you can see in Figure 17-5.

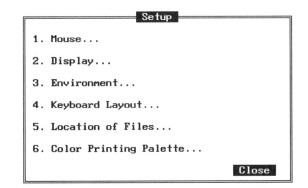

Figure 17-5: The Setup screen.

SETUP OPTIONS

1 (Mouse): Lets you set the characteristics of your mouse (if you have one).

2 (Display): Lets you change the way your screen looks (explained in detail below).

3 (Environment): Lets you set various features including cursor speed and backup options.

4 (Keyboard Layout): Lets you reassign the actions performed by keys and key combinations.

5 (Location of Files): Lets you tell WordPerfect where to find special files such as macros, styles and printer files. It allows you to put each group of files into a separate subdirectory. If you choose not to do this, WordPerfect will look for these files in the current directory.

6 (Color Printing Palette): Lets you make color choices for color printing.

Note: If you're using WordPerfect 5.1, your Setup menu options are different.

CHANGING THE WAY YOUR SCREEN LOOKS

WordPerfect lets you set up the way text attributes (like underline and italic) will look on your screen. If you have a monochrome monitor, you can use combinations of Bold, Underline, Reverse video and Blinking. But if you have a color monitor, you can use different colors for each type of format.

HANDS-ON   Check the "Screen Type/Colors" screen.

Press: **Shift-F1** (Setup) or select *File/Setup*

Select: **2** (Display), **2** (Text Mode Screen Type/Colors),
2 (Color Schemes)

(In WordPerfect 5.1, the sequence is Shift-F1, 2, 1.)

```
╔══════════════ Text Mode Screen Type/Colors ══════════════╗
║                                                           ║
║   1. Screen Type...  Auto Selected                        ║
║                                                           ║
║   ┌2. Color Schemes─────────────  Screen Font─┐           ║
║   │*black and white              Normal       │↑ 1. Select║
║   │ [Deep Blue Sea]              Normal        │  2. Create...║
║   │ [Gettysburg]                 Normal        │  3. Edit...║
║   │ [Winter Wonderland]          Normal        │  4. Delete║
║   │ [WP Default]                 Normal        │  5. Copy...║
║   │                                            │  N. Name Search║
║   │                                            │           ║
║   │                                            │           ║
║   │                                            │↓          ║
║   └────────────────────────────────────────────┘          ║
║                                            ▐Close▌        ║
╚═══════════════════════════════════════════════════════════╝
```

Figure 17-6: The Text Mode Screen Type/Colors screen.

The screen shown in Figure 17-6 allows you to select an existing color scheme or create a new one. To select a color scheme from the list, move the highlight bar to it and choose 1 (Select). If you want to create a new color scheme, choose 2 (Create). You will then see the screen shown in Figure 17-7.

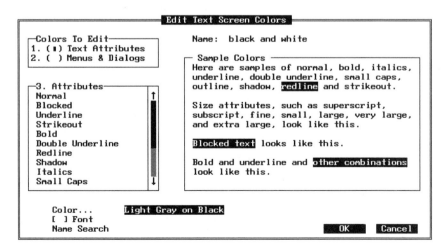

Figure 17-7: The Edit Text Screen Colors screen.

At the Edit Text Screen Colors screen, you have to decide how you want each text attribute to look on your screen as you edit your documents.

The current appearance of each text attribute is shown in the Sample Colors portion of the screen. To change a text attribute, select 3 (Attributes). Move the highlight bar to the desired attribute–for example, Bold–and press Enter. You will then see a table of different foreground/background color combinations. Use the arrow keys to move the selection box to the combination you want, and then press Enter. Then repeat the procedure for other text attributes you want to change. When you are finished, select the OK button.

When you've returned to the Screen Type/Colors screen, move the highlight bar to the name of the color scheme that you just created. Then turn it on by selecting 1 (Select). When you return to the editing screen, your new color scheme will be in effect.

GRAPHICS MODE

In WordPerfect 6.0, you have the option of running the program in either text mode, described in the preceding section, or in graphics mode. If you choose graphics mode, the appearance of text onscreen will be similar to its appearance on a printout. This type of display is called WYSIWYG, short for What You See Is What You Get.

To set up the program to run in graphics mode, you would

Press: **Shift-F1** (Setup) or select *File/Setup*

Select: **2** (Display), **1** (Graphics Mode Screen Type/Colors)

Then you would see a screen that allows you to choose the color scheme you want to use in the editing screen.

WORDPERFECT & DOS

In the DOS section of *Office Companion*, you learned that your PC software programs work within the DOS environment. Even so, most programs require that you exit the program to use DOS commands. But not WordPerfect. It lets you temporarily go to the DOS prompt without leaving the program.

GOING TO DOS

HANDS-ON Go to the DOS prompt temporarily.

Press: **Ctrl-F1** (Shell) or select *File/Go to Shell*

Select: **1** (Go to DOS)

```
Microsoft(R) MS-DOS(R) Version 6
           (C)Copyright Microsoft Corp 1981-1993.

Enter 'EXIT' to return to WordPerfect
C:\WP
```

Figure 17-8: Result of the Go to DOS command.

Figure 17-8 shows the DOS prompt. At this point, you can perform file management operations such as listing and copying files. When you're ready to return to WordPerfect, type **EXIT** and press Enter.

Option 6 (DOS Command) on the Shell menu is useful when running a macro that uses DOS commands (see Chapter 30, "Letting WordPerfect Do the Typing," for information on macros). (In Word-Perfect 5.1, it's Option 2.)

CHAPTER SUMMARY

■ In WordPerfect, the function keys give you access to 40 or more operations and menus.

■ You can select a menu option by typing either its number or its highlighted letter. With a mouse, you simply point to the option and click the left button.

■ Pressing the Esc key terminates an operation; F7 will exit a menu or exit the program. With a mouse, clicking the middle button (or the left and right buttons together) will terminate an operation; clicking the right button will exit a menu.

■ Paired codes indicate the beginning and end points for text formatting. Open codes indicate document characteristics that remain in effect until conflicting codes are encountered.

■ From the Shift-F1 (Setup) or *File/Setup* menu, you can change certain default settings that affect the way your screen will look and the way the program will operate.

■ From the Ctrl-F1 (Shell) or *File/Go to Shell* menu, you can select 1 (Go to DOS) to go to the DOS prompt without exiting WordPerfect. To return to the editing screen, type **EXIT** and press Enter.

Learning
the Basics

WordPerfect
18

The first step in becoming comfortable with WordPerfect is to learn some basic skills–such as moving the cursor, saving and retrieving files and getting help. So in this chapter you'll learn how to

■ Move the cursor to specific locations.

■ Save and retrieve files.

■ Make WordPerfect save your file automatically at regular intervals.

■ Protect a file by adding a password.

■ Work on a non-WordPerfect file.

■ Get help on specific topics.

You'll be able to use these practical techniques almost every time you work in WordPerfect.

BASIC SKILLS

Here's an overview of the basic WordPerfect skills you'll learn in this chapter.

CURSOR MOVEMENT

As you saw in the last chapter, the position of the cursor is very important. If it's not where you think it is, you might format new text in a way you didn't intend. Fortunately, WordPerfect provides several ways to move the cursor quickly–to skip words, lines, screens and pages.

SAVING & RETRIEVING A DOCUMENT

WordPerfect provides two ways to save a document: you can save it and remain in the document, or save it and exit. And when you make changes, you can either update the old version or save the new version under a different name, thus retaining both versions of the document.

The program gives you *three* ways to retrieve a document. You can retrieve it either as you start up WordPerfect or after you're in the program. And if you're already in the program, you can save keystrokes by retrieving from the File Management screen.

WORKING WITH ASCII FILES

You can create and edit ASCII text files, such as your AUTOEXEC.BAT file and other batch files, while you're in WordPerfect. You simply retrieve them like any other file, and specify the ASCII format when you save them. In WordPerfect 5.1, you must use special retrieve and save commands in the Ctrl-F5 (Text In/Out) or *File/Text In (Out)* menu.

GETTING HELP

WordPerfect has an online help feature that gives information about functions and features. To use HELP, you don't have to exit your document. The help screens come up on top of your document and don't affect it.

INCLUDING TODAY'S DATE

If you want the current date to appear on this (or any) document, you press Shift-F5 (Date/Outline) or select *Layout*, then 2 (Insert Date Code). (In WordPerfect 5.1, the sequence is Shift-F5, 2.) The date code will be inserted at the cursor's position. Now each time you retrieve the document, it will show the current date.

A SAMPLE DOCUMENT

Most of the exercises in this section of *Office Companion* will be based on the sample document shown in Figure 18-1. If you create this document, you'll be able to do the exercises exactly as described. If you decide to use one of your own documents, you can simply "adapt" the exercises to fit your text.

If you've never used a word processing program before, be aware that you don't press Enter at the end of each line. The program automatically wraps the text from one line to the next. You press Enter only when you want to create a new paragraph.

The illustration shows the way the sample document will look onscreen if the font is Courier 10-cpi (ten characters per inch). With a different font, your lines may be longer than the ones shown here (that's OK). In Chapter 19, "Formatting Text," you'll learn how to change the font.

```
Acne Widget Company
Fourth Quarter Report (Executive Summary)


Summary

This has been a very good year for Acme Widget.  Sales of standard
widgets have exceeded our expectations, and all of our new widget
product lines have been well received.  Our success has created
great opportunities for growth not only here but abroad as well.


Quarterly Breakdown

Both of our plants showed increases in sales throughout the year.
As shown below, Chicago outpaced St. Louis by about 10% each
quarter.  As usual, we saw a large increase in widget demand at the
end of the year.  Note: Figures are in thousands.

Chicago
First Quarter: 970
Second Quarter: 1135
Third Quarter: 1200
Fourth Quarter: 1508

St. Louis
First Quarter: 850
Second Quarter: 995
Third Quarter: 1046
Fourth Quarter: 1350


Message from J. E. Quattlebaum, President

At our last board meeting, our president gave a brief but inspiring
account of the state of the company:

"We at Acme are proud of our position as the third largest supplier
of quality widget products in the midwest.  I believe that our
increased efforts in research and development will help to ensure
our continued success in this very competitive market.  The future
looks bright indeed at Acme."
```

Figure 18-1: A sample document you can use to do the hands-on exercises in this section of *Office Companion*.

MOVING THE CURSOR

WordPerfect provides a number of ways to instantly move the cursor to specific locations, as shown in the table below.

Key	Result
Right/Left arrow	One character to the right/left.
Up/Down arrow	One row up/down.
End	To the end of the line.
Home, Left arrow	To the beginning of the line.
–/+	Up/down one screen. Be sure to use the minus – and plus + keys on your number keypad. (Be sure the Num Lock key is turned off.)
Home, Up/Down arrow	To the top/bottom of the current screen.
PgUp/PgDn	To the top of the previous/next page.
Home, Home, Up/Down arrow	To the beginning/end of the document.
Home, Home, Home, Up arrow	To the top of the document above all codes.
Ctrl-Home, number, Enter	To the specified page. For example, Ctrl-Home, 12, Enter would move the cursor to page 12.

If you're using a mouse, just point to the desired location and click the left button.

CREATING NEW PAGES

When you type more text than one page can contain, WordPerfect automatically continues the text on a new page. This type of page division is a *soft* page break, indicated on the screen with a single horizontal line and by the code [SPg]. (In older versions of the program, a dashed line is used.) If you delete some text, the new page may no longer be needed, and the page break will disappear.

A hard page break is one you create manually by pressing Ctrl-Enter or selecting *Layout/Alignment/Hard Page.* A hard page break stays in place regardless of changes made in the amount of text before or after it.

> **TIP** Any time text must begin at the top of a new page, always use the hard break. This page division is represented onscreen by a double line and by the code [HPg]. (See Figure 18-2.)

Soft page break
_____

Hard page break
_____

Figure 18-2: Comparison of a soft page break and a hard page break.

HOW A PAGE BREAK AFFECTS HARD RETURNS

Normally you enter two hard returns at the end of a paragraph to provide a blank line for separation between paragraphs. If you enter the two returns on the *last line* of a page, WordPerfect will make the second one a "dormant" hard return. The result will be that your next paragraph will start on the *first*, not second, line of the next page (in other words, the blank line will be suppressed). Later, if the page break between those paragraphs is removed, the dormant hard return will be converted into a normal hard return, and a blank line will once again separate the two paragraphs.

SAVING FILES

When you save a document, you can either exit the document or remain in it to do further editing.

SAVING

To save a *new* document, press F10 (Save) or select *File/Save*. Word-Perfect will prompt you to type the file name. If you're saving it in the default directory, you don't have to specify the file's directory path.

HANDS-ON Save the current document as "4Q.RPT."

Press: **F10** (Save) or select *File/Save*

Type: **4Q.RPT** Enter

To *update* a file that's already been saved, press F10 (Save) or select *File/Save*. WordPerfect will show the current file name, as shown in Figure 18-3. If you want to replace the old version with the new, press Enter. WordPerfect will then ask you to confirm your decision by typing Y (Yes). If you don't want to replace the old version with the new, press Enter or type N (No).

Figure 18-3: Prompt to replace a file with an updated version.

```
Replace C:\WP\4Q.RPT?

        Yes        No
```

SAVING & EXITING

To exit a document, press F7 (Exit) or select File/Exit. WordPerfect will ask if you want to save the document. If you've made changes since your last save, select Yes. WordPerfect will then ask if you want to exit the program. To remain in WordPerfect, select No. But to exit the program, select Yes.

AUTOMATIC BACKUPS

WordPerfect has two automatic file backup options: you can choose Timed or Original.

The Timed Backup option instructs WordPerfect to save your document automatically at regular intervals as you work on it. The Timed Backup file for Document 1 is named WP{WPC}.BK1, and for Document 2, WP{WPC}.BK2. (In 5.1, they're named WP{WP}.BK1 and WP{WP}.BK2.) When you exit WordPerfect properly, these files are deleted. But if you are forced to exit the program because of a power outage, these files will be saved and can be retrieved when you reenter the program, just like any other file.

The Original Backup option instructs WordPerfect to save the most recent previous version of each file. So let's say you create and save a file named PROPOSAL. If you then make changes to the file and save it again, the updated file will have the same name–PROPOSAL. However, the previous version of the file will also exist, saved under the name PROPOSAL.BK! If you decide you need the previous version, you can retrieve it just like any other file.

To turn on the Timed Backup,

Press: **Shift-F1** (Setup) or select *File/Setup*

Select: **3** (Environment), **1** (Backup Options)

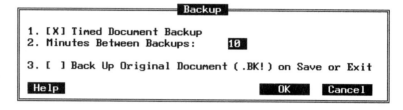

Figure 18-4: The WordPerfect
Backup options.

If Timed Document Backup is not marked (Figure 18-4), select option 1. Then select option 2 and enter the number of minutes between backups.

(In WordPerfect 5.1, the sequence is Shift-F1, 3, 1, 1, Y.)

To turn on the Original Backup, you would go to the same Backup Options screen and select option 3 (Back Up Original Document). (In Version 5.1, it's option 2.)

RETRIEVING FILES

WordPerfect gives you three ways to retrieve a WordPerfect document. One way is to retrieve a file as you start up the program. The other two ways can be used when you're already in the program: you can either type the file name or select it from a list of files.

RETRIEVING DURING START-UP

If you want to go directly into a document when you start Word-Perfect, you can include the file name in the start-up command. For example, to retrieve the file PICNIC.MEM as you start WordPerfect, you would enter WP PICNIC.MEM at the DOS prompt.

If the file is in a subdirectory, you have to enter the full path, like this: WP WP\MEMOS\PICNIC.MEM.

> **TIP** The WordPerfect program can be started from any directory provided your AUTOEXEC.BAT file contains a PATH command that includes the path to your WordPerfect directory. For a refresher on this topic, see Section 1, Chapter 6, "Understanding Directories." Also see Chapter 13, "Increasing the Power of Your PC."

RETRIEVING BY TYPING

From a blank screen, you can retrieve a file by using Shift-F10 (Retrieve) or File/Open. WordPerfect will prompt you to enter the name of the file.

> **TIP** If your file is not in the current directory, you'll have to include its full path; for example, \WP\LETTERS\PICNIC.MEM.

RETRIEVING WITHOUT TYPING

The easiest way to retrieve a file (the way that eliminates typing) is to select F5 (File Manager) or *File/File Manager* to see a list of your files. Be sure to type in the directory you want and press Enter. (Otherwise you'll get the default directory.) Then use the Up and Down arrow keys to move the selection bar to the file you want and press 1 (Open into New Document). For more detail about the File Management screen, see Chapter 24, "Managing Your Files."

PROTECTING A FILE

If you want to prevent other people from opening a particular file, you can protect it by adding a password to it. But to retrieve the file, you must give the password; if you can't remember the password, there's no way to open the file. So use a name you can easily remember, or keep a record of it.

HANDS-ON Add the password "widget" to the current document.

> Press: **F10** (Save As) or select *File/Save As*
>
> Press: **F8** (Password)
>
> Type: **widget** K
>
> Type: **widget** K (to verify)
>
> (In WordPerfect 5.1, the sequence is Ctrl-F5, 2, 1.)

> You won't be able to see the letters as you type them, so be careful.

To remove password protection,

Press: **F10** (Save As) or select *File/Save As*

Press: **F8** (Password)

Press: **F6** (Remove)

(In WordPerfect 5.1 the sequence is Ctrl-F5, 2, 2.)

WORKING WITH NON-WORDPERFECT FILES

In Chapter 12 of Section 1, "Letting DOS Do the Typing," you learned how to create several useful files including AUTOEXEC.BAT, CONFIG.SYS and special-purpose batch files. You may recall that these files can be created using COPY CON, EDITOR OR EDLIN (the DOS line editors) or WordPerfect.

Regardless of the method you use, these are *ASCII* (pronounced ask'-ey) files—plain, unformatted text files. To work on an ASCII file in WordPerfect, you can retrieve it and save it as you would a regular WordPerfect file, specifying ASCII as the file format. (In Version 5.1, you use the Ctrl-F5 Text in/Out or *File/Text In Out* function.)

RETRIEVING A NON-WORDPERFECT FILE

To retrieve an ASCII file,

Press: **Shift-F10** (Retrieve) or select File/Retrieve

Type: **the file name** Enter

Select: **ASCII Text (Standard)**

Be sure to include the file's complete path if it is outside the current directory.

(In WordPerfect 5.1, the sequence is Ctrl-F5, 1, 2.)

If you're bringing in a Lotus 1-2-3 spreadsheet, you can use the command sequence shown above. But to bring in a named range, press Alt-F7 (Columns/Tables) or select *Tools*, then 5 (Spreadsheet) and 1 (Import).

In WordPerfect 5.1, you press Ctrl-F5 or select *File/Text In*, then 5 (Spreadsheet), and then 1 (Import).

SAVING A NON-WORDPERFECT FILE

To save a document as an ASCII file,

Press: F10 (Save As) or select *File/Save As*

WordPerfect will automatically specify ASCII format for the file.

(In WordPerfect 5.1, the sequence is Ctrl-F5, 1, 1.)

> **TIP** If you also want to save the file as a WordPerfect file, use F10 (Save) or File/Save As. Be sure to use a different name than the one you gave to the ASCII version of the file.

GETTING HELP

When you get stuck using a function or feature, WordPerfect is ready to help. The program has detailed screens that explain everything from aligning text to macros to word-searching.

HOW IT WORKS

To get help with a topic, press F1 (Help) or select *Help* (in Word-Perfect 5.1, Help is F3).

You will then see the first Help screen, shown in Figure 18-5.

```
┌──────────────────────────────[ Help ]──────────────────────────────┐
│                                                                  ↑  │
│ Contents                                                            │
│ ─────────────────────────────────────────────────────────────────  │
│ Welcome to WordPerfect Help.                                        │
│                                                                     │
│ Choose                  For information about                       │
│ ─────────────────────────────────────────────────────────────────  │
│ Index                   features listed alphabetically              │
│ How Do I                performing tasks                            │
│ Glossary                meanings of terms                           │
│ Template                function keys and their actions             │
│ Keystrokes              keystrokes and their actions                │
│ Shortcut Keys           quickly accessing features                  │
│ Error Messages          causes and solutions for common error messages │
│                                                                     │
│ Double-click on this → Using Help, if you need information about     │
│ Help.                                                            ↓  │
│ ───────────────────────────────────────────────────────────────── │
│ Name Search   Contents   Coaches   Look   Previous        Cancel   │
└─────────────────────────────────────────────────────────────────────┘
```

Figure 18-5: The first screen of the WordPerfect Help feature.

The highlight bar, initially on Index, lets you select the type of help you need. If you select Index, you will see a long list of WordPerfect features and commands. To get help with a topic, move the highlight bar to it and press Enter.

If you're using version 5.1, you have two options after pressing F3 (Help). You can

a) Press the key you want to find out about.

b) Type the initial letter of the topic you're interested in. Word-Perfect will show a list of topics beginning with that letter so that you can choose.

> **TIP** When you are ready to return to the editing screen after using the Help feature, you can select the Cancel button or press the Esc key, or click the left and right mouse buttons together. If you're using version 5.1, you must press Enter to exit a Help screen.

CHAPTER SUMMARY

■ Cursor movement keys allow you to move the cursor by character, line, screen and page.

■ A hard page break remains in a document, regardless of the amount of text added or deleted bove it.

■ To save a document, use F10 (Save) or *File/Save*. To save and exit the document, use F7 (Exit) or *File/Exit WP*.

■ Timed Backup saves your document at regular intervals as you work. You control it through the Shift-F1 (Setup) or *File/Setup* menu.

■ A password can be added to any document by using F10 (Save As) or *File/Save* and then F8 (Password).

■ To work on non-WordPerfect (ASCII) files in Version 5.1, retrieve and save them using the Retrieve and Save commands found in the Ctrl-F5 (Text In/Out) or *File* menu.

■ To get help with a function or feature, press F1 (Help) or select *Help* (in Version 5.1, it's F3).

Formatting Text

WordPerfect 19

The key to effective written communication lies not only in the content of a document but in its appearance as well. Readers are strongly influenced by the way text looks. So in this chapter, you'll learn how to

- Choose text formatting options.
- Format text as you type it or after you've typed it.
- Convert uppercase letters to lowercase, and vice versa.
- Distinguish between initial and base fonts.
- Adjust word and letter spacing for special effects.
- Create nonstandard characters.

WordPerfect gives you a great deal of control over the way text looks. By changing the type size, style (appearance) or font, you can draw attention, create emphasis or even change the feeling of a document. Handled judiciously, such changes can enhance the appearance of your document.

SIZE & APPEARANCE OPTIONS

Text is measured in points, with 72 points equaling one inch. The variety of sizes available to you depends on your printer and the fonts you have installed. Most documents use 10- or 12-point type. Appearance (or style) options are independent of size and include Bold, Underline, Small Caps and other styles.

TYPEFACE/FONT OPTIONS

A typeface (such as Courier or Times Roman) consists of a family of sizes and styles. Each member of the family is a font. So while Helvetica is a typeface, Helvetica 10-point italic is a font. Typefaces and their fonts have two characteristics that affect document design:

■ Letters are either equally spaced or proportionally spaced.

■ Letters have serifs (small decorative strokes at the ends of the main character stems), or they don't. Fonts without serifs are called sans-serif.

To get a feel for these characteristics, compare Courier, Dutch Roman and Helvetica:

`Courier is an equal-spaced, serif typeface.`

Dutch Roman is a proportional-spaced, serif typeface.

Helvetica is a proportional-spaced, sans-serif typeface.

CHANGING THE FONT

The *initial font* is the default font that WordPerfect uses when you begin a new document. A *base font* is one you insert in a specific document to override the default font.

> **TIP** The number of font choices you have depends on your printer and the fonts you've purchased and installed.

CHANGING FONTS

WordPerfect lets you change fonts in the following ways:

To change the initial font for the *current* document only,

Press: **Shift-F8** (Format) or select *Layout*

Select: **4** (Document), **3** (Initial Font), **1** (Font)

Then select a new initial font.

(In WordPerfect 5.1, the sequence is Shift-F8, 3, 3.)

To change the font of text below the cursor in the *current* document,

Press: **Ctrl-F8** (Font) or select *Font*

Select: **1** (Font)

Then select a base font.

(In WordPerfect 5.1, the sequence is Ctrl-F8, 4.)

> **TIP** Because choosing a base font inserts an open code, the font will affect all text that follows the code until you enter another base-font code.

To change the initial font for *all* new documents (WordPerfect 5.1 and higher),

Press: **Shift-F8** (Format) or select *Layout*

Select: **4** (Document), **3** (Initial Font), **1** (Font)

Select a new initial font.

Select: **4** (All New Documents)

(In WordPerfect 5.1, the sequence is Shift-F1, 4, 5, Ctrl-F8, 4.)

FORMATTING TEXT

Regardless of the font you've chosen, you can format the text with underlining, boldface and other techniques.

FORMATTING AS YOU TYPE

To format text as you type, first turn on the format (for example, select F6 (Bold) and then type the text. To turn off the bold and continue with normal text, move the cursor to the right of the formatting code by pressing the function key again or by pressing the Right arrow key.

FORMATTING TEXT AFTER YOU'VE TYPED IT

To format text after you've typed it, you must first *block* the text. To block text, select Alt-F4 (Block), then stretch the block as far as needed using cursor movement keys. With a mouse, hold down the left button to activate Block, and then drag the block to the desired size. After you format a block, the cursor will automatically move to the right of the format codes.

WRITER'S BLOCK

Using the arrow keys to stretch the block can take time. So Word-Perfect lets you use the standard cursor movement techniques to stretch a block quickly. It also provides a shortcut: typing a character (such as M or m) stretches the block to that character in the text. Here are a few useful ways to stretch a block after you've selected Alt-F4 (Block):

To block:	Press:
An entire word	Ctrl-Right arrow or Space bar
	Note: Both methods include the space following the word. To overcome this, just use the Left arrow key to shorten the block by one character.
An entire sentence	. (period)
An entire paragraph	Enter
To the next page break	PgDn
To a particular page	Ctrl-Home, page number [Enter]

To extend the block to include more text, just press the key again. For example, to block two sentences, select Alt-F4 (Block) and press the period key (.) twice.

REPEATING THE LAST BLOCK

When you block text, the block turns off as soon as you select a formatting option. So if you want to add other formatting to the same text, you have to block it again. A quick way is to press Alt-F4 (Block) and then press Ctrl-Home (Go To) twice (WordPerfect 5.1 only).

REMOVING FORMATTING

To remove text formatting, you press Alt-F3 (Reveal Codes) or *View/Reveal Codes* (in Version 5.1, it's *Edit/Reveal Codes*). Then move the cursor to either the beginning or ending code and press Del (Delete).

GOING BEYOND BOLD & UNDERLINE

Bold and Underline are the only two text formatting functions available through the function keys. To turn on other formats, you must go to the Ctrl-F8 (Font) or *Font/Font* menu (in WordPerfect 5.1, it's *Font/Appearance*). As with Bold and Underline, you can format either as you type or after you type.

THE FONT MENU

Pressing Ctrl-F8 (Font) or selecting *Font/Font* brings up the Font menu as shown in Figure 19-1.

```
                            ┌─Font─┐
   Type   Built-In                  HP LaserJet Series II
  ┌─────────────────────────────────────────────────────────────┐
  │ 1. Font [ Courier 10cpi               ↓] 2. Size [ 12pt    ↓  │
  └─────────────────────────────────────────────────────────────┘
  ┌─3. Appearance──────────────────────────────┐ ┌─5. Position─────┐
  │   [ ] Bold        [ ] Italics   [ ] Small Caps │ │ (■) Normal      │
  │   [ ] Underline   [ ] Outline   [ ] Redline    │ │ ( ) Superscript │
  │   [ ] Dbl Undline [ ] Shadow    [ ] Strikeout  │ │ ( ) Subscript   │
  └────────────────────────────────────────────┘ └─────────────────┘
  ┌─4. Relative Size────────────────────────────┐ ┌─6. Underline────┐
  │   (■) Normal    ( ) Small    ( ) Very Large    │ │ [X] Spaces      │
  │   ( ) Fine      ( ) Large    ( ) Extra Large   │ │ [ ] Tabs        │
  └────────────────────────────────────────────┘ └─────────────────┘
  ┌─Resulting Font──────────────────────────────────────────────┐
  │ Courier 10cpi                                                │
  └─────────────────────────────────────────────────────────────┘
  [ Setup... Shft+F1 ]  [ Normal ]  [ Color... ]      [ OK ]  [ Cancel ]
```

Figure 19-1: The Font menu, showing the various options.

At the Font menu, you have a variety of options for modifying text size and appearance. When you select a main option–for example, 3 (Appearance)–the options within that box become available. So Bold will then become option 1, Underline will become option 2, and so on.

Some of the size and appearance formats may not be available to you. It depends on your printer and the fonts you have. For example, if your base font is 12-point Times, you would need to have a larger font available (such as 14-point Times) to use Option 4 (Large) as the Relative Size.

CASE CONVERSION

Converting text from lowercase to uppercase (or vice versa) is one formatting operation you can't do at the Ctrl-F8 (Font) menu. You have to block the text, then press Shift-F3 (Switch) or select *Edit/Convert Case*. WordPerfect then gives you three choices: 1 (Uppercase), 2 (Lowercase) or 3 (Initial Caps). (Option 3 isn't available in Version 5.1.)

WORD & LETTER SPACING

If you're interested in exercising some fine control over the appearance of text, you can adjust the spacing of letters and words. This technique is most appropriate for headlines, announcements and other small sections of text. The spacing adjustment can range from 50 to 250 percent of normal.

ADJUSTING WORD & LETTER SPACING

WordPerfect chooses spacing for words and their letters based on the font you're using. When you adjust spacing, you have the option of controlling both word and letter spacing or setting one and letting WordPerfect set the other.

The spacing options are

1 (Normal): The spacing recommended by the font designer.

2 (Optimal): The spacing recommended by WordPerfect (often the same as Normal).

3 (Percent of Optimal): Reduced or expanded spacing, relative to the Optimal setting.

4 (Set Pitch): Reduced or expanded spacing to fit the number of characters per inch that you specify.

To change word spacing or letter spacing, you would

Press: **Shift-F8** (Format) or select *Layout*

Select: **7** (Other), **9** (Printer Functions), **6** (Word/Letter Spacing)

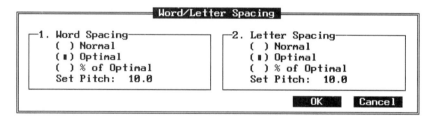

Figure 19-2: The Word/Letter spacing menu.

You'll see the screen shown in Figure 19-2. Then you would select either 1 (Word Spacing) or 2 (Letter Spacing) and make the desired changes.

(In WordPerfect 5.1, the sequence is Shift-F8, 4, 6, 3.)

> **TIP** Changes to word and letter spacing insert open codes into the document. To return to normal text, you have to change spacing back to Optimal below the altered text.

CREATING NONSTANDARD CHARACTERS

Depending on the type of document you're writing, you may need to use special characters such as ·, → or ©. With the Ctrl-W (Compose) or *Font/Characters* feature, you can create over 1,000 special characters not available on your keyboard. Your WordPerfect manual appendix shows these characters.

> **TIP** The number of characters available to you depends on your printer and fonts. To find out what these characters are, retrieve and print the CHARACTR.DOC file that came with your program.

USING COMPOSE

To insert a special character into your document, press Ctrl-W or select *Font/WP Characters* to see the screen shown in Figure 19-3.

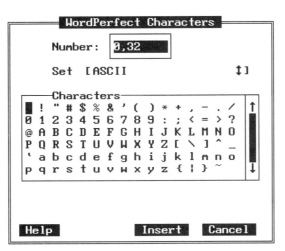

Figure 19-3: The WordPerfect Characters screen.

At the Characters screen, you see a particular set of characters displayed—ASCII characters, in this illustration. To insert a character, press Tab twice to move the cursor to the Characters box. Then move the cursor to the character you want using the arrow keys, and press Enter.

To make other character sets available, tab to the Set box and press Enter. Then select another set from the ones shown in the list. For example, you might want to use a character from the Typographic Symbols set to give your document a typeset look.

If you're using WordPerfect 5.1, each special character is identified by its *set* and *number*. (You'll need to refer to the tables in your *User's Guide* to determine a particular character's set and number). To insert a character, select Ctrl-W or *Font/Characters*. Then type the character's set, a comma or space, and its number. For example, to insert the bullet (·) character (set 4, number 3), you would select Ctrl-W and then type 4, a comma or space, and 3.

> **TIP** To save yourself time and keystrokes, you can automate the commands needed to create special characters with macros (see Chapter 30, "Letting WordPerfect Do the Typing").

CHAPTER SUMMARY

■ The initial font is the default font used for all new documents. You select a base font to override the initial font in a document.

■ You can format text either as you type it or after you've typed it.

■ When you've turned on Alt-F4 (Block), you can stretch the block to the end of a sentence by pressing . (period), and to the end of a paragraph by pressing Enter.

■ Most text formatting options are listed in the Ctrl-F8 (Font) or *Font/Font* menu.

■ Word and letter spacing can be adjusted independently to create visual interest in small blocks of text.

■ The Ctrl-W (Compose) or *Font/Characters* feature lets you insert special characters that aren't available on the keyboard.

Formatting Lines & Paragraphs

A well-designed document takes into account not only the appearance of words, but also the appearance of lines and paragraphs. Attending to the shape and overall layout of text can result in more visually forceful documents. In this chapter, you'll learn how to

- Adjust line spacing.
- Align text left, right and center.
- Use tabs and indents.
- Align numbers on their decimal points.
- Hyphenate words automatically.
- Print text at any place on a page.

In the previous chapter, you learned how to format words. This chapter focuses on formats and format changes relating to entire lines and paragraphs.

> **TIP** Line and paragraph formatting options can affect the impression your readers get when they first look at your document.

FORMATTING OPTIONS

Here's an overview of the line and paragraph formatting techniques you'll learn in this chapter.

LINE SPACING

The distance between lines of text affects the density of a page. For example, if spacing is too close, text can look cramped and be hard to read. So WordPerfect gives you complete control over line spacing.

TEXT ALIGNMENT

WordPerfect normally aligns text fully justified (with even left and right margins). But you can change this default alignment to left, right or centered.

TABS & INDENTS

With tabs and indents, you can change the starting position of the first line of a paragraph or all lines of a paragraph.

HYPHENATION

The decision to hyphenate will affect the way your pages look. Without hyphenation, pages may have awkward spaces either within lines or at the ends of lines.

POSITIONING TEXT

One special feature you'll want to take advantage of is Advance, which lets you position a block of text anywhere on a page. It's useful for skipping over letterheads and for printing text on standard business forms.

ALTERING LINE SPACING

The default line spacing for WordPerfect documents is 1 (single-spaced lines). The easy way to change the spacing is to adjust it in terms of lines. For example, using a 2 would double-space the lines. You can also specify fractional spacing, such as 1.2.

To increase the line spacing of a document slightly, you'd

Press: **Shift-F8** (Format) or select *Layout*

Select: **1** (Line), **3** (Line Spacing)

The cursor will then be at the Line Spacing option on the Line Format menu (see Figure 20-1).

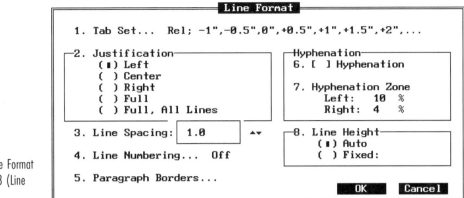

Figure 20-1: The Line Format screen, with option 3 (Line Spacing) selected.

Then enter the new line spacing, for example, 1.2.

(In WordPerfect 5.1, the sequence is Shift-F8, 1, 6.)

ADJUSTING THE LEADING

Another way to achieve the same result is to use single spacing and adjust the leading (the blank space between lines of text). This method of adjusting line spacing is available in WordPerfect 5.1 and higher.

WordPerfect lets you adjust line spacing and paragraph spacing independently. In other words, it lets you treat soft returns differently from hard returns. To adjust within-paragraph leading in version 6.0, you would

Press: **Shift-F8** (Format) or select *Layout*

Select: **7** (Other), **9** (Printer Functions), **4** (Leading Adjustment)

Then you would enter the leading (in inches).

And to adjust the between-paragraph leading, you would:

Press: **Shift-F8** (Format) or select *Layout*

Select: **2** (Margins), **8** (Paragraph Spacing)

Then you would enter the paragraph spacing (in line units).

In WordPerfect 5.1, within-paragraph leading is called Primary leading, and the between-paragraph leading is called Secondary leading. To adjust them, you would

Press: **Shift-F8** (Format) or select *Layout*

Select: **4** (Other), **6** (Printer Functions), **6** (Leading),
     2 (Set Leading)

Then enter the Primary leading (affecting lines within a paragraph) and the Secondary leading (determining spacing between paragraphs). You can enter the leading in points (72 points make one inch). For example, entering 3p would change the leading to 3 points.

ALIGNING TEXT

The most obvious appearance factor in a document is text alignment. Text can be aligned in four ways:

Fully justified (with even left and right margins).

Left aligned (with an uneven right margin).

Right aligned (with an uneven left margin).

Centered.

THE DEFAULT ALIGNMENT

In WordPerfect 6.0, the default is left justification (in Version 5.1, it's full justification).

To change the alignment of text below the cursor, you'd

Press: **Shift-F8** (Format) or select *Layout*

Select: **1** (Line), **2** (Justification)

(In WordPerfect 5.1, the sequence is Shift-F8, 1, 3.)

Then select the alignment you want.

TIP Because an alignment change inserts an open code, the alignment stays in effect until the end of the document or until you enter another alignment code.

ALIGNING TEXT WITH FUNCTION KEYS

You can align text right and center with function keys Alt-F6 (Right) and Shift-F6 (Center) or by selecting *Layout/Alignment* and then either Flush Right or Center. As with other formatting options, you can align text either as you type or after you've typed.

If you format as you type, the Right and Center alignments will affect all text only until you press Enter. So if you want to format text that includes hard returns, you'll have to type the text, then block it and then apply the format (WordPerfect 6.0 doesn't prompt you to confirm your choice).

ALIGNING TEXT AT A TAB

WordPerfect's Ctrl-F6 (Tab Align) feature allows you to align a group of words or numbers on a character they have in common. (With a mouse, the command sequence is *Layout/Alignment/Decimal Tab*.) Since this feature is most useful for aligning numbers, the default alignment character is a period (decimal). When using the default character, the Tab Align feature has the same effect as a Decimal tab (explained in the next section).

SETTING TABS

Tabs allow you to align words or numbers vertically. If you set *relative* tabs, distances are relative to the left margin; so making changes to your margins won't affect the tab settings. If you select *absolute* tabs, distances are measured from 0" on the Tabs Ruler.

    If you want to align text, always use tabs. If you don't, text may look aligned on the screen but print quite differently.

THE TABS RULER

To set tabs, you need to bring up the Tabs Ruler.

HANDS-ON   Display the Tabs Ruler.

    Press: **Shift-F8** (Format) or select *Layout*

    Select: **1** (Line), **1** (Tab Set)

    (In WordPerfect 5.1, the sequence is Shift-F8, 1, 8.)

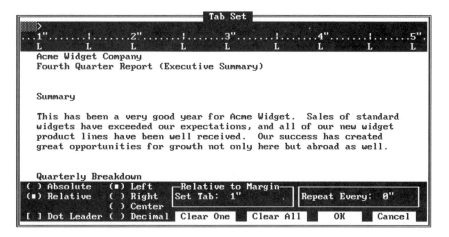

Figure 20-2: The Tabs Ruler

> **TIP** As you can see in Figure 20-2, WordPerfect's default tabs are set at every half-inch. To delete a tab, move the cursor to it and press Delete. To delete all tabs and start from scratch, press Ctrl-End, or select A (Clear All).

To set a tab, position the cursor and type L, R, C or D to create a Left, Right, Center or Decimal tab. You may also enter a number (for example, 2.5) to set a tab at a specific location on the ruler.

HANDS-ON Delete the tabs at 2.0" and 2.5" using the Delete key. Then type D at the 2.5" mark to create a Decimal tab. Use the Tab key to move the cursor to the OK button, and then press Enter.

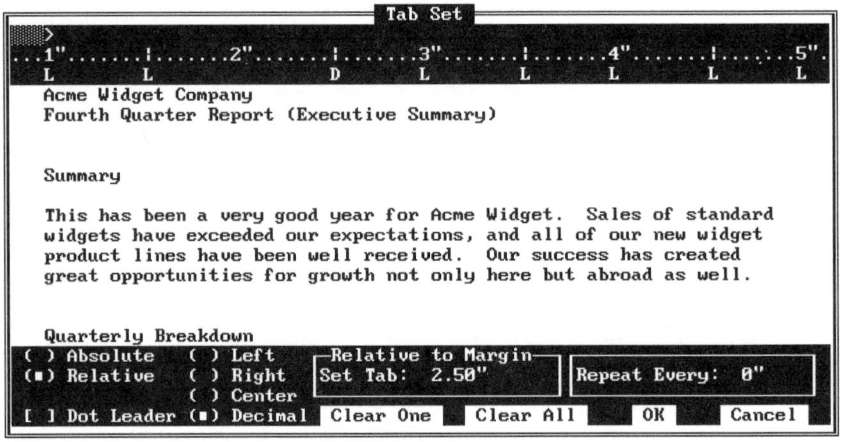

Figure 20-3: A decimal tab set at 2.5" from the left margin.

Figure 20-3 shows the new decimal tab at the 2.5" mark.

HANDS-ON To improve the appearance of the sample document, move the cursor to the first digit of each sales figure and press the Tab key. (*Note*: The F4 (Indent) key won't have the same effect.)

```
Chicago
First Quarter:          970
Second Quarter:         1135
Third Quarter:          1200
Fourth Quarter:         1508

St. Louis
First Quarter:          850
Second Quarter:         995
Third Quarter:          1046
Fourth Quarter:         1350


Message from J. E. Quattlebaum, President

At our last board meeting, our president gave a brief but inspiring
account of the state of the company:

"We at Acme are proud of our position as the third largest supplier
of quality widget products in the midwest.  I believe that our
```

Figure 20-4: Numbers aligned using a decimal tab.

Figure 20-4 shows the column of numbers properly aligned on their (implied) decimals.

DOT LEADERS

A dot leader is a horizontal dotted line that leads to a tab. It's useful for connecting one item of text with another across a page; for example, chapter titles and their page numbers in a table of contents. To create a dot leader for a tab, simply type period (.) on the Tabs Ruler where you've already set a tab with L, R, C or D.

USING TABS & INDENTS

Once your tabs are set, you can use the Tab key, F4 (Indent) or Shift F4 (Double Indent) to move text. If you're using a mouse, select *Layout/Alignment* and then the option you want.

USING THE TAB KEY

To move text over to the next tab stop, position the cursor on the first letter of the text and press the Tab key. The tab affects only the first line of the paragraph.

USING F4 (INDENT)

Unlike a tab, an indent affects the entire paragraph. Using F4 (Indent) or *Layout/Alignment/Indent* moves the left margin of a paragraph to the next tab stop.

THE DOUBLE INDENT

You know that if you use a simple indent, only the left margin of the paragraph moves in. But if you use Shift-F4 (Double Indent) or *Layout/Alignment/Double Indent*, both left and right margins move in the same distance. This technique is useful for setting off a quote or other special paragraph to which you want to draw attention.

HANDS-ON Double-indent the sample report's quote from the president. First, move the cursor to the start of that paragraph.

> Press: **Shift-F4** (Double Indent) or
> select *Layout/Alignment/Double Indent*

```
Third Quarter:        1046
Fourth Quarter:       1350


Message from J. E. Quattlebaum, President

At our last board meeting, our president gave a brief but inspiring
account of the state of the company:

          "We at Acme are proud of our position as the third
          largest supplier of quality widget products in the
          midwest.  I believe that our increased efforts in
          research and development will help to ensure our
          continued success in this very competitive market.
          The future looks bright indeed at Acme."
```

Figure 20-5: A paragraph indented on the left and right sides.

USING HYPHENATION

Depending on your base font and the number of columns you're using, you may end up with awkward spaces at the end of some text lines. If you justify the text, the spaces are simply spread throughout the line, which may create unsightly gaps in lines. To overcome this problem, you can instruct WordPerfect to hyphenate words that can't fully fit at the end of a line.

HANDS-ON Turn on automatic hyphenation. First, move the cursor to the top of the document.

> Press: **Shift-F8** (Format) or select *Layout*
>
> Select: **1** (Line), **6** (Hyphenation)
>
> (In WordPerfect 5.1, the sequence is Shift-F8, 1, 1, Y.)

If the program encounters a word it doesn't know how to hyphenate, it will prompt you to position the hyphen (using the Left and Right arrow keys) and then press Esc (Escape).

POSITIONING TEXT

WordPerfect's Advance feature makes your printer advance the paper to a specific location before printing text, taking the guesswork out of placing text on a page. This technique has two practical uses:

- To skip over your company letterhead at the top of a sheet of paper.
- To precisely place text on a preprinted business form.

To advance text, you would

Press: **Shift-F8** (Format) or select *Layout*

Select: **7** (Other), **6** (Advance)

(In WordPerfect 5.1, the sequence is Shift-F8, 4, 1.)

```
┌──────────────────Advance─────────────────┐
│  ┌Horizontal Position────────────────┐    │
│  │ 1. ( ) Left from Cursor:          │    │
│  │ 2. ( ) Right from Cursor:         │    │
│  │ 3. ( ) From Left Edge of Page:    │    │
│  └───────────────────────────────────┘    │
│  ┌Vertical Position──────────────────┐    │
│  │ 4. ( ) Up from Cursor:            │    │
│  │ 5. ( ) Down from Cursor:          │    │
│  │ 6. ( ) From Top of Page:          │    │
│  └───────────────────────────────────┘    │
│                      ▌  OK  ▌  ▌ Cancel ▌  │
└───────────────────────────────────────────┘
```

Figure 20-6: The Advance menu, showing horizontal and vertical placement options.

In the Advance menu (Figure 20-6), options 1, 2, 4 and 5 let you place text at positions relative to the cursor's current position. Options 3 and 6 let you place text at absolute distances from the edges of your paper (not from the margins).

PRINTING ON FORMS

The Advance feature also enables you to accurately print text on preprinted business forms. This technique requires a little patience and experimentation to get it just right.

To print text on a pre-printed form, follow these steps:

1. Determine the horizontal and vertical placement point for each item to be entered on the form.

2. Type each entry as a separate paragraph.

3. Enter an Advance code at the beginning of each paragraph that specifies the absolute vertical and horizontal placement points.

4. If the form is not $8\frac{1}{2}$ x 11 inches, change the paper size:

Press: **Shift-F8** (Format) or select *Layout*

Select: **3** (Page), **4** (Paper Size/Type)

(In WordPerfect 5.1, the sequence is Shift-F8, 2, 7.)

Then select the paper size you want.

CHAPTER SUMMARY

- You can change the default line spacing from 1 to any other number.

- The default alignment for text is left justification. But you can change the alignment to full, right or center.

- You can set four types of tabs: Left, Right, Center and Decimal.

- To align numbers on their decimals at a tab, use Ctrl-F6 (Tab Align) or *Layout/Alignment/Decimal Tab*, or create a decimal tab.

- The Tab key affects the first line of a paragraph. F4 (Indent) or *Layout/Alignment/Indent* affects the entire paragraph. Shift-F4 (Double Indent) or *Layout/Alignment/Double Indent* brings in both the left and right margins.

- The Advance feature can be used to place text anywhere on the page.

Formatting Pages

WordPerfect
21

Some formatting decisions you make affect particular words, lines and paragraphs. Other choices apply to every page of a document and therefore deserve some special attention. So in this chapter, you'll learn how to

- Set the page margins.
- Number pages either consecutively or by section.
- Add headers and footers to a document.
- Format when the first page is not page 1.

For a new document, WordPerfect automatically sets some formatting specifications such as one-inch margins, single-spaced lines and fully justified text. Other page format items, such as page numbers, headers and footers, must be entered for each document.

PAGE LAYOUT ELEMENTS

Here's an overview of the page formatting techniques you'll learn in this chapter.

MARGINS

Even though WordPerfect's default margins are set at one inch, you can change each margin—top, bottom, left and right—to suit your document. And if you're going to bind your document, WordPerfect will shift the text of each page slightly to leave room for the binding.

PAGE NUMBERS

Page numbers can be separate from headers and footers or included in them. One useful WordPerfect feature is the option to use sectional page numbers, which makes it easy to add or delete pages without having to reprint an entire document.

HEADERS & FOOTERS

Headers and footers are text lines at the top and bottom of the page. They're useful for showing document title, chapter title, page number and date. WordPerfect allows you to place different headers and footers on left and right facing pages.

SETTING MARGINS

The influence of text margins on your document's appearance is obvious. The difference between a "clean" document and a "busy" one is often a matter of choosing margin sizes that work well with your base font and the type of document you're formatting.

CHANGING LEFT & RIGHT MARGINS

Your choice for left and right margins should depend on several factors, including the characteristics of the font. For example, if you use a proportionally spaced font (like Times Roman) or a small text size, the standard 6.5-inch-wide text column will probably be too wide. Each line will contain too many characters, making reading difficult.

To change the left and right margins,

Press: **Shift-F8** (Format) or select *Layout*

Select: **2** (Margins), **1** (Left Margin)

Type: **new margin** Enter

Select: **2** (Right Margin)

Type: **new margin** Enter

(In WordPerfect 5.1, the sequence is Shift-F8, 1, 7.)

WordPerfect also gives you the option of setting left and right margins for individual paragraphs (options 5 and 6 at the Margin Format menu).

CHANGING TOP & BOTTOM MARGINS

To change top and bottom margins, start at the Shift-F8 (Format) or *Layout* menu and select 2 (Margins). Then select 3 (Top Margin) and 4 (Bottom Margin) in turn, typing the new margins for each. In WordPerfect 5.1, you'd select option 2 and then 5.

MAKING OTHER MARGIN ADJUSTMENTS

WordPerfect gives you two other ways to alter document margins. One technique centers a page of text, and the other shifts text to allow for binding.

Centering a Page

You can adjust top and bottom margins by centering the text on a page. This technique is typically used with a short one-page document or a title page to give a balanced look.

To center the current page of text top to bottom,

Press: **Shift-F8** (Format) or select *Layout*

Select: **3** (Page), **2** (Center Current Page)

(In Version 5.1, the sequence is Shift-F8, 2, 1, Y.)

Adding a Binding Area

Adding a binding area will affect the left and right margins. This operation shifts the text toward the outer edge of the document so that a binding won't interfere with the left margin of right-side pages or the right margin of left-side pages. To add a binding area,

Press: **Shift-F8** (Format) or select *Layout*

Select: **7** (Other), **9** (Printer Functions), **2** (Binding Offset), **1** (Binding Offset)

Type: **the binding offset** Enter

(In WordPerfect 5.1, the sequence is Shift-F7, B.)

USING HEADERS & FOOTERS

Headers and footers are text lines that lie outside the text area (but still within the margins). Placed at the top and bottom of a page, they usually display information such as document title, chapter title and page number. The same rules apply to both headers and footers, so I'll talk about only footers to simplify matters.

TIP Since your documents can be designed for either one-sided pages or facing pages, WordPerfect lets you use either a single footer (A) or two footers (both A and B).

You are allowed to have as many A and B footers as you need in your document. For example, in a document with five chapters, you may want a different footer in each chapter. So, you would simply create a different Footer A on the first page of each chapter. A footer is represented by an open code, and remains in effect until you enter another one.

OPTIONS

You can use any available text font, style and size in a footer. For example, to make the footer less intrusive, you might make it smaller than the document text. And you can choose the justification as well (left, right, center or full).

SINGLE FOOTERS

If your document is printed on one side of the paper, you'll probably want the same footer on every page of each section. So you can create a new Footer A on the first page of each section.

Creating a Footer

To create a footer, position the cursor at the top of the first page of a section. Make sure the cursor is not inside a format code. If it is, the footer will have that format characteristic.

HANDS-ON Add a footer that will appear on every page of the sample document. First, move the cursor above all codes by pressing Home, Home, Home, Up arrow.

Press: **Shift-F8** (Format) or select *Layout*

Select: **5** (Header/Footer/ Watermark), **2** (Footers)

Select: **1** (Footer A), **C** (Create)

Type: **Acme Widget -- 4th Quarter**

(In WordPerfect 5.1, the sequence is Shift-F8, 2, 4, 1, 2.)

Don't press Enter after typing the footer. Exit the screen by pressing F7 (Exit) or clicking the right mouse button.

```
Acme Widget Company
Fourth Quarter Report (Executive Summary)


Summary

This has been a very good year for Acme Widget.  Sales of standard
widgets have exceeded our expectations, and all of our new widget
product lines have been well received.  Our success has created
great opportunities for growth not only here but abroad as well.


Quarterly Breakdown

Both of our plants showed increases in sales throughout the year.
As shown below, Chicago outpaced St. Louis by about 10% each
quarter.  As usual, we saw a large increase in widget demand at the
end of the year.  Note: Figures are in thousands.
[Open Style:InitialCodes;[Just:Full]][Footer A:All Pages;Acme Widget [- Hyphen]
4th Quarter][Rgt Mar][Booknark][Bold On][Tab Set]Acme Widget Company[HRt]
Fourth Quarter Report (Executive Summary)[Bold Off][HRt]
```

Figure 21-1: The revealed codes, showing the insertion of a footer.

 The footer code in Figure 21-1 indicates you've created Footer A and that it appears on all pages.

Creating a Header

Single and double headers are created in the same way as footers. On the Format menu, select 5 (Header/Footer/Watermark) and then 1 (Headers).

DOUBLE FOOTERS

If your document will be presented on facing pages (like a book), you might want a different footer on each side. You could create Footer A for the right-hand pages and Footer B for the left-hand pages.

TIP An example of double footers: Footer A (for odd-numbered pages) could be "4th Quarter Report" and Footer B (for even-numbered pages) could be "Acme Widget."

SKIPPING THE TITLE PAGE

If you want all pages of your document except the title page to have a footer, you can insert the footer code on the title page, but suppress the footer on that page. To do this, you would

Press: **Shift-F8** (Format) or select *Layout*

Select: **3** (Page), **9** (Suppress), **3** (Footer A)

(In WordPerfect 5.1, the sequence is Shift-F8, 2, 8, 1.)

EDITING A HEADER & FOOTER

To edit a header or footer, begin by positioning the cursor on or to the right of its code. Then

Press: **Shift-F8** (Format) or select *Layout*

Select: **5** (Header/Footer/Watermark), **1** or **2** (Headers or Footers)

Select: **1** or **2** (A or B), **E** (Edit)

After changing the header or footer, press F7 (Exit) to return to the editing screen.

(In WordPerfect 5.1, the sequence is Shift-F8, 2, 3 or 4, 1 or 2, 5.)

INCLUDING PAGE NUMBERS IN HEADERS & FOOTERS

If you want to include page numbers in a header or footer, use the Formatted Page Number option. (In Version 5.1, just press Ctrl-B. This character will appear as ^B onscreen.)

HANDS-ON Edit Footer A so that it includes the page number on the *right side* of every page.

Press: **Shift-F8** (Format) or select *Layout*

Select: **5** (Header/Footer/Watermark), **2** (Footers)

Select: **1** (Footer A), **E** (Edit)

Press: **End**

Press: **Shift-F6** (Flush Right)

Press: **Shift-F8** (Format) or select *Layout*

Select: **3** (Page), **1** (Page Numbering), **7** (Insert Formatted Page Number)

(In WordPerfect 5.1, the page number code is inserted by pressing Ctrl-B.)

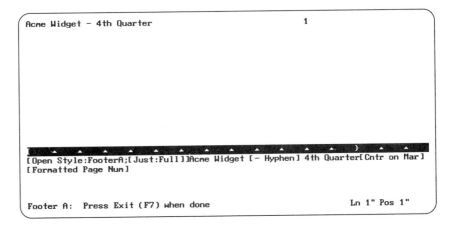

Figure 21-2: The result of inserting a formatted page number code in a footer.

Figure 21-2 shows the formatted page numbering code in a footer.

Using Sectional Page Numbers

In a longer document, it's usually more practical to number pages according to section. For example, you might want pages in Chapter 1 to be numbered 1-1, 1-2, 1-3 and so on.

To create sectional page numbers, insert a new footer (or header) at the beginning of each section. To use a sectional page number in a header or footer, insert a formatted page number as explained in the previous exercise. Then, when you exit the Page Numbering screens, the page number code will be shown in your header or footer (as in Figure 21-2). Type the chapter number, followed by a dash or period, in front of the page number. If this header or footer belongs at the beginning of chapter 4, for example, you would type 4- in front of the page number code. Then when you exit the header or footer editing screen, your document will have sectional page numbers.

Now you have to tell WordPerfect that the first page of each section is page 1. If you don't, WordPerfect will number the pages consecutively without regard to your sectional divisions. To specify a page as page 1,

Press: **Shift-F8** (Format) or select *Layout*

Select: **3** (Page), **1** (Page Numbering)

Select: **2** (Page Number), **1** (New Number)

Type: **1** Enter

(In WordPerfect 5.1, the sequence is Shift-F8, 2, 6, 1.)

After repeating the sequence on the first page of each section, each first page will have the [Pg Num Set] code.

Numbering Front Matter Pages

At the beginning of a document, the title page, preface and table of contents are called *front matter*. The usual custom is to number these pages with small Roman numerals (i, ii, iii, iv and so on) to distinguish them from the body of the document. To create this type of page numbering, you would open the header or footer and

Press: **Shift-F8** (Format) or select *Layout*

Select: **3** (Page), **1** (Page Numbering), **2** (Page Number)

Select: **2** (Numbering Method), **O** (Lower Roman)

If you're using WordPerfect 5.1, you would press Ctrl-B to insert the ^B code in a header or footer. Then you would select 1 (New Page Number) as described above, but type i as the page number.

INDEPENDENT PAGE NUMBERS

If you don't have headers or footers, you can still include page numbers in your document, but you must tell WordPerfect where to place the number on each page.

For example, to add a page number,

Press: **Shift-F8** (Format) or select *Layout*

Select: **3** (Page), **1** (Page Numbering)

Select: **1** (Page Number Position)

(In WordPerfect 5.1, the sequence is Shift-F8, 2, 6, 4.)

```
┌──────────────────── Page Number Position ────────────────────┐
│                                                               │
│ Page Number Position                              ┌─Page─┐    │
│ 1. ( ) Top Left              Every                │1 2 3 │    │
│ 2. ( ) Top Center            Page                 │      │    │
│ 3. ( ) Top Right                                  │5 6 7 │    │
│ 4. ( ) Alternating, Top                           └──────┘    │
│ 5. ( ) Bottom Left                             ┌─Page┐ ┌─Page┐ │
│ 6. ( ) Bottom Center         Alternating       │4    │ │    4│ │
│ 7. ( ) Bottom Right          Pages             │Even │ │ Odd │ │
│ 8. ( ) Alternating, Bottom                     │8    │ │    8│ │
│ 9. (■) None                                    └─────┘ └─────┘ │
│                                                               │
│ A. Font/Attribute/Color...                                    │
│                                                               │
│                                          [  OK  ]  [ Cancel ] │
└───────────────────────────────────────────────────────────────┘
```

Figure 21-3: Choices for placement of page numbers.

Figure 21-3 shows how to select the position for the page number. For example, to select "upper right" for every page, you'd select 3.

CHAPTER SUMMARY

■ You can change WordPerfect's default margins for an individual document with the Shift-F8 (Format) or *Layout* menu.

■ The Center Current Page command centers a page of text from top to bottom.

■ A binding area shifts the text so that a binding won't encroach on the text.

■ Headers and footers lie outside the text area but within the margins.

■ Page numbers can be included in headers or footers.

■ Sectional page numbers can be created by inserting a header or footer on the first page of each section, and then designating each of those first pages as page number 1.

Making Changes

One of the most valuable qualities of a word processing program is its ability to let you change your mind. You can make major or minor modifications quickly and easily until you get it "just right." So in this chapter, you'll learn how to

- Delete and undelete text.
- Replace one word with another.
- Move and copy blocks of text.
- Correct spelling errors.
- Add new words to WordPerfect's dictionary.
- Add variety and precision to your writing.

Before automated word processing, making changes to a document was something you tried hard to avoid. It involved cutting and pasting and whiting-out or retyping words, paragraphs or entire pages. But now, making changes is easy.

WAYS TO MAKE CHANGES

This chapter covers several ways of making changes: correcting typing mistakes, relocating text, replacing one word with another, and changing words with the Spelling Checker and Thesaurus.

CORRECTING MISTAKES

WordPerfect lets you delete a letter, word or block of text. But the comforting part is that if you change your mind, you can bring back deleted text. The program keeps your last three deletions, just in case you want them back.

RELOCATING TEXT

WordPerfect makes it easy to move and copy text (sometimes called cutting and pasting). You can move and copy within a document or from one document to another.

REPLACING WORDS

WordPerfect's Search and Replace features let you locate text and change words. These techniques can save considerable time and extra typing.

THE SPELLING CHECKER & THESAURUS

WordPerfect's Spelling Checker is a wonderful feature that ferrets out those inevitable misspellings. And the Thesaurus provides alternatives for a chosen word to help give variety to a document. If you need a better word—friendlier, stronger or whatever—the Thesaurus can help to find the right shade of meaning.

DELETING & RESTORING TEXT

WordPerfect not only lets you delete text, but also lets you retrieve it if you change your mind. This safety net can help reduce your anxiety as you edit your documents.

DELETING

To delete one character at a time, use the Backspace key. To delete sections of text, first block the text then press Backspace or Del. WordPerfect 5.1 asks you to confirm your decision by typing Y (Yes).

> **TIP** Another way to delete blocked text is to press Ctrl-X (with a mouse, select Edit/Cut). But you won't be able to undelete it using the technique explained in the next section.

UNDELETING

When text has been deleted, it's gone, right? Well, not exactly. Word-Perfect retains the *last three* deletions that you made. So you can make up to three consecutive mistakes without penalty.

For example, to restore the last deletion, press Esc (Escape). (In WordPerfect 5.1, you'd select F1.) With a mouse, select *Edit/Undelete*. WordPerfect then inserts the last deleted text at the cursor's position. If you want to restore it, select 1 (Restore).

But to choose another block of deleted text, select 2 (Previous Deletion) to insert it into the document, and then select 1 (Restore). If you decide not to restore any text, just press Esc.

LOCATING & REPLACING TEXT

If you want to change a particular word, you have to find it first. In a large document, this can sometimes be a problem. But WordPerfect makes it easy with the Search function.

> **TIP** Search works through your document from the cursor to find the word or characters you specify. So, to check an entire document, first move the cursor to the top and then do the search.

SEARCHING FOR TEXT

To search for a text string, press F2 (Search), type the text, press Enter and then press F2 again. (In Version 5.1, don't press Enter after typing the text.) To include a WordPerfect code in the search string, press F5 to display a list of codes. Then move the highlight bar to the desired code and press Enter.

HANDS-ON Locate the word "abroad."

Press: **F2** (Search) or select *Edit/Search*

Type: **abroad** Enter

Select: **F2** (Search) or press the right mouse button

WordPerfect moves the cursor to the first occurrence of "abroad." To search for the next occurrence, press F2 (Search) twice: once to bring up the current search word ("abroad"), and again to initiate the search.

> **TIP** WordPerfect also lets you search for text from the cursor backward through the document. Just select Shift-F2 (Backward Search), or enter the text and press F2. With a mouse, select Edit/Search, and then mark "Backward Search" at the Search screen.

REPLACING TEXT

If you want to replace one word with another word, you can simply locate and retype it. But if you want to change all (or most) occurrences of a word, use the Replace feature. It's similar to Search, but here WordPerfect will automatically change all occurrences of the specified word. Alternatively, you may select 3 (Confirm Replacement) at the Search and Replace screen. Then you will be prompted to confirm each replacement.

HANDS-ON Replace all occurrences of "abroad" with "in Europe." Start with the cursor at the top of the document. (In Version 5.1, you press F2, not Enter, after typing the text.)

Press: **Alt-F2** (Replace) or select *Edit/Replace*

Type: **abroad** (the text to be replaced) Enter

Type: **in Europe** (the new text) Enter

Select: **F2** (Search)

Summary

This has been a very good year for Acme Widget. Sales of standard widgets have exceeded our expectations, and all of our new widget product lines have been well received. Our success has created great opportunities for growth not only here but in Europe as well.

Quarterly Breakdown

Both of our plants showed increases in sales throughout the year. As shown below, Chicago outpaced St. Louis by about 10% each

---

Figure 22-1: Illustration of the replacement of "abroad" with "in Europe."

Figure 22-1 shows that "abroad" has been replaced with "in Europe." You can also use this technique to simplify typing a document. If you need to use a long word or phrase several times, you can abbreviate it when you type the document. For example, instead of typing "Acme Widget Company" a number of times, you could type "AC" each time and later do a Replace operation.

EXTENDING THE SEARCH

Normally, WordPerfect doesn't include headers, footers or notes during a Search or Replace operation. To extend the Search or Replace to all text in a document, first move the cursor above all codes by pressing Home, Home, Home, Up arrow. Then select 5 (Extended Search) at the Search screen, or 7 (Extended Search) at the Search and Replace screen.

MOVING & COPYING TEXT

WordPerfect allows you to move or copy a block of text and its accompanying codes. And by making use of the Doc 2 editing screen, you can copy and move text from one document to another.

> You can get to Doc 2 and then return to Doc 1 by pressing Shift-F3 (Switch) or selecting Window/Switch. (In Version 5.1, it's Edit/Switch Document.)

MOVING TEXT

To move text, block it and then

>Press: **Ctrl-F4** (Move) or select *Edit*

>Select: **1** (Cut and Paste)

>(In Verson 5.1, the sequence is Ctrl-F4, 1, 1.)

At this point, you're free to move the cursor to the point where you want to insert the text. Then press Enter to complete the move operation.

COPYING TEXT

Copying text is similar to moving text. First you block the text, then

>Press: **Ctrl-F4** (Move) or select *Edit*

>Select: **2** (Copy and Paste)

>(In Version 5.1, the sequence is Ctrl-F4, 1, 2.)

Then position the cursor and insert the text by pressing Enter just as you did with Move.

COPYING TEXT TO ANOTHER DOCUMENT

You can copy (or move) text to another document using another editing screen, Doc 2. After initiating the Copy or Move operation in your first document, press Shift-F3 (Switch) or select *Window/Switch* to switch to the Doc 2 screen. Retrieve your second document. Then position the cursor and press Enter to complete the Copy or Move operation. To return to Doc 1, press Shift-F3 (Switch) or select *Window/Switch*.

There's more information on the Doc 2 editing screen in Chapter 26, "Working With More Than One Document."

REPEATING A COPY OR MOVE COMMAND

If you want to insert the moved or copied text again in another location, you don't have to repeat the Move and Copy routines. Just press Shift-F10 (Retrieve) or select *File/Open*, and instead of typing a file name, press Enter or click the right mouse button and press Enter or click on OK.

THE SPELLING CHECKER

The Spelling Checker is one of the most useful features ever developed for word processors. It provides you with a built-in dictionary.

WordPerfect checks spelling by comparing a word first to its Common Word List and then, if necessary, to its Main Word List.

> **TIP** If you routinely use words that aren't in WordPerfect's dictionary, you can create a supplemental dictionary. WordPerfect will then skip those words when you run a spelling check.

The Spelling Checker is extremely useful, but it does have several limitations. First, if you make a mistake—such as transposing letters—that creates a legitimate word, WordPerfect won't notice it. For example, if you type "form" when you meant "from," the error will go unnoticed.

The second limitation is that WordPerfect doesn't know all of the rules about capitalization. For example, if you write "i LIKE my bOSS," it will identify only "bOSS" as being irregular case. So the Spelling Checker isn't a substitute for careful proofreading.

CHECKING YOUR SPELLING

The Spelling Checker can check the current word, the current page, the entire document or a block of text.

HANDS-ON Check the spelling of the entire sample document. The cursor may be anywhere in the document.

Press: **Ctrl-F2** (Spell) or select *Tools/Writing Tools/Speller*

Select: **3** (Document)

When WordPerfect encounters a word that's not in its dictionary, it displays a menu. If the unrecognized word is similar to words that are in its dictionary, WordPerfect will list those words. The illustration in Figure 22-2 shows what WordPerfect's response would be if you had misspelled the word "market."

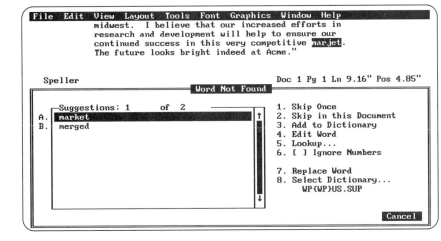

File Edit View Layout Tools Font Graphics Window Help
              midwest. I believe that our increased efforts in
              research and development will help to ensure our
              continued success in this very competitive market.
              The future looks bright indeed at Acme."

         Speller   Doc 1 Pg 1 Ln 9.16" Pos 4.85"
                                    ┌─ Word Not Found ─┐
         ┌─Suggestions: 1   of   2 ─────────┐   1. Skip Once
         A. market   ↑   2. Skip in this Document
         B. merged   3. Add to Dictionary
                                                      4. Edit Word
                                                      5. Lookup...
                                                      6. [ ] Ignore Numbers

                                                      7. Replace Word
                                                      8. Select Dictionary...
                                                         WP{WP}US.SUP
                                                 ↓

                                                              Cancel

Figure 22-2: WordPerfect's response to locating a word it doesn't recognize.

TIP If you want to substitute one of the similar words for the word in your text, type the letter shown beside the list word.

Your other options are listed in the menu. (The WordPerfect 5.1 menu doesn't include options 7 and 8.)

1 (Skip Once): Skips this occurrence of the word.

2 (Skip in this Document): Skips all occurrences of the word.

3 (Add to Dictionary): Adds the word to the supplementary dictionary (explained below).

4 (Edit Word): Lets you edit the word. When you're finished, press F7 (Exit) to continue with the spell check.

5 (Lookup): Lets you look up a word.

6 (Ignore Numbers): Tells WordPerfect not to check words containing numbers.

7 (Replace Word): Replaces the incorrect word with the highlighted word in the list.

8 (Select Dictionary): Lets you select a supplemental dictionary for use during the spell check.

TEACHING NEW WORDS TO WORDPERFECT

WordPerfect's dictionary contains more than 100,000 words, but it can't possibly contain every word you need. You probably use proper names, professional jargon and abbreviations unique to your work.

Fortunately, the program lets you add frequently used words to the dictionary.

When you run a spell check, you can introduce WordPerfect to a word it doesn't recognize by selecting 3 (Add to Dictionary). Each word you add is saved in a supplemental dictionary file called WP{WP}US.SUP. Every time you run a spelling check, WordPerfect will recognize the words in that file.

> **TIP** The WP{WP}US.SUP file can be retrieved just like any other file. So, if you need to add other words to the list, you can simply edit the file instead of going through the spelling-check operation again.

THE THESAURUS

Choosing the right words can mean the difference between a document that persuades and one that merely communicates. Occasionally, you know there must be a better way to say something, but you don't know how. This is where a thesaurus comes in handy.

> **TIP** WordPerfect's Thesaurus lists synonyms and sometimes antonyms for words. It can help you add clarity and variety to your work.

USING WORDPERFECT'S THESAURUS

To use the Thesaurus, position the cursor anywhere in a word and then press Alt-F1 (Writing Tools) or select *Tools/Writing Tools*. Then select 2 (Thesaurus). If the cursor isn't in a word, WordPerfect will display "Word not found" and prompt you to type a word.

HANDS-ON Find alternatives for the word "great." First, move the cursor to the word in the text.

Press: **Alt-F1** (Writing Tools) or select *Tools/Writing Tools*

Select: **2** (Thesaurus)

(In Version 5.1, the sequence is Alt-F1.)

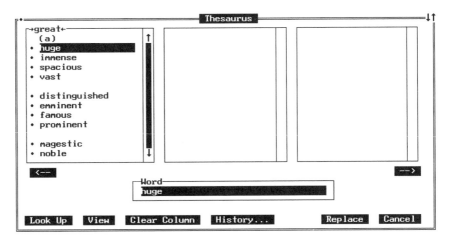

Figure 22-3: Thesaurus alternative for the word "great."

As you can see in Figure 22-3, WordPerfect lists alternatives for the word. To replace the word in your document with a word on the list, move the highlight bar to it and select R (Replace).

You can leave these words in view if you want. WordPerfect allows you to display up to three words and their references side by side. But if you want to clear the column, select C (Clear Column).

To look up another word, select L (Look Up) and then enter the word. When you have words in more than one column, use the Left or Right arrow key to move the highlight bar to another column.

(In WordPerfect 5.1, Replace is option 1, Clear Column is 4 and Look Up Word is 3.)

To return to the editing screen, press Esc or click the left and right mouse buttons.

Moving Through the Document

Above the Thesaurus screen, WordPerfect displays part of your document. If you want to choose words from another section of your document, you don't have to exit the Thesaurus. You can select V (View), use the cursor keys to move to another word, then press Enter. Each time you select a word this way, WordPerfect clears the previously checked word.

CHAPTER SUMMARY

■ You can bring back your last three deletions by pressing Esc or by clicking the middle mouse button (or left and right buttons at the same time).

■ To search for text, use F2 (Search) or *Edit/Search*, or Shift-F2 (Backward Search).

■ To replace text with other text, use Alt-F2 (Replace) or *Edit/ Replace*.

■ To extend a Search or Replace operation to headers, footers and notes, select the Extended Search option.

■ To move or copy blocked text, start with Ctrl-F4 (Move) or *Edit*. To repeat a copy or move, press Shift-F10 (Retrieve) or select *File/Open* and then press Enter or click the right mouse button.

■ To check your spelling, press Ctrl-F2 (Spell) or select *Tools/ Writing Tools/Speller*.

■ To find alternatives for a word, press Alt-F1 (Writing Tools) or select *Tools/Writing Tools*, and then 2 (Thesaurus).

Printing Your Documents

WordPerfect 23

You can take great care in designing a document—choosing the fonts, margins and other features. But it's only when you print your document that you really see how it looks on the page. So in this chapter, you'll learn how to

- Check the accuracy of a document before printing.
- Print a page or an entire document.
- Print a block of text.
- Print several documents in sequence.
- Change the default printer settings.
- Save printing time by downloading fonts.

WordPerfect gives you a great deal of control over what you print and how you print it. By learning a few simple techniques, you can save yourself time and effort.

OVERVIEW

Here's an overview of WordPerfect's most important printing options.

VIEWING YOUR DOCUMENT

If your PC can display graphics, WordPerfect's Print Preview feature will show you approximately what your pages will look like when they're printed. Since printing consumes time and paper, using this feature lets you make sure everything is all right before printing.

PRINTING

WordPerfect gives you considerable flexibility in printing. You can print a page, a block of text, a document or several documents. And if you change your mind, you can cancel a print job.

Print Options

WordPerfect's Print options let you change certain default print settings. For example, you can change the number of copies, the print quality and the printer (if you have two printers).

Downloading

If you use a laser printer, printing takes time because your PC has to send font information to the printer for each job. But you can speed printing by using a special technique called downloading. This technique sends font information to the printer only once at the beginning of your work session. So when you print, the fonts are already in the printer's memory, and your work is printed faster.

CHECKING A DOCUMENT BEFORE PRINTING

Before you print a document, you can save time, frustration and printer paper by doing a few simple things:

- If your PC is capable of displaying graphics, use the Print Preview feature to check your page layout.
- Do a test print of a couple of pages to check headers, footers, page numbers and other details before printing the entire document.
- Save the document—just in case. You never know when some unusual problem might occur.
- Check the spelling. Even on a draft copy, spelling errors can be annoying.

VIEWING THE DOCUMENT

Unless you're running WordPerfect in graphics mode, it's hard to visualize exactly how a page will look when it's printed. So, before printing, use the Print Preview feature to get a better idea of how a page will look. Just press Shift-F7 (Print) and then select 7 (Print Preview). (In Version 5.1, Print Preview is option V.) With a mouse, select *File/Print Preview*.

TIP By looking at one page or two facing pages, you can see how the text is positioned on the page to determine balance, text density and general organization.

To see the document close up, select 1 (100%) or 2 (200%). If you zoom in, you can use the Up and Down arrow keys to display other parts of the page. To return to the editing screen after viewing, press F7 (Exit) or click the right mouse button.

PRINTING YOUR DOCUMENT

WordPerfect provides four ways to print your work. You can print the current page, a specified block of text, the entire document or several documents.

THE PRINT MENU

The Shift-F7 (Print) or *File/Print* menu (Figure 23-1) displays the choices for printing and also for printer settings. (*Note*: the Word-Perfect 5.1 menu is different.)

```
╔════════════════════ Print ════════════════════╗
║  ┌─Current Printer─────────────────────────────┐
║  │ HP LaserJet Series II              Select... │
║  ├─Print─────────────────┬─Output Options───────┤
║  │ 1. (■) Full Document  │ [ ] Print Job Graphically
║  │ 2. ( ) Page           │ Number of Copies: 1
║  │ 3. ( ) Document on Disk...│ Generated by     [WordPerfect ↕]
║  │ 4. ( ) Multiple Pages...│ Output Options...
║  │ 5. ( ) Blocked Text   │ No Options
║  ├─Options───────────────┼─Document Settings────┤
║  │ 6. Control Printer... │ Text Quality     [High    ↕]
║  │ 7. Print Preview...   │ Graphics Quality [Medium  ↕]
║  │ 8. Initialize Printer │ Print Color      [Black   ↕]
║  │ 9. Fax Services...    │
║  └───────────────────────┴──────────────────────┘
║  Setup... Shft+F1          Print   Close   Cancel
╚════════════════════════════════════════════════╝
```

Figure 23-1: The Print menu printing and printer settings options.

1 (Full Document): Prints the entire document.

2 (Page): Prints the current page (the one the cursor is on).

3 (Document on Disk): Lets you print a document without retrieving it. When you enter the file name, be sure that you use the complete path.

4 (Multiple Pages): Lets you print groups of pages (available in WordPerfect 5.1 and higher).

5 (Blocked Text): Prints only text that has been blocked.

6 (Control Printer): Most useful for canceling a print job.

7 (Print Preview): Shows one or two complete pages (if your PC can display graphics).

8 (Initialize Printer): Downloads fonts to your printer. See "Downloading Fonts" in this chapter for an explanation.

9 (Fax Services): Faxes a WordPerfect document from your PC using a fax modem.

PRINTING A SECTION OF TEXT

To print a section of text, first block it. Press Shift-F7 (Print) or select *File/Print* and then 5 (Blocked Text). (In WordPerfect 5.1, you won't see the Print menu. Instead, WordPerfect will ask if you want to print the block. Type Y (Yes) to confirm your decision.)

EXITING THE DOCUMENT

After initiating a print, you may immediately exit the document. But if you want to exit WordPerfect as well, you need to wait until your PC has had time to send the necessary information to the printer. If you try to leave the program too soon, WordPerfect will ask if you want to cancel all print jobs. If you answer Y (Yes), WordPerfect will terminate the printing.

PRINTING FROM THE FILE MANAGEMENT SCREEN

If you're in another document or in a blank screen, you can press F5 (File Manager) or select *File/File Manager* and print selected pages from the File Management screen. You can also mark several files and print them all with one command. For more details on the File Management screen, see Chapter 24, "Managing Your Files."

PRINT OPTIONS

The Current Printer, Options, Output Options and Document Settings portions of the Print menu allow you to change the default printer and the characteristics of the printout.

(Again, the WordPerfect 5.1 menu is different.)

S (Select): Lets you switch to another printer, change the default initial font and select fonts for downloading (see "Downloading Fonts" in this chapter).

N (Number of Copies): Sets the number of copies to be printed. If you change this setting, be sure to change it back to 1 after you have printed.

T (Text Quality): Determines the print quality of text. The options are shown in Figure 23-2.

G (Graphics Quality): Determines the print quality of graphics. The choices are the same as with text.

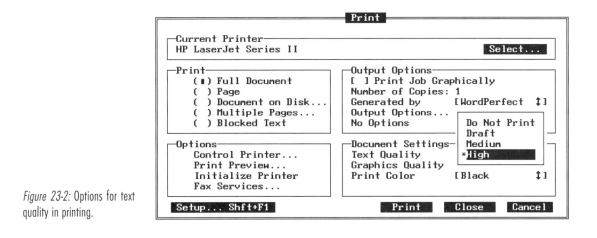

Figure 23-2: Options for text quality in printing.

TIP You might use the G and T options if you need a draft copy of a report. To speed printing, you could set Graphics Quality to Do Not Print and Text Quality to Draft.

DOWNLOADING FONTS

Each time you print a document on a laser printer, WordPerfect has to send the necessary fonts to the printer's memory. So, if your document requires several fonts, printing can take a while. And each time you print, the process has to be repeated.

The solution to this problem is to have WordPerfect send (or download) the most frequently used fonts to the printer once per work session. When this has been done, documents that use any of these fonts can be printed more quickly. This technique doesn't limit you to just those fonts. Others can be sent temporarily to the printer as you need them.

SELECTING DOWNLOADABLE FONTS

To mark fonts for downloading,

Press: **Shift-F7** (Print) or select *File/Print*

Select: **S** (Select Printer), **3** (Edit)

Select: **6** (Font Setup), **2** (Select Graphics Fonts)

(In WordPerfect 5.1, the sequence is Shift-F7, S, 3, 4.)

WordPerfect will now show a list of the available fonts. Mark the fonts you use most often with an asterisk (*). In WordPerfect 5.1, also mark fonts you use *occasionally* with a plus (+). Figure 23-3 shows a list of fonts.

```
┌───────────────────── Select Graphics Fonts ─────────────────────┐
│  ┌─DRS Fonts──────────────────────────────────────────────┐     │
│  │*BitstreamCharter Roman (Speedo)                        │↑│   │
│  │*Bodoni-WP Bold (Type 1)                                │ │   │
│  │ Century-WP,Greek (Type 1)                              │ │   │
│  │ CommercialScript-WP (Type 1)                           │ │   │
│  │*Courier 10 Bold (Speedo)                               │ │   │
│  │*Courier 10 Bold Italic (Speedo)                        │ │   │
│  │*Courier 10 Italic (Speedo)                             │↓│   │
│  └────────────────────────────────────────────────────────┘     │
│  →* (Un)mark DRS Font    N. Name Search    Home,* (Un)mark All Fonts │
│                                                                  │
│  ┌─Font Information──────────────────────────────────────────┐  │
│  │ Font Data File:      C:\BTFONTS\BX000648.SPD    (File Found)│  │
│  │ Rasterizer Driver:   Bitstream Speedo Rasterizer (Internal)│  │
│  └───────────────────────────────────────────────────────────┘  │
│                                            ▐ OK ▌  ▐ Cancel ▌    │
└──────────────────────────────────────────────────────────────────┘
```

*Figure 23-3: A list of laser fonts, showing the available ones marked with *.*

INITIALIZING THE PRINTER

To download the fonts you've marked with asterisks, you have to initialize your printer. You need to do this each time you turn on your printer. And because it ties up some of your printer's memory, be sure to do it only once. To download fonts,

Press: **Shift-F7** (Print) or select *File/Print*

Select: **8** (Initialize Printer)

(In WordPerfect 5.1, the sequence is Shift-F7, 7.)

CHAPTER SUMMARY

■ The Print Preview feature shows one or two complete pages from your document.

■ Shift-F7 (Print) or *File/Print* allows you to print one or more pages of a document. If you block text first, pressing Shift-F7 (Print) or selecting *File/Print* will print just the block.

■ You can print one or more documents from the File Management screen.

■ The Print menu lets you change the number of copies, the print quality and the default printer.

■ Fonts marked with * will be downloaded when you select 8 (Initialize Printer) on the Print menu. You need to initialize your printer only once per work session.

Managing Your Files

In the DOS section of *Office Companion*, you learned how to manage your files using commands such as Copy, Erase and Rename. WordPerfect lets you do all of these operations and more, without leaving the program. So in this chapter, you'll learn how to

■ List WordPerfect files contained in any subdirectory.

■ List selected files.

■ Copy and move files.

■ Delete files.

■ Look at a file without retrieving it.

You know that at the DOS prompt you can erase, copy and perform other actions on your files. But you can also do many of these operations in WordPerfect at the File Management screen, where you can manipulate your WordPerfect files. Even though you're not at the DOS prompt, the same rules and guidelines apply.

THE DEFAULT DIRECTORY

The default directory is the directory you're currently working in (probably \WP60). (Because I don't know which version of Word-Perfect you use, I'll call it \WP.) When you press F5 (File Manager) or select *File/File Manager*, the program will indicate with C:\WP*.* that it's about to show you all files in the default directory. You may recall that * is a wildcard character that represents other characters. So *.* means any file with any extension.

At this point, you can do one of four things:

■ Press Enter to see all the files in the default directory.

■ Display a subset of files by entering in place of *.* a more specific file name. (For example, *.RPT would display all files with the .RPT extension.)

■ Look in another directory temporarily by deleting the default directory and typing another.

■ Change the default directory by pressing = (equals sign) and typing the new directory name. If you'll be working mostly in another directory, changing the default directory will make getting to your files a little easier. (The new directory you specify will remain the default directory until you exit WordPerfect.)

THE FILE MANAGEMENT SCREEN

Pressing F5 (File Manager) displays your WordPerfect files and allows you to perform a variety of file management activities, including copying, erasing and renaming.

DISPLAYING THE FILE MANAGEMENT SCREEN

To see the File Management screen, press F5 (File Manager) or select *File/File Manager*.

Figure 24-1: Result of pressing F5 (File Manager).

```
┌──────────── Specify File Manager List ────────────┐
│                                                     │
│   Directory:  C:\WP\*.*                             │
│                                                     │
│    Quick List... F6     Use QuickFinder.... F4      │
│                                                     │
│    Directory Tree.... F8      Redo F5    OK   Cancel│
└─────────────────────────────────────────────────────┘
```

As you can see in Figure 24-1, WordPerfect indicates that it's going to show you all files (*.*) in the current directory (C:\WP). Press Enter or click the right mouse button to see the list. If you want, you can enter a different directory—for example, \WP\LETTERS.

Figure 24-2: Files in the \WP\LETTERS subdirectory.

```
┌──────────────────────── File Manager ────────────────────────┐
│ Directory:  C:\WP\LETTERS\*.*                   03-10-93  03:04p│
│ ┌Sort by: Filename──────────────┐                              │
│ │.    Current    <Dir>         │↑ 1. Open into New Document    │
│ │..   Parent                    │  2. Retrieve into Current Doc │
│ │ACME1    .LET    1174  05-26-93 10:32a│  3. Look...            │
│ │ACME2    .LET    5316  03-08-93  3:55p│  4. Copy...            │
│ │DR_SMITH.JUN     9028  06-09-93  2:41p│  5. Move/Rename...     │
│ │DR_SMITH.MAR     1190  03-30-93 12:14p│  6. Delete             │
│ │DR_SMITH.MAY     1898  05-26-93 10:52a│  7. Print...           │
│ │EASTERLY.LET     3556  05-01-93  1:41p│  8. Print List         │
│ │JUDY     .MEM     450  04-07-93  9:53a│                        │
│ │OFFICE1  .MEM    1898  05-26-93 10:52a│  9. Sort by...         │
│ │PICNIC   .MEM    1174  05-26-93 10:32a│  H. Change Default Dir...│
│ │PURCHASE.LET     7301  03-14-93  4:39p│  U. Current Dir...  F5 │
│ │REEVES   .LET    3216  05-24-93 10:47a│  F. Find...            │
│ │SURVEY   .LET    4972  05-13-93  3:30p│  E. Search...          │
│ │TOM      .MEM     886  05-25-93  2:36p│  N. Name Search        │
│ │                              │↓ *(Un)mark                     │
│ └ Files:   15 ─── Marked:    0 ─┘ Home,* (Un)mark All           │
│   Free:  8,692,629   Used:   42,059                            │
│                              Setup... Shft+F1   Close           │
└───────────────────────────────────────────────────────────────┘
```

The File Management screen, shown in Figure 24-2, displays your files in alphabetical order. The selection bar indicates the file that will be affected when you select a function from the menu.

> **TIP** To move the selection bar, use the Up and Down arrows and other cursor movement keys.

LOOKING IN SUBDIRECTORIES

If you've organized your files into subdirectories, you'll see them at the top of the list designated <DIR>. To display the files in a subdirectory, move the selection bar to it and press Enter. WordPerfect will indicate that it's about to show you all files (*.*) in that subdirectory. To see the files, press Enter.

LISTING SELECTED FILES

If you don't want to see all files in a directory, you can specify a subset of files. When you press F5 (File Manager) or select *File/File Manager*, WordPerfect says it's going to show you all files (*.*). Simply replace the file name *.* with a more specific file name.

HANDS-ON   List just the files that have the .LET extension.

Press: **F5** (File Manager) or select *File/File Manager*

Then replace *.* in the prompt with *.LET, and press Enter.

```
┌─────────────────────────────── File Manager ───────────────────────────────┐
│ Directory:  C:\WP\LETTERS\*.LET                              03-10-93  03:04p │
│ ┌─Sort by: Filename──────────────────────────┐ ↑  1. Open into New Document  │
│ │ .       Current    <Dir>                    │ █  2. Retrieve into Current Doc│
│ │ ..      Parent                              │    3. Look...                 │
│ │ ACME1   .LET    1174  05-26-93 10:32a       │    4. Copy...                 │
│ │ ACME2   .LET    5316  03-08-93  3:55p       │    5. Move/Rename...          │
│ │ EASTERLY.LET    3556  05-01-93  1:41p       │    6. Delete                  │
│ │ PURCHASE.LET    7301  03-14-93  4:39p       │    7. Print...                │
│ │ REEVES  .LET    3216  05-24-93 10:47a       │    8. Print List              │
│ │ SURVEY  .LET    4972  05-13-93  3:30p       │                               │
│ │                                             │    9. Sort by...              │
│ │                                             │    H. Change Default Dir...   │
│ │                                             │    U. Current Dir...   F5     │
│ │                                             │    F. Find...                 │
│ │                                             │    E. Search...               │
│ │                                             │    N. Name Search             │
│ │                                             │ ↓                             │
│ │                                             │    *(Un)mark                  │
│ └─ Files:    6 ──── Marked:    0 ─────────────┘    Home,* (Un)mark All        │
│    Free:  8,676,105  Used:   25,535                                          │
│                                             Setup... Shft+F1    Close        │
└──────────────────────────────────────────────────────────────────────────────┘
```

Figure 24-3: Files with the .LET extension.

Figure 24-3 shows that only the files with the .LET extension were listed. This technique also works when you select a subdirectory from the File Management screen.

CHANGING THE DEFAULT DIRECTORY

When you use F5 (File Manager) or *File/File Manager*, WordPerfect always shows the default directory. If you'll be working mostly in some other directory during this session, you can change the default directory to make getting to the files a lot easier.

> **TIP** To change the default directory, press F5 (File Manager) or select File/File Manager and then press = (equals). Edit the directory name and press Enter.

THE FILE MANAGEMENT MENU

The menu on the right side of the File Management screen allows you to perform many of the operations you learned to do at the DOS prompt, such as copying, renaming and erasing files.

Although you don't see the DOS prompt, these functions are using standard DOS commands. So the rules and suggestions you learned about manipulating files apply here.

SELECTING A MENU OPTION

To manipulate a file, move the selection bar to it. Then select the menu option you want (the menu is described below). Or, if you want to work with several files, move the light bar to each and type *. For example, you could delete several files with one command by first marking them with *, then selecting the Delete option. If you want to mark all files, press Home, *.

1 (Open into New Document): Retrieves the file into a new document.

2 (Retrieve into Current Doc): Retrieves the file into the current document.

3 (Look): Lets you look at the file without leaving the File Management screen. You cannot edit the file when you're using this option.

4 (Copy): Copies the file. If you're copying within the current directory, just type the new name. If you're copying to another directory, you must type the full path.

5 (Move/Rename): Renames or moves a file. To rename it, simply type the new name. To move it, type the full path indicating the new directory location and name.

6 (Delete): Deletes the file.

7 (Print): Prints the pages you specify. If you then select 1 (*Page/Label Range*), you can specify pages as shown below:

All pages:	Enter
A single page:	12
Single pages:	12, 23, 26
A group of pages:	12 17
Several groups:	12 17, 21 22, 30

From a page to the end: 12

8 (Print List): Prints the current file list.

9 (Sort by): Lets you sort the file listing in several ways, including by filename extension and date/time.

H (Change Default Dir): Changes the default directory for this session and for future sessions.

U (Current Directory): Changes the current directory for this session only.

F (Find): Searches for a specified word or words in the file(s). If WordPerfect finds the word in a file, it marks the file with an asterisk (*).

E (Search): Locates file names in the list that contain a text string you specify. For example, if you enter MA, it will find 15MAY93.RPT, MARK.MEM, and other file names containing the letters MA.

CHAPTER SUMMARY

■ F5 (File Manager) or *File/File Manager* displays all files (*.*) in the default directory and allows you to copy, delete and perform other routine operations.

■ To list a subset of files, use F5 (File Manager) or *File/File Manager* and replace *.* in the prompt with a more specific file name.

■ To change the default directory, press F5 (File Manager) or select *File/File Manager* and then press = (equals). Then enter the new directory.

■ On the File Management screen, you can work with several files at once by first marking them with an asterisk (*).

Using Columns

A multicolumn format can enhance the organization and readability of certain types of documents such as newsletters and schedules. So in this chapter, you'll learn how to

- Set up parallel columns for organizing information.
- Create newspaper-style columns for newsletters and other documents.
- Protect a paragraph from being split between two columns.

TWO TYPES OF COLUMNS

TIP WordPerfect provides two ways of organizing text into columns: newspaper-style and parallel.

Newspaper columns present text in short lines to make reading easier. These columns are characterized by the text-wrap feature: text at the bottom of one column automatically continues at the top of the next column.

Parallel columns are used to organize pieces of related information. These columns would be appropriate in a document such as a conference agenda. The time for each meeting could be in column 1, the meeting room in column 2 and the meeting topic in column 3.

TIP You can use columns throughout an entire document or in selected portions only.

DEFINING TEXT COLUMNS

Regardless of the type of columns you want to use, start at the Text Columns definition screen. Here, you tell WordPerfect the type and characteristics of the columns you want.

THE COLUMN DEFINITION SCREEN

To define columns,

> Press: **Alt-F7** (Columns/Tables) or select *Layout*

> Select: **1** (Columns)

> (In WordPerfect 5.1, the sequence is Alt-F7, 1, 3.)

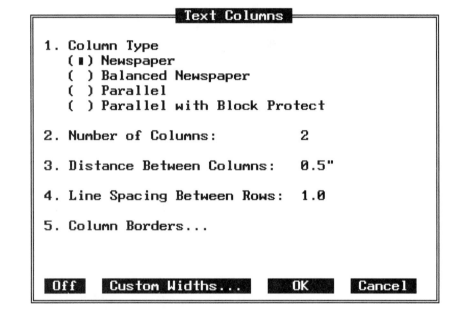

```
┌─────────────────  Text Columns ──────────────────┐
│                                                   │
│  1. Column Type                                   │
│     (■) Newspaper                                 │
│     ( ) Balanced Newspaper                        │
│     ( ) Parallel                                  │
│     ( ) Parallel with Block Protect               │
│                                                   │
│  2. Number of Columns:          2                 │
│                                                   │
│  3. Distance Between Columns:   0.5"              │
│                                                   │
│  4. Line Spacing Between Rows:  1.0              │
│                                                   │
│  5. Column Borders...                             │
│                                                   │
│                                                   │
│  ▐ Off ▌  ▐ Custom Widths... ▌   ▐ OK ▌  ▐ Cancel ▌ │
└───────────────────────────────────────────────────┘
```

Figure 25-1: The column definition screen.

On the column definition screen, shown in Figure 25-1, you can enter the type of columns (newspaper is the default) and the number of columns (2 is the default). WordPerfect will then automatically create the spacing between columns. The defaults are equal-width columns separated by a half-inch space. Use option 3 (Distance Between Columns) to adjust spacing.

TURNING COLUMNS ON & OFF

Once you've defined the columns, you have to turn on the Columns feature by selecting OK (in Version 5.1, "On" is option 1). After formatting your text, turn off the columns by selecting F (Off) on the same menu. In Version 5.1, select 2 (Off).

Now that you know what's required, try the exercise that follows.

PARALLEL COLUMNS

Parallel columns are useful for arranging related pieces of information side by side. An important feature here is Block Protect (also available for newspaper columns). By using it, you ensure that WordPerfect will not break a paragraph between the bottom of one page and the top of the next.

USING PARALLEL COLUMNS

HANDS-ON In the sample document, arrange the two groups of sales figures on the sample report into a two-column format. First, move the cursor to the beginning of the word "Chicago."

Press: **Alt-F7** (Columns/Tables) or select *Layout*

Select: **1** (Columns), **1** (Column Type), **4** (Parallel with Block Protect)

Select: **OK**

(In WordPerfect 5.1, the sequence is Alt-F7, 1, 3, 1, 3.)

The code [Col Def] is now inserted into the document. (When highlighted, the code expands to [Col Def: Parallel with Protect;2].)
The screen should now look like Figure 25-2:

```
quarter.  As usual, we saw a large increase in widget demand at the
end of the year.  Note: Figures are in thousands.


Chicago                               St. Louis
First Quarter:        970             First Quarter:        850
Second Quarter:      1135             Second Quarter:       995
Third Quarter:       1200             Third Quarter:       1046
Fourth Quarter:      1500             Fourth Quarter:      1350


                                      Message from J. E.
                                      Quattlebaum, President

                                      At our last board meeting, our
                                      president gave a brief but
                                      inspiring account of the state
                                      of the company:

                                              "We at Acme
                                              are proud of
```

Figure 25-2: Text formatted into two columns.

TIP To move the cursor from one column to another, press Ctrl-Home (Go To) and then the Left or Right arrow key. With a mouse, just point to one of the columns and click the left button.

TURNING OFF COLUMNS

To return to the normal one-column format, position the cursor and turn off the columns feature.

HANDS-ON Turn off the column format. First, move the cursor to the end of the line containing the last sales figure.

Press: **Alt-F7** (Columns/Tables) or select *Layout*

Select: **1** (Columns), **F** (Off)

(In WordPerfect 5.1, the sequence is Alt-F7, 1, 2.)

The screen should now look like Figure 25-3.

```
quarter.  As usual, we saw a large increase in widget demand at the
end of the year.  Note: Figures are in thousands.


Chicago                            St. Louis
First Quarter:        970          First Quarter:        850
Second Quarter:      1135          Second Quarter:       995
Third Quarter:       1200          Third Quarter:       1046
Fourth Quarter:      1508          Fourth Quarter:      1350



Message from J. E. Quattlebaum, President

At our last board meeting, our president gave a brief but inspiring
account of the state of the company:

        "We at Acme are proud of our position as the third
        largest supplier of quality widget products in the
        midwest.  I believe that our increased efforts in
```

Figure 25-3: Text below the sales figures is formatted into a single column.

The code [Col Def] is now inserted into the document. (When highlighted, the code expands to [Col Def:Off].) If you need to add other items in the column format, just move your cursor above the [Col Off] code to work in the columns.

If you're using three or more columns, you might want to turn off the full text justification. Making the text left-aligned will eliminate the large spaces between words that can sometimes occur with narrow columns. You could also use automatic hyphenation to minimize the awkward spaces.

NEWSPAPER COLUMNS

Newspaper columns are "connected" because text flows (wraps) from the bottom of one column to the top of the next.

USING NEWSPAPER COLUMNS

To set up newspaper columns, you start at the column definition screen, just as you do with parallel columns. But here, you would select 1 (Column Type) and then 1 (Newspaper). Another option is the Balanced Newspaper format, where text is adjusted so that all columns are of equal length. Then you would exit the screen and turn on the columns by selecting OK.

> **TIP** To move from one column to another, you can use the same method you used with parallel columns. Press Ctrl-Home (Go To) and then either the Left or Right arrow key.

When you're ready to turn off the columns, open the column definition screen and select F (Off).

PROTECTING A BLOCK

To make use of the Block Protect feature with newspaper columns, you must block the paragraph you want to protect. Then press Shift-F8 (Format) or select *Layout.* Then select 7 (Other) and 1 (Block Protect). In WordPerfect 5.1, simply press Shift-F8 and type Y (Yes), or select *Edit/Protect Block.*

CHAPTER SUMMARY

■ Parallel columns arrange related pieces of information side by side. Newspaper columns arrange text in a continuous "page" that wraps from column to column.

■ To set up columns, press Alt-F7 (Columns/Tables) or select *Layout/Columns,* and then select 1 (Columns).

■ WordPerfect automatically controls column width and spacing unless you choose to enter those measurements yourself.

■ The Block Protect feature prevents a paragraph from being split between the bottom of one page or column and the top of the next page or column.

■ To move the cursor from column to column, press Ctrl-Home (Go To) and then the Right or Left arrow key.

Working With More Than One Document

Creating a document sometimes involves using or referring to other documents. For example, you might want to move or copy text from another document, or combine a number of small documents into a larger one. So in this chapter, you'll learn how to

- Display two different documents on one screen.
- Open two different documents at the same time on two different editing screens.
- Simplify the creation of large documents using the Master Document feature.

OPTIONS

WordPerfect provides two ways to work on two or more documents. The first way is to open two or more editing screens at once. The second is to combine several documents into one file using WordPerfect's Master Document feature.

WORKING WITH MULTIPLE DOCUMENTS

At times, you might need to refer to a section of one document while writing another. Or you might need to copy text from one document to another. WordPerfect allows you to open up to nine documents on one screen using the Window feature. (In Version 5.1, you can open only two.) Or, if you prefer, you can have two documents open in two separate, full-size editing screens.

USING MASTER DOCUMENTS

To simplify the writing of long documents, WordPerfect lets you create the parts of the document as separate files. Then you can combine them into one master document for operations such as spell checking, text replacement and printing. The procedure saves time because you need to perform the operations only once instead of many times.

SEEING TWO DOCUMENTS ON THE SCREEN

WordPerfect's Window feature lets you divide the screen into two or more parts. Because each part is a separate editing screen, you can have a document open in each.

SPLITTING THE SCREEN

To split the screen into two editing windows, use the Tile feature.

HANDS-ON   Display two editing windows on the screen.

      Press: **Shift-F3** twice

      Press: **Ctrl-F3** (Screen) or click *Window*

      Select: **1** (Window), **4** (Tile)

```
 File  Edit  View  Layout  Tools  Font  Graphics  Window  Help
                              1-(Untitled)



Courier 10cpi                                    Doc 1 Pg 1 Ln 1" Pos 1"
                              2-(Untitled)



Courier 10cpi                                    Doc 2 Pg 1 Ln 1.19" Pos 1"
```

Figure 26-1: Two editing screens displayed together.

    (In WordPerfect 5.1, press Ctrl-F3 or select Edit. Then select 1 (Window) and type 12.)

    As you can see in Figure 26-1, you can now create a new document in the new window or retrieve an existing document into it. To move the cursor from one window to the other, press Shift-F3 (Switch), or select *Window/Switch*, or click the mouse inside the window.

OPENING THE SAME DOCUMENT IN BOTH WINDOWS

If you're working on a long document, you might occasionally need to refer to some earlier text while you're writing—to check key words, organization or other information. To continually page up and down through the document would be time-consuming and frustrating. But by opening the document in both the Doc 1 and Doc 2 windows, you can leave an earlier page in view while you create a later page. Just be careful not to make changes in both of the windows.

RETURNING TO ONE WINDOW

To return to a normal screen, move the cursor to the Doc 1 window and then press Ctrl-F3 (Screen) or select *Window.* Then select 1 (Window) and 3 (Maximize).

> **TIP** If you're using Version 5.1, change the Doc 1 window size back to 24 lines using Ctrl-F3 (Screen) or Edit/Window.

USING TWO FULL-SIZE EDITING SCREENS

What if you want to have two documents open but don't want them on the same screen? WordPerfect can accommodate you because it has two separate editing screens. It calls the first Doc 1 and the second Doc 2. By switching to Doc 2, you can retrieve and edit a second document without exiting the first. By using Shift-F3 (Switch) or *Window/Switch,* you can move from one document to the other.

USING THE DOC 2 SCREEN

HANDS-ON

Go to the Doc 2 screen.

Press: **Shift-F3** (Switch) or select *Window/Switch*

Figure 26-2: Status line indicating the Doc 2 editing screen.

```
Courier 10cpi                                    Doc 2 Pg 1 Ln 1" Pos 1"
```

In the Status Line at the bottom right of the screen, you see "Doc 2" (Figure 26-2). Now you can retrieve a document into this editing screen or create a new one without affecting the document in the Doc 1 screen.

> **TIP** If you're using the Timed Backup feature (explained in Chapter 18), the temporary backup file for Doc 2 will be named WP{WP}.BK2.

MASTER DOCUMENTS

A master document is a WordPerfect file composed of other smaller files called subdocuments. A subdocument is no different from any other WordPerfect document. It functions as a subdocument only when you identify it as such in a master document.

Creating a master document gives you the advantage of working on several smaller (and more manageable) documents instead of a large, unwieldy one. When the time comes to use the complete document, you tell WordPerfect to combine the subdocuments into a single file.

THINKING AHEAD

Before creating a master document, decide how you'll divide your document. Let's say you have four reports—one for each quarter of the year—and you want to assemble them into one document. In your master document, you'd include four subdocuments.

You have other matters to consider, also. First, will each subdocument have its own formatting codes, or will you have the codes only in the master document? You'll probably want each subdocument to have its own codes. This way, each one will look right (that is, have the correct margins, tabs and other features) as you work on it. And to ensure consistent features in all subdocuments, you can use WordPerfect styles (see Chapter 30, "Letting WordPerfect Do the Typing").

Second, how will you number pages? If you want sectional page numbers, you'll have to designate the first page of each subdocument as page 1. Then you'll need to add the sectional page number to your headers or footers the way you learned in Chapter 21, "Formatting Pages." But if you want continuous page numbering, don't put any page numbers in the subdocuments. Instead, put the page numbering code at the top of the master document.

CREATING A MASTER DOCUMENT

To create a master document, bring up a blank screen (or go to Doc 2). Then insert codes that identify each subdocument. If all your subdocuments are in the same subdirectory, creating your master document in that subdirectory will save you some typing. If they're not, you'll have to enter the complete path for each subdocument.

> **TIP** By the way, you can create a master document before you have created the subdocuments.

HANDS-ON In the Doc 2 screen, create a master document called 1993.RPT that begins with a blank page (for a table of contents). Then include four subdocuments: 1Q.RPT, 2Q.RPT, 3Q.RPT and 4Q.RPT. Add a page break after each subdocument.

Press: **Ctrl-Enter** (to create a blank page)

Press: **Alt-F5** (Mark Text) or select *File*

Select: **3** (Master Document), **3** (Subdocument)

Type: **1Q.RPT** Enter

Press: **Ctrl-Enter**

(In WordPerfect 5.1, the sequence is Alt-F5, 2.)

Now add the other subdocuments in the same manner. Save the file as 1993.RPT. The document should look like Figure 26-3.

```
Subdoc: 1Q.RPT

Subdoc: 2Q.RPT

Subdoc: 3Q.RPT

Subdoc: 4Q.RPT
```

Figure 26-3: A master document containing subdocuments.

Now you can put the master document aside and work on your subdocuments. You won't need the master document again until you're ready to assemble the complete document.

EDITING A MASTER DOCUMENT

If you need to make a change to the master document, you can't edit it like normal text. To change a subdocument code, you have to delete it with the Backspace key and insert a new one in its place. You can also add other subdocuments if necessary.

WORKING WITH MASTER DOCUMENTS

To work on the series of subdocuments as if they were one file, you have to expand the master document. When you do, WordPerfect retrieves the subdocuments. Once you've expanded the master document, you can perform document-wide operations such as search and replace, spell check and print.

Expanding the Master Document

HANDS-ON Expand the master document 1993.RPT.

Press: **Alt-F5** (Mark Text) or select *File*

Select: **3** (Master Document), **1** (Expand)

(In WordPerfect 5.1, the sequence is Alt-F5, 6, 3.)

You'll then see a list of the subdocuments that will be expanded. You may unmark any one by removing the * that appears next to its name. Select OK and then Y (Yes).

> **TIP** If a subdocument doesn't yet exist, WordPerfect will prompt you to press Enter to skip it.

```
┌──────────────────────────────────────────────────────────┐
│  ════════════════════════════════════════════════════    │
│                                                           │
│  ┌─────────────────────────────────────────────────────┐ │
│  │ Subdoc Begin: 4Q.RPT                                 │ │
│  └─────────────────────────────────────────────────────┘ │
│  Acme Widget Company                                       │
│  Fourth Quarter Report (Executive Summary)                 │
│                                                           │
│  Summary                                                  │
│                                                           │
│  This has been a very good year for Acme Widget.  Sales of │
│  standard widgets have exceeded our expectations, and all of our │
│  new widget product lines have been well received.  Our success │
│  has created great opportunities for growth not only here but │
│  abroad as well.                                          │
│                                                           │
│  Courier 10cpi                          Doc 2 Pg 2 Ln 1" Pos 1" │
└──────────────────────────────────────────────────────────┘
```

Figure 26-4: An expanded master document.

Each expanded subdocument is now bound by two markers (see Figure 26-4). These markers are necessary, so don't delete them.

Closing a Master Document

When you're ready to leave the expanded master document, condense it into subdocuments once again.

HANDS-ON   Condense the master document 1993.RPT.

> Press: **Alt-F5** (Mark Text) or select *File*
>
> Select: **3** (Master Document), **2** (Condense)
>
> (In WordPerfect 5.1, the sequence is Alt-F5, 6, 4.)

```
┌──────────────────────── Condense Master Document ────────────────────────┐
│ ┌─1. Subdocuments───────────────────Save─┐↑     1. Save Subdoc            │
│ │ *1Q.RPT                                 │      2. Save All               │
│ │ *2Q.RPT                                 │      3. Name Search            │
│ │ *3Q.RPT                                 │                                │
│ │ *4Q.RPT                                 │      *  (Un)mark               │
│ │                                         │↓  Home,*  (Un)mark All         │
│ └─────────────────────────────────────────┘                              │
│                                                      OK      Cancel        │
└───────────────────────────────────────────────────────────────────────────┘
```

Figure 26-5: Prompt to condense expanded subdocuments.

You'll see a list of subdocuments that will be condensed (see Figure 26-5). If you made any changes to a subdocument when it was expanded, highlight its name and select 1 (Save Subdoc).

CHAPTER SUMMARY

■ WordPerfect's Window feature lets you split the screen into two or more separate editing screens named Doc 1, Doc 2 and so on.

■ Doc 2 is a second editing screen.

■ To switch between Doc 1 and Doc 2, use Shift-F3 (Switch) or *Window/Switch*.

■ The master document feature simplifies creating large documents by letting you work on individual subdocuments.

■ A master document must be expanded before you can perform operations such as spell checking or printing.

Creating
Access Aids

WordPerfect
27

In a long document, readers often skip around to find information on specific topics. To help your readers, you'll want to provide access aids that guide them to chapters, figures, special topics and other items of interest. So in this chapter, you'll learn how to create

- A table of contents.
- An index.
- A list of figures or tables.
- Page references.

Access aids—such as tables of contents, indexes and lists—help your readers find what they're looking for in your document. Each of these aids is a list of items and their page locations.

> **TIP** The problem with locating a topic is that it might move around as you add or delete sections of text. To overcome the problem, WordPerfect automatically keeps track of a topic's location regardless of how much it moves around.

THREE STEPS

All the access aids mentioned above require the same three steps: marking the entries, defining the list and generating the list.

1. To create an entry for a list, you block it, then *mark* it as a particular type of entry (for example, an index entry). Once it's been marked, WordPerfect will always keep up with its page location and the type of list to which it belongs.

2. Once you've marked the appropriate items, you need to *define* the list by telling WordPerfect where to create it and what it should look like.

3. After you've defined the list, you can have WordPerfect *generate* it. If you generate a draft version of the list, be sure to regenerate it when you've finished creating and editing the document.

CREATING A TABLE OF CONTENTS

A table of contents quickly gives your readers an idea of how your document is organized and where to find major topics. WordPerfect can accommodate up to five heading levels in a table of contents.

MARKING TEXT FOR THE TABLE

The first step in creating a table of contents is to mark the topics that will be included in the table. When you mark an entry, you have to specify the level (from one through five) to which it belongs.

For the following exercise, go back to the sample report in Doc 1 by pressing Shift-F3 (Switch) or selecting *Window/Switch*.

HANDS-ON Mark "Fourth Quarter Report" for Level 1 of the table of contents. First, block the phrase.

Press: **Alt-F5** (Mark) or select *Tools*

Select: **1** (Table of Contents)

Type: **1** (Level 1) [Enter]

(In WordPerfect 5.1, the sequence is Alt-F5, 1, 1.)

```
Acne Widget Company
Fourth Quarter Report (Executive Summary)


Summary

This has been a very good year for Acne Widget.  Sales of standard
widgets have exceeded our expectations, and all of our new widget
product lines have been well received.  Our success has created
great opportunities for growth not only here but abroad as well.


Quarterly Breakdown

Both of our plants showed increases in sales throughout the year.
As shown below, Chicago outpaced St. Louis by about 10% each
quarter.  As usual, we saw a large increase in widget demand at the
end of the year.  Note: Figures are in thousands.

[Mrk Txt ToC Begin]Fourth Quarter Report[Mrk Txt ToC End] (Executive Summary)[Bo
ld Off][HRt]
```

Figure 27-1: Codes showing that text has been marked for the table of contents.

Figure 27-1 shows the document's codes. Mark and End Mark codes indicate that the phrase "Fourth Quarter Report" is an entry for Level 1 of the table of contents. If you wanted a more detailed table, you could block and mark the document's subheadings for Level 2 of the table.

DEFINING THE TABLE

After marking all entries for the table, the second step is to define the table. Here, you tell WordPerfect where to create the table and what its format should be. For this exercise, you can define the table of contents in the master document that you created in the Doc 2 screen.

HANDS-ON At the top of the master document 1993.RPT, define the table of contents with one level. First, type TABLE OF CONTENTS at the top of the document. Press Enter a few times to add a little space between this title and the table.

Press: **Alt-F5** (Mark) or select *Tools*

Select: **2** (Define), **1** (Table of Contents)

(In WordPerfect 5.1, the sequence is Alt-F5, 5, 1.)

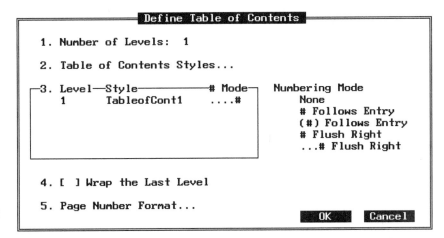

Figure 27-2: Definition screen for a table of contents.

The Table of Contents Definition screen is shown in Figure 27-2. If you exit this menu without making a choice, WordPerfect will set up one level using the default page-numbering scheme: flush-right with a dot leader. If you want to choose a different page-numbering method, you can select option 3 and select a numbering mode.

When you're finished defining the table, WordPerfect inserts the table definition mark [Def Mark] into your document at the cursor. (When expanded, the code is [Def Mark: ToC, 1: Dot Ldr #].) The numbers mean you have one level in the table that uses the Flush Right with Leader numbering option.

GENERATING THE TABLE

If you've marked the entries and defined the table of contents, you can now generate the table. The cursor may be anywhere in the document when you do this. If a subdocument is missing, WordPerfect will prompt you to press Enter to skip it.

HANDS-ON   Generate the table of contents.

Press: **Alt-F5** (Mark) or select *Tools*

Select: **4** (Generate)

Select: **OK**

(In WordPerfect 5.1, the sequence is Alt-F5, 6, 5, Y.)

```
TABLE OF CONTENTS

First Quarter Report. . . . . . . . . . . . . . . . . . . . . . . 3

Second Quarter Report . . . . . . . . . . . . . . . . . . . . . . 4

Third Quarter Report. . . . . . . . . . . . . . . . . . . . . . . 5

Fourth Quarter Report . . . . . . . . . . . . . . . . . . . . . . 6


Subdoc: 1Q.RPT


Subdoc: 2Q.RPT
C:\WP\1993.RPT                              Doc 1 Pg 1 Ln 1" Pos 1"
```

Figure 27-3: A generated table of contents.

Figure 27-3 shows how the generated table looks onscreen.

> **TIP** Keep in mind that if you make changes to your subdocuments, you'll have to regenerate the table.

CREATING AN INDEX

An index lists specific words and topics that readers may want to locate and usually provides more detail than a table of contents. WordPerfect gives you two ways to create entries for an index:

- You can block and mark each individual entry in your document, designating it as an index item. If the entry is a single word, you don't have to block it first—just position the cursor in the word.
- You can list and mark all words you want in the index in a separate concordance file and let WordPerfect do the rest of the work.

MARKING INDEX ITEMS

To mark an item for the index, block it and then

Press: **Alt-F5** (Mark) or select *Tools*

Select: **4** (Index)

You'll then see a box showing the blocked text as an index heading. If you want it to be a heading, press Enter three times. But if you want the text to be a subheading, type the correct heading and press Enter. WordPerfect will make the original blocked text a subheading. At that point, press Enter twice to return to the editing screen.

USING A CONCORDANCE

A *concordance* is a document in which you list words and phrases you want included in the index. You mark items in a concordance just as you mark them in a document (as described in the previous section). WordPerfect will locate every occurrence of each item and keep track of its page locations. When you define the index in your current document, WordPerfect will allow you to enter the name of the concordance file.

DEFINING THE INDEX

To define an index, create a new page at the end of your document. Then type INDEX and press Enter several times to add some space. Then define the index.

Defining an index is similar to defining a table of contents:

Press: **Alt-F5** (Mark) or select *Tools*

Select: **2** (Define), **4** (Index)

(In WordPerfect 5.1, the sequence is Alt-F5, 5, 3.)

```
╔══════════════════ Define Index ══════════════════╗
║ ┌Level────────Current Style─┐ ┌Numbering Mode──────┐ ║
║ │ Heading       Index1       │ │ 1. ( ) None        │ ║
║ │ Subheading    Index2       │ │ 2. ( ) # Follows Entry │ ║
║ └────────────────────────────┘ │ 3. ( ) (#) Follows Entry │ ║
║                                 │ 4. ( ) # Flush Right │ ║
║   6. Index Level Styles...      │ 5. (▪) ...# Flush Right │ ║
║                                 └────────────────────┘ ║
║   7. [X] Combine Sequential Page Numbers (Example: 51-62) ║
║                                                    ║
║   8. Page Number Format...                         ║
║                                                    ║
║   9. Concordance Filename:                         ║
║                                                    ║
║ ▐File List... F5▌ ▐Quick List... F6▌    ▐ OK ▌ ▐Cancel▌ ║
╚════════════════════════════════════════════════════╝
```

Figure 27-4: The index definition screen.

At the Define Index screen (Figure 27-4), you can select the page-numbering method and other options. If you're using a concordance, select option 9 and enter the name of the file.

When you're finished defining the index, WordPerfect inserts the definition mark code [Def Mark] at the cursor. (When expanded, the code is [Def Mark:Index, Dot Ldr #].)

GENERATING THE INDEX

After defining the index, you can generate it. The cursor may be anywhere in the document. To generate an index,

Press: **Alt-F5** (Mark) or select *Tools*

Select: **4** (Generate)

Select: **OK**

(In WordPerfect 5.1, the sequence is Alt-F5, 6, 5, Y.)

> **TIP** To give your index a more professional look, you could format it into two newspaper-style columns. You might also want to use a font smaller than the one used in the document.

CREATING A LIST

In a complex document, it's customary to include lists of figures, tables and illustrations. WordPerfect lets you have ten different lists per document. Lists one through five use text that you mark using the method explained below. Lists six through ten use captions you've entered for graphics boxes (see Chapter 28, "Using Graphics").

MARKING THE LIST ENTRIES

To mark an item for a list, block the text. Then

Press: **Alt-F5** (Mark) or select *Tools*

Select: **2** (List)

Then enter the number of the list to which this text belongs.

DEFINING THE LIST

After marking all entries for a list, you can define the list:

Press: **Alt-F5** (Mark) or select *Tools*

Select: **2** (Define), **2** (List)

(In WordPerfect 5.1, the sequence is Alt-F5, 5, 2.)

After you've defined and named the list, WordPerfect inserts the definition mark code [Def Mark] into the document at the cursor. When expanded, the code is [Def Mark: List, name: Dot Ldr #].

GENERATING THE LIST

After you mark items and define the list, you may generate the list:

Press: **Alt-F5** (Mark) or select *Tools*

Select: **4** (Generate)

Select: **OK**

(In WordPerfect 5.1, the sequence is Alt-F5, 6, 5, Y.)

CREATING A PAGE REFERENCE

Unlike the other access aids, a page reference isn't a list. A page reference simply refers the readers to another topic (the target) in the document. Since the target topic may move around as you edit your document, you want WordPerfect to keep up with its location.

For example, let's say that on page 12 of a document you want to make a reference to a topic that appears earlier. On page 12, you would type your reference text, for example

(See "Creating an Index," page)

Because you want WordPerfect to keep up with the page number, you leave it off. Now position the cursor on the parenthesis after the word "page." Then

Press: **Alt-F5** (Mark) or select *Tools*

Select: **1** (Mark Text), **6** (Both Reference & Target)

```
┌──────────── Mark Cross Reference and Target ────────────┐
│                                                         │
│  1. Tie Reference to                                    │
│     ( ∎ ) Page                                          │
│     ( ) Secondary Page                                  │
│     ( ) Chapter                                         │
│     ( ) Volume                                          │
│     ( ) Paragraph/Outline                               │
│     ( ) Footnote                                        │
│     ( ) Endnote                                         │
│     ( ) Caption Number                                  │
│     ( ) Counter...                                      │
│                                                         │
│  2. Target Name:                                        │
│                                                         │
│  ▌ Targets... F5 ▐              ▌ OK ▐    ▌ Cancel ▐     │
└─────────────────────────────────────────────────────────┘
```

Figure 27-5: Options that let you identify reference and target text for a cross-reference.

Select: **2** (Target Name)

Type: **Creating an Index** [Enter]

Select: **OK**

(In WordPerfect 5.1, the sequence is Alt-F5, 1, 3.)

WordPerfect will then prompt you to mark the target text in your document. So move the cursor to the target text and press Enter. When you return to the editing screen, you'll find that the page reference has been inserted at the cursor's position.

If your editing causes target text to change locations, you'll need to regenerate the cross-references so the page numbers are correct.

Press: **Alt-F5** (Mark) or select *Tools*

Select: **4** (Generate)

Select: **OK**

(In WordPerfect 5.1, the sequence is Alt-F5, 6, 5, Y.)

CHAPTER SUMMARY

■ Common access aids are tables of contents, indexes, lists and page references. To create them, press Alt-F5 (Mark) or select *Tools.*

■ To create a table of contents, index or list, you must mark the text, define the access aid, then generate it.

■ For an index, an alternative to marking each entry is creating a concordance file that lists all entries.

■ If you make changes to your document, you'll need to regenerate the tables, indexes and lists to make sure the page number references are correct.

■ To create a page reference, you must indicate the reference text and mark the target text.

Using Graphics

While text conveys ideas over a period of minutes, pictures convey ideas almost instantaneously. Adding charts and illustrations can greatly enhance the visual interest and effectiveness of a document. So in this chapter, you'll learn how to

- Draw horizontal and vertical lines in various widths and shades of gray.
- Place an image in a document.
- Reposition an image on the page.
- Change the proportions of an image.

WordPerfect's graphics capabilities create great opportunities for creative expression. No longer do your documents have to look dull and average–now, you can be your own graphic designer.

GRAPHICS OPTIONS

Here's an overview of the graphics options in WordPerfect.

LINES

WordPerfect lets you draw vertical and horizontal lines on a page. But to fully appreciate this feature, you'll need to broaden your conception of what a line is. In WordPerfect, a line can be narrow or as wide as the page. And it doesn't have to be black. WordPerfect allows shades of gray from 0 percent (white) to 100 percent (black).

TEXT

WordPerfect allows you to treat text as graphics. This feature is useful for displaying quotes from the text (pull-quotes), creating headlines and using other text blocks as design elements.

IMAGES

In your WordPerfect document, you can make use of images from a variety of sources, including drawing programs, painting programs and scanned photographs. You can also use Lotus 1-2-3 graphs.

DRAWING LINES

Horizontal and vertical lines can give a document an organized appearance by cleanly separating areas of text or images. WordPerfect gives you control over a line's position, length and width, and shading density.

CREATING A LINE

HANDS-ON   Draw a horizontal line under the title of the sample report. First, move the cursor to the blank line below the title.

Press: **Alt-F9** (Graphics) or select *Graphics*

Select: **2** (Graphics Lines), **1** (Create)

(In WordPerfect 5.1, the sequence is Alt-F9, 5, 1.)

```
┌──────────────────────┤ Create Graphics Line ├──────────────────────┐
│                                                                      │
│   1. Line Orientation      [Horizontal      ↕]                       │
│                                                                      │
│   2. Horizontal Position   [Full            ↕]                       │
│   3. Vertical Position     [Baseline        ↕]                       │
│                                                                      │
│   4. Thickness             [Auto            ↕]                       │
│                                                                      │
│   5. Length:               6.5"                                      │
│                                                                      │
│   6. Line Style...         Single Line                               │
│                                                                      │
│   7. Color                                                           │
│         (■) Use Line Style Color                                     │
│         ( ) Choose Color...                                          │
│                                                                      │
│   8. Spacing...            0", 0"                                    │
│                                                              OK   Cancel │
└──────────────────────────────────────────────────────────────────────┘
```

Figure 28-1: The line definition screen.

As shown in Figure 28-1, the defaults are

■ Horizontal line.

■ Full horizontal position (the line will extend to the left and right margins).

■ Baseline vertical position (the line's vertical position is determined by the cursor's position).

■ Single line style.

You may change any of the settings, or select the OK button to accept the defaults.

Although the line won't appear on the editing screen, you will see it when you either view the document or print the page.

EDITING A LINE

To edit an existing graphics line, position the cursor to the right of the line code and

Press: **Alt-F9** (Graphics) or select *Graphics*

Select: **2** (Graphics Lines), **2** (Edit), **E** (Edit Line)

(In WordPerfect 5.1, the sequence is Alt-F9, 5.)

GRAPHIC IMAGES

Drawing lines is a simple way of adding flair to a document. But to get really creative, you'll want to make use of WordPerfect's ability to handle graphic images.

GRAPHICS BOXES

To insert an image into a document, you first have to create a *graphics box* that indicates the intended size and location of the image. WordPerfect provides eight types of boxes. Four of the box types—Figure, Table, Text and User—are "general-purpose" boxes and can contain text or graphics. By offering different types of boxes, WordPerfect can create separate lists of the different types of graphics. For example, if you put your tables in Table boxes and your illustrations in Figure boxes, WordPerfect can create separate lists of your tables and illustrations.

FOUR WAYS TO ATTACH A BOX TO THE TEXT

To create a graphics box, you have to decide how it will be attached to the text. (In Version 5.1, it's called anchoring.) You have four choices:

- If you want an image to appear on a particular page, regardless of subsequent text editing, use the Page option.
- If you want an image to always be in a particular paragraph, use the Paragraph option.

■ If you want an image to appear in a fixed location, unaffected by text editing, use the Fixed Page Position option (not available in Version 5.1).

■ If you want an image to be treated just like a word in a sentence, use the Character Position option.

CREATING A GRAPHICS BOX

The first step in using images is to create a graphics box. The image you bring into WordPerfect will be scaled to fit the box you create. Later, you can move the box or scale it to different proportions.

HANDS-ON Create a graphics box containing a Lotus 1-2-3 bar graph. Here, the graph file being used is called BAR1.PIC in the \123 directory on Drive C. First, move the cursor below the sales figures (and below the [Col Def:Off] code).

Press: **Alt-F9** (Graphics) or select *Graphics*

Select: **1** (Graphics Boxes), **1** (Create)

```
════════════════════ Create Graphics Box ════════════════════
  1. Filename...
 ┌──────────────────────────────────────────────────────────┐
 │                                                            │
 └──────────────────────────────────────────────────────────┘
  2. Contents  [None            ↕│ 7. Attach To [Paragraph            ↕]
  3. Create Text...                 8. Edit Position...
                                       Horiz.  Right (Margin)
  4. Create Caption...                 Vert.   0"
 ┌──────────────────────────────┐  9. Edit Size...
 │                              │     Width   2.2" (Forced)
 └──────────────────────────────┘     Height  2.2" (Automatic)
  5. Options
     Content Options...           T. Text Flow Around Box
     Caption Options...              Text Flows [On Larger Side ↕]
  6. Edit Border/Fill...             [ ] Contour Text Flow
 ┌──────────────────────────────────────────────────────────┐
 │ Y. Based on Box Style...  Figure Box                       │
 └──────────────────────────────────────────────────────────┘
  Help                                      OK      Cancel
```

Figure 28-2: The graphics box definition screen.

On the definition screen (Figure 28-2), enter the file name and how you want the graphics box attached to the text. You can also enter a caption for the figure, change the size of the box, or reposition the box.

Select: **1** (Filename)

Type: **C:\123\BAR1.PIC**

Select: **7** (Attach To), **P** (Paragraph)

Select: **8** (Edit Position), **1** (Horizontal Position)

Select: **C** (Centered)

(In WordPerfect 5.1, option 4 (Anchor Type) is the same as 7 (Attach To).)

If you ever make a change to the file used for a box (in this example, BAR1.PIC), you'll need to come to this screen again and replace the old file name with the new one.

Viewing the Image

When you create a graphics box and specify a file, WordPerfect automatically inserts the image into the box. You can't see the image on the editing screen; you see only the graphics box (see Figure 28-3). But you can see it when you view or print the document.

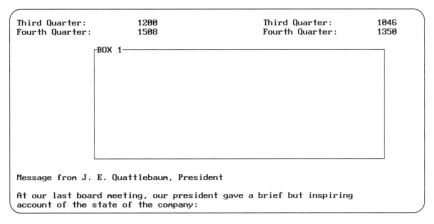

```
Third Quarter:        1200              Third Quarter:        1046
Fourth Quarter:       1508              Fourth Quarter:       1350
                ┌BOX 1─────────────────────────────────┐
                │                                       │
                │                                       │
                │                                       │
                │                                       │
                │                                       │
                │                                       │
                │                                       │
                └───────────────────────────────────────┘

Message from J. E. Quattlebaum, President

At our last board meeting, our president gave a brief but inspiring
account of the state of the company:
```

Figure 28-3: A document that contains a graphic image.

EDITING A GRAPHICS BOX

As you create a graphics box, you can specify its location, size and proportions. You can also edit a graphics box after you've created it. When you modify a box, WordPerfect will scale the image to make it fit the box.

To edit an existing graphics box, move the cursor to the right of its code. Then

Press: **Alt-F9** (Graphics) or select *Graphics*

Select: **1** (Graphics Boxes), **2** (Edit), **E** (Edit Box)

(In Version 5.1, the sequence is Alt-F9, 1, 2.)

At this point, you would see the original Graphics Box Definition screen for the selected box.

Removing a Box

To remove a graphics box, press Alt-F3 (Reveal Codes) or select *View/Reveal Codes*, and delete the code for the box.

EDITING AN IMAGE

When you modify the size and shape of a graphics box, WordPerfect adjusts the image to fit the box. But you can also edit the image itself, independent of its box. By modifying the image, you can create some interesting visual effects, such as rotation and distortion.

The modifications you make don't affect the original graphics file. The image you're working with here is part of your WordPerfect document.

The Graphics Editing Screen

To bring up the graphics editing screen, you have to identify the type and number of the box containing the image.

HANDS-ON Bring up the graphics editing screen for the Figure box you created.

Press: **Alt-F9** (Graphics) or select *Graphics*

Select: **1** (Graphics Boxes), **2** (Edit)

Select: **E** (Edit Box), **3** (Image Editor)

(In WordPerfect 5.1, the sequence is Alt-F9, 1, 2, box number, 9.)

The menu at the bottom of the screen lists the editing options. (Version 6.0 has additional options at the top of the screen.) The options shown in the first line let you quickly edit the image:

■ The arrow keys move the image within the box.

■ The PgUp and PgDn keys scale the image larger or smaller.

■ The + and – keys rotate the image.

■ The Insert key determines the percent of change brought about by the keys described above. The choices are 1, 5, 10 or 25 percent.

■ The options on the second line of the menu give you finer control over your image by letting you move the image to any position, scale the X- and Y-axes independently and rotate the image any number of degrees.

■ If you don't like the changes you've made, you can revert to the original image by pressing Ctrl-Home (Go To) or selecting *Edit/Go To*.

USING GRAPHICS OPTIONS

WordPerfect provides several options for enhancing the appearance of your graphic images and their boxes.

HANDS-ON   Bring up the options screen.

Press: **Alt-F9** (Graphics) or select *Graphics*

Select: **1** (Graphics Boxes), **2** (Edit), **E** (Edit Box)

Select: **5** (Options), **2** (Caption Options)

(In WordPerfect 5.1, the sequence is Alt-F9, 1, 4.)

```
┌──────────────────────────────── Caption Options ────────────────────────────────┐
│  ┌─Caption Position──────────────────┐  ┌─Caption Format────────────────────┐    │
│  │ 1. Side of Box        [Bottom  ↕] │  │ 6. Caption Width                  │    │
│  │                                   │  │    (■) Auto (Based on Caption)    │    │
│  │ 2. Relation to Border [Outside ↕] │  │    ( ) Set:                       │    │
│  │                                   │  │    ( ) Percent:                   │    │
│  │ 3. Position           [Left    ↕] │  │                                   │    │
│  │                                   │  │ 7. Rotation           [None    ↕] │    │
│  │ 4. Offset from Position           │  │                                   │    │
│  │    ( ) Set:                       │  └───────────────────────────────────┘    │
│  │    (■) Percent:        0      ▼▲  │  ┌─Caption Counter───────────────────┐    │
│  │ 5. Offset Direction   [Right   ↕] │  │ 8. Counter...  Figure Box         │    │
│  └───────────────────────────────────┘  └───────────────────────────────────┘    │
│                                                          ▐ OK ▌   ▐ Cancel ▌      │
└───────────────────────────────────────────────────────────────────────────────────┘
```

Figure 28-4: Options for a graphics box caption.

At the Caption Options screen (Figure 28-4), you can choose the side of the box on which the caption appears, the location of the caption (inside or outside), and other characteristics.

CHAPTER SUMMARY

■ Pressing Alt-F9 (Graphics) or selecting *Graphics* lets you create and edit lines, boxes and images.

■ A graphics line may be any width and length and any shade of gray.

■ To insert an image into a document, you have to first create a graphics box.

■ Graphics boxes can contain text or images.

■ A box can be attached to the text in four ways: to a page, to a particular position on a page, to a paragraph or to a character.

■ If you edit the size and shape of a box, WordPerfect will scale the image to fit.

■ An image may be edited independent of its graphics box.

Merging
& Sorting

An important part of any business is correspondence. To make this activity a little easier, WordPerfect lets you automatically create business letters and mailing labels. So in this chapter, you'll learn

- How to create a database file in WordPerfect.
- What records and fields are.
- What form and data files are and how to use them.
- How to automatically merge one file into another.
- How to print mailing labels.

DATABASES

WordPerfect goes beyond simple word processing by allowing you to set up information in a *database* format. A database is simply a collection of information arranged in a specific way. Your telephone book is an example of a database. Each line is one complete *record*. Each record consists of three *fields*: name, address and phone number.

In an electronic database, you can do some useful things, like sort the records alphabetically and select certain records that meet a criterion.

MERGING

In WordPerfect, you can also merge records into a document. For example, you can create mailing labels (the records) in one file and a business letter in another. When you're ready, WordPerfect will take each record and insert the information into the letter. If you're sending the same letter to more than a few people, this technique can save a great deal of time and effort.

In using the Merge feature, you'll make use of special codes that are available by pressing Shift-F9 (Merge Codes) or selecting *Tools/Merge/Define*. These codes give WordPerfect important information about the way you've set up the database and the way you want to perform the merge. Only a few of the most important codes will be covered here.

CREATING MERGE FILES

To use WordPerfect's Merge feature, you create a *form* file and a *data* file. Typically, the form file is a business letter, and the data file contains name/address records. When you're ready to create and print the letters, you open a *new* document and give the command to merge the data file into the form file. In this new document, WordPerfect creates a letter addressed to each person listed in the data file.

Creating a Data File

To create a data file containing names and addresses, type each record as shown in Figure 29-1. Here, you're breaking the information into individual fields. So the salutation is field 1, the person's first name is field 2, and so on. (You can break a record into as many fields as you find practical. For example, you might have a need to use the state and ZIP Code as separate fields.) After you type each field, press F9 (End Field) to insert the ENDFIELD code (in version 5.1, the code is {END FIELD}). This action automatically inserts a hard return and moves the cursor to the next line.

After typing the final field of each record, you need to insert the ENDRECORD code. To insert this code, press Shift-F9 (Merge Codes) or select *Tools/Merge/Define*. Then select 2 (Data [Text]) and 2 (End Record). This action will insert the ENDRECORD code and insert a hard page break.

HANDS-ON Create the data file, like the one shown below, and save it as NAMES.DAT. Include as much data as you want.

```
Mr.ENDFIELD
JamesENDFIELD
P.ENDFIELD
SmithENDFIELD
PresidentENDFIELD
Acme ManufacturingENDFIELD
100 Technology Ave.ENDFIELD
Newark, NJ   10999ENDFIELD
ENDRECORD

Ms.ENDFIELD
AndreaENDFIELD
J.ENDFIELD
RestonENDFIELD
Sales ManagerENDFIELD
Unitied Industries, Inc.ENDFIELD
1200 Pineview Rd.ENDFIELD
San Francisco, CA   98888ENDFIELD
ENDRECORD
```

Figure 29-1: Records in a data file.

Creating a Form File

In your letter (the form file), you need to insert codes that indicate where to use the fields from the data file. So if you want your letter to have "Dear Mr. Smith:" as the greeting, you would have to type "Dear FIELD(1) FIELD(4):" because the salutation is field 1 and the last name is field 4.

To insert a field code into your form file, position the cursor and press Shift-F9 (Merge Codes) or select *Tools/Merge/Define.* Select 1 (Form) as the document type. Then select 1 (Field), type the number of the field, and press Enter. WordPerfect will then insert the code for that field.

HANDS-ON   Open a new document and create the form file shown in Figure 29-2. Save it as 15MAY93.FRM.

```
                                      15 May 1993

                                      L. L. Greene
                                      Director of Marketing
                                      Acme Widget Company
                                      100 Widget Way
                                      St. Louis, MO  65500

FIELD(2) FIELD(3) FIELD(4)
FIELD(5)
FIELD(6)
FIELD(7)
FIELD(8)


Dear FIELD(1) FIELD(4):

Acme Widget, in an effort to supply its customers with the newest
and the best, has begun production of a new Euro-style widget.
As one of our valued customers, you will soon be receiving a
brochure that outlines the technical specifications of the product.
```

Figure 29-2: Part of a form file, including field markers.

Here, fields 1 through 8 of the data file are represented with the markers FIELD(1) through FIELD(8). (In Version 5.1, you'll see {FIELD}1~ through {FIELD}8~.) But keep in mind that you don't have to use all your data fields in the form file.

MERGING FILES

After you've created and saved the form and data files, you're ready to open a new document and merge those two files. In this example, the form file is 15MAY93.FRM and the data file is NAMES.DAT.

HANDS-ON Print a copy of the form file letter for every person in the data file.

Press: **Ctrl-F9** (Merge/Sort) or select *Tools*

Select: **1** (Merge)

Type: **15MAY93.FRM** (the form file) `Enter`

Type: **NAMES.DAT** (the data file) `Enter`

Select: **Merge**

WordPerfect will now create identical letters (except for the addressees), with each letter beginning on a new page (see Figure 29-3). At this point, you can print or view the letters at the Shift-F7 (Print) menu.

Figure 29-3: Result of merging the data and form files.

```
                                              15 May 1993

                                              L. L. Greene
                                              Director of Marketing
                                              Acme Widget Company
                                              100 Widget Way
                                              St. Louis, MO  65500


        James P. Smith
        President
        Acme Manufacturing
        100 Technology Ave.
        Newark, NJ  10999


        Dear Mr. Smith:

        Acme Widget, in an effort to supply its customers with the newest
        and the best, has begun production of a new Euro-style widget.
        As one of our valued customers, you will soon be receiving a
```

There's no need to save this merged file since you can easily re-create it whenever you need it.

SELECTING RECORDS

What if you want to send the letter to just a few people listed in the data file? You need to *select* the records you want from the original data file and save them in a new file. This new file then becomes the data file for the merge operation.

USING THE SORT FEATURE

To select records from your data file, you'll need to

(1) Identify the data file. (2) Create the sort specifications. (3) Enter the criterion for selecting records. (4) Perform the sort.

Identifying the Files

At the first Sort screen, you have to specify the file containing the name and address records (the data file).

HANDS-ON Identify NAMES.DAT as the file containing the name/address records.

Press: **Ctrl-F9** (Merge/Sort) or select *Tools*

Select: **2** (Sort), **2** (File)

Type: **NAMES.DAT** Enter

Figure 29-4 shows the completed screen.

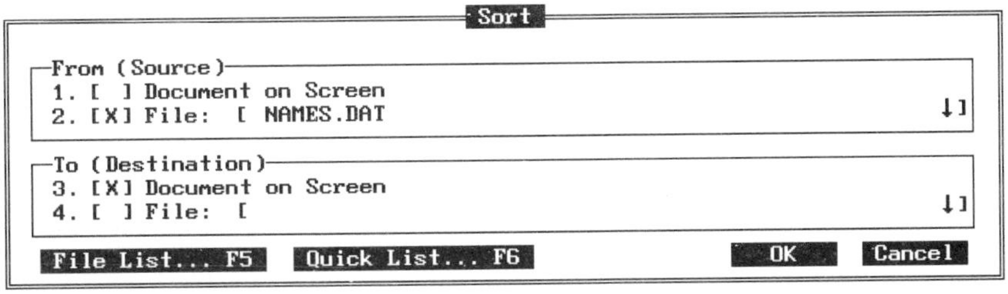

Figure 29-4: The Sort screen with NAMES.DAT specified as the data file.

Creating the Sort Specifications

At the next Sort screen, you need to tell WordPerfect how to sort the data file records (see Figure 29-5). On the right side of the screen, you see the default specifications:

Key: The number of this particular sort specification (you may have up to nine keys).

Type: The type of sort (alphabetic or numeric).

Order: The order in which the selected records will be arranged (ascending or descending).

Field: The field which contains the information that's relevant for the sort (here, it's field 5, which contains each person's job title).

Line: The line in the field on which the Word appears (if the field consists of more than one line).

Word: The word number within the field (if the field contains more than one word).

```
Mr.ENDFIELD
JamesENDFIELD
P.ENDFIELD
SmithENDFIELD
PresidentENDFIELD
Acme ManufacturingENDFIELD                          Doc 2 Pg 1 Ln 1" Pos 1"
┌─────────────────────────────────Sort────────────────────────────────┐
│  1. Record Type  [Merge Data File ↓]                                  │
│                                                                       │
│  2. Sort Keys (Sort Priority)      ┌Key Type  Ord  Field  Line  Word┐ │
│                        1. Add       1   Alpha  ↑      1     1     1 │↑│ │
│                        2. Edit                                     │ │ │
│                        3. Delete                                   │ │ │
│                        4. Insert                                   │↓│ │
│                                                                       │
│  3. Select Records:                                                   │
│  4. [ ] Select Without Sorting                                        │
│  5. [ ] Sort Uppercase First    [Perform Action] [View] [Close] [Cancel] │
└───────────────────────────────────────────────────────────────────────┘
```

Figure 29-5: The second Sort screen, showing the default selections.

For this example, only one item needs to be changed: the Field. Right now, it's shown as field 1; but the field containing the person's job title is field 5. So you need to edit the specifications box.

HANDS-ON Change the sort Field to field 5.

Select: **2** (Sort Keys), **2** (Edit), **4** (Field)

Type: **5** [Enter]

Select: **OK**

Figure 29-6 shows the completed screen.

```
Mr.ENDFIELD
JamesENDFIELD
P.ENDFIELD
SmithENDFIELD
PresidentENDFIELD
Acme ManufacturingENDFIELD
┌─────────────Edit Sort Key─────────────┐         Doc 2 Pg 1 Ln 1" Pos 1"
│  1. Key Number:  1     4. Field:  5    │
│                                        │
│  2. Type               5. Line:   1    │ Key Type  Ord  Field  Line  Word
│     (■) Alpha                          │ 1   Alpha  ↑      1     1     1 │↑│
│     ( ) Numeric        6. Word:   1    │
│                                        │
│  3. Order                              │
│     (■) Ascending  [A-Z]               │                              │↓│
│     ( ) Descending [Z-A]               │
│  [Help]          [ OK ]  [Cancel]      │ Action   View   Close   Cancel
└────────────────────────────────────────┘
```

Figure 29-6: The Edit Sort Key box, showing that the field has been changed to field 5.

Entering the Criterion

Finally, you need to indicate the criterion for selecting records. Let's say that you want to use all records for people who are presidents of their companies. So the person's title (field 5) needs to contain the word "President."

HANDS-ON Specify the criterion for using only those records with "President" in the key field (field 5).

> Press: **Esc**
>
> Select: **3** (Select Records)
>
> Type: **key1=President** [Enter]
>
> Figure 29-7 shows how the Sort screen should now look.

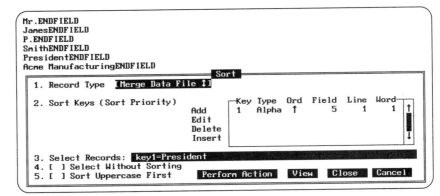

Figure 29-7: The completed Sort screen, showing the criterion for selecting records.

Sorting the Records

After completing the Sort screen, you're ready to select the records that meet your criterion.

HANDS-ON Sort the data file.

> Select: **P** (Perform Action)

The records that meet the criterion—people who are Presidents of companies—will be inserted into the current document.

PRINTING MAILING LABELS

Creating and printing letters are only half the job. The other part is printing mailing labels. If you have a data file like the one described above, you can use it to print mailing labels for all your letters.

LASER PRINTERS

If you use a laser printer, you're most likely using a full page of labels (either two or three across). To print on these labels, you'll want to create a special form file into which the existing data file names and addresses will be merged.

STEP 1. Open a new document and set up two parallel columns with block protect. You'll probably have to adjust the column width and spacing to match the layout of your labels on the page. Then turn on the columns.

STEP 2. Insert the field code in this new form file for each field that you're using from the data file. To insert a field code:

Press: **Shift-F9** (Merge Codes) or select *Tools/Merge/Define*

Select: **1** (Field)

Type: field number [Enter]

Insert the codes for all of the fields you're using. Don't press Enter after the final field code.

STEP 3. Press Ctrl-Enter to go to the second column. Insert the NEXTRECORD code by selecting it from a list of merge codes:

Press: **Shift-F9** (Merge Codes) or select *Tools/Merge/Define*

Select: **M** (Merge Codes)

Select: **NEXTRECORD**

Then enter the field codes as you did in the first column. Don't press Enter after the final field code.

STEP 4. Turn off the columns.

STEP 5. If you need to add blank lines (to fill up the space on the labels), press Enter. After doing a test print, you will see whether you need to add more blank lines or adjust the line spacing.

STEP 6. Insert the PAGEOFF code:

Press: **Shift-F9** (Merge Codes) or select *Tools/Merge/Define*

Select: **3** (Page Off)

The screen should now look like Figure 29-8.

Figure 29-8: The completed form file for creating mailing labels.

```
FIELD(2) FIELD(3) FIELD(4)        NEXTRECORD FIELD(2) FIELD(3) FIELD(4)
FIELD(5)                          FIELD(5)
FIELD(6)                          FIELD(6)
FIELD(7)                          FIELD(7)
FIELD(8)                          FIELD(8)

PAGEOFF
```

The form file is now complete. After you save it, you can open a new document and merge your name/address records using Ctrl-F9 (Merge) and print your two-across labels.

DOT-MATRIX PRINTERS

If you use a dot-matrix printer, you're probably using one-across continuous labels. Here, the procedure is a little easier. What you want to do is treat each label as a separate page (a very small page). So, in your form file, you'll have to set new margins and a new paper size—at the Shift-F8 (Format) or Layout menu—to match the size of your labels.

CHAPTER SUMMARY

- A database consists of records, which in turn are composed of fields.
- Merging involves inserting fields from a data file into a form file (called secondary and primary, respectively, in Version 5.1).
- In a WordPerfect data file, the code ENDFIELD indicates the end of a field, and ENDRECORD indicates the end of a record.
- A form file contains markers that indicate where to use fields from the data file.
- To merge a data file and a form file, open a new document and press Ctrl-F9 (Merge/Sort) or select *Tools*, and then 1 (Merge).
- Records can be sorted and selected by using Ctrl-F9 (Merge/Sort) or *Tools* and then 2 (Sort).

Letting WordPerfect Do the Typing

WordPerfect 30

Entering formatting codes can be tedious when you're working on a long document. But for most operations, WordPerfect will do the typing for you. So in this chapter, you'll learn how to

- Save a group of formatting codes in a file.
- Use open and paired styles.
- Save a series of keystrokes in a file.
- Perform complex operations by pressing only two keys.

STYLES & MACROS

To take full advantage of WordPerfect, you'll want to learn how to automate text formatting and other operations. The program offers two techniques: *styles* and *macros*.

For each, you simply enter the commands once and save them in a file. Then when you're ready to execute the commands, you insert the style or activate the macro, and WordPerfect does the rest.

STYLES

A WordPerfect *style* is a set of codes saved in a file. Any time you want to apply those codes, you insert the style. The main advantages in using styles are that they

- Save you keystrokes.
- Ensure a consistent look to a document.
- Make document-wide format changes quickly and easily.

MACROS

A WordPerfect *macro* is a file that contains a series of keystrokes (commands and/or text). When you activate the macro, WordPerfect will execute all the operations listed in the file. Macros automate typing and save you keystrokes. They also reduce the incidence of errors.

WHAT'S THE DIFFERENCE?

Both styles and macros can be used to insert codes. What's the difference? The most important difference has to do with changing your mind. If you don't like the way your text looks after you apply a style, you can simply edit the style, and WordPerfect will automatically change all text affected by the style. But if you had applied formatting with macros, you'd have to replace every occurrence of the macro codes yourself. So, for formatting applied throughout a document, use styles.

UNDERSTANDING STYLES

WordPerfect allows you to create three types of styles: open, paragraph and character.

An *open style* consists of open codes. When you insert an open style, its codes remain in effect until other conflicting codes are encountered. Open styles can include codes such as base font, margins, tabs and page numbering. An open style could be used to set up the overall format of a document.

A *paragraph style* (called a *paired style* in Version 5.1) consists of paired codes such as Bold or Underline. Unlike an open style, a paired style is applied only to a specific block of text. Paragraph styles are useful for formatting frequently used items in a document, such as chapter titles, subheadings and quotes.

Styles are initially available only in the document in which they were created. But later in this chapter, you'll learn how to use a list of styles in any document.

CREATING AN OPEN STYLE

Open styles are useful for setting up the characteristics of a document, such as margins, tabs and font.

HANDS-ON Create an open style called LETTER that sets up your standard business letter. Include codes for the Courier 10-cpi (ten characters per inch) font, and left and right margins at two inches.

Press: **Alt-F8** (Style) or select *Layout/Styles*

Select: **2** (Create)

Type: **LETTER** Enter

Select: **2** (Style Type), **O** (Open Style)

Select: **OK**

Select: **4** (Style Contents)

Figure 30-1 shows the Edit Style screen with option 4 selected.

```
                          ▌Edit Style▐

     1. Style Name:    LETTER
     2. Description:
     3. Style Type     [Open        ↕]

    ┌4. Style Contents──────────────────────────────────┐
    │                                                    │
    │                                                    │
    │                                                    │
    │                                                    │
    │                                                    │
    └────────────────────────────────────────────────────┘

     5. [ ] Show Style Off Codes
     6. Enter Key Action...                    ▌  OK  ▐  ▌Cancel▐
```

Figure 30-1: The Edit Style screen with option 4 selected.

In the Style Contents box, insert the margin code by pressing Shift-F8 (Format) or selecting *Layout*, 1 (Line), 2 (Margins), then 1 (Left Margin) and 2 (Right Margin). Insert the font code by pressing Ctrl-F8 (Font) or selecting *Font*, 1 (Font), then the Courier font. Press F7 (Exit) when you're finished inserting the codes. The completed style is shown in Figure 30-2.

```
                          ▌Edit Style▐


     Font... Ctrl+F8    Format... Shft+F8    Based on Style... Alt+F8

    ┌──Style Contents───────────────────────────────────┐
    │▌Lft Mar▐[ Rgt Mar ][ Font:Courier 10cpi ]          │
    │                                                    │
    │                                                    │
    │                                                    │
    │                                                    │
    └─Press F7 when done. ───────────────────────────────┘
                                              ▌  OK  ▐  ▌Cancel▐
```

Figure 30-2: The completed style with codes for new margin settings and a new base font.

Saving the Style

When you exit the Edit Style screen by selecting OK, your style is automatically saved.

Applying the Style

Creating an open style doesn't turn it on. To apply an open style in a document, position your cursor where you want the style to begin. Then press Alt-F8 (Style) or select *Layout/Styles*. You'll see the screen shown in Figure 30-3. Move the highlight bar to the style you want, and select 1 (Select).

```
                          ┌─── Style List ───┐
 List Styles from: (■) Document  ( ) Personal Library  ( ) Shared Library
 ┌Name────────── Type────── Description──────────────────────────────┐
  Heading 1      •Paragraph  Title                                   ↑
  Heading 2      •Paragraph  Main Heading
  Heading 3      •Paragraph  Subheading
  LETTER          Open
  None            Paragraph   No Paragraph Style
                                                                     ↓
 ──────────────────────────────────────────────────────────────────
 1. Select    3. Edit...   5. Copy...    7. Save...    9. Mark
 2. Create... 4. Delete... 6. Options... 8. Retrieve... N. Name Search
              "•" Denotes Library Style              │ Close │
```

Figure 30-3: The list of available styles.

Editing a Style

When you modify a style, the text to which that style has been applied is automatically updated.

CREATING A PARAGRAPH STYLE

A paragraph style is used to apply formatting codes to blocks of existing text. Whereas an open style uses open codes, a paragraph style uses paired codes.

In WordPerfect 6.0, you create a paragraph style on the same screen used for creating open styles. However, for a paragraph style, you insert the *first part* of a paired code. For example, if you want the style to make text bold, you would press F6 (Bold). The code will be displayed as the first part of the paired code, like this: [Bold On]. Later, when you apply the style to blocked text, WordPerfect will insert the code [Bold On] at the beginning of the block, and code [Bold Off] at the end.

MAKING A STYLE LIST

A style is initially available only in the document in which it originated. But you might create styles that you want to use in other documents. To simplify using styles, you can put several styles in a list, then retrieve the list into any document. You may even have several lists, each containing a group of related styles—for example, a list called NEWSLTR.STY could contain formatting styles for various parts of a newsletter.

Creating a Style List

First, create within the current document all styles you want to include in your list. Then select 7 (Save) at the Style List screen and enter the name of the list. It's a good idea to use the extension .STY so the list will be easy to find.

For example, to save the current list of styles as NEWSLTR.STY,

Press: **Alt-F8** (Style) or select *Layout/Styles*

Select: **7** (Save)

Type: **NEWSLTR.STY** Enter

(In WordPerfect 5.1, the sequence is Alt-F8, 6.)

To retrieve the style list in another document,

Press: **Alt-F8** (Style) or select *Layout/Styles*

Select: **8** (Retrieve)

Type: **NEWSLTR.STY** Enter

(In WordPerfect 5.1, the sequence is Alt-F8, 7.)

When you save the document, the style list will be saved with it.

MACROS

A macro is a sequence of codes and/or text you save in a file. When you want to enter those codes, you activate the macro and WordPerfect does the typing for you.

TWO TYPES OF MACROS

WordPerfect lets you name and use macros in two ways:

- If you name the macro ALT followed by a letter (for example, ALTB), you can execute the macro by pressing ALT and the appropriate letter (Alt-B). Using ALT in the macro name has the advantage of convenience.

- If you choose any other name, you'll have to select Alt-F10 (Macro Play) or *Tools/Macro/Play* and then type the name of the macro to activate it. These character macros have the advantage of letting you use names that sound like the operation.

HOW TO USE MACROS

Macros can be used to automate any series of keystrokes. Typical applications include

■ Applying frequently used size or appearance formatting to a word or sentence. For example, you might create a macro that italicizes one word.

■ Inserting "boilerplate" text. For example, create a macro that types a standard copyright notice.

CREATING A MACRO

Before trying to create a macro, make a list of the exact keystrokes you need to enter. This method will help eliminate mistakes.

HANDS-ON Create a macro called ALTB that will make one word bold.

Press: **Ctrl-F10** (Macro Record) or select *Tools/Macro/Record*

You'll be prompted to enter the name of the macro, as shown in Figure 30-4.

Figure 30-4: The Record Macro screen.

Record Macro
Macro: _____ ↓
[ ] Edit Macro
File List... F5   Quick List... F6   OK   Cancel

Type: **ALTB** [Enter]

At this point, you'll see "Recording Macro" at the bottom of the editing screen. Now enter the keystrokes for this macro:

Press: **Alt-F4** (Block)

Press: **Ctrl-Right arrow**

Press: **Left arrow**

Press: **F6** (Bold)

To save the macro and stop recording keystrokes, press Ctrl-F10 (Macro) or select *Tools/Macro*.

The macro is saved as ALTB.WPM in the default directory. If you want to save your macros in their own subdirectory (for example, \WP\MACROS), you need to tell WordPerfect where to find the files. You do this at the Shift-F1 (Setup) or *File/Setup* menu.

ACTIVATING THE MACRO

To activate this macro, position the cursor at the beginning of a word and press Alt-B. To activate a character macro, you would need to select Alt-F10 and then type its name.

EDITING A MACRO

To edit a macro, you would press Ctrl-F10 (Macro Record) or select *Tools/Macro/Record*, enter the macro's name (or press Alt and the letter name), and select E (Edit Macro). When you edit a macro, WordPerfect displays the codes and commands (see Figure 30-5).

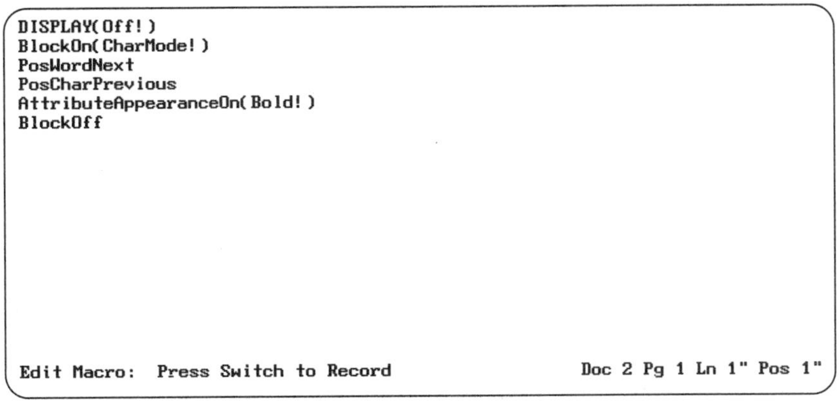

```
DISPLAY(Off!)
BlockOn(CharMode!)
PosWordNext
PosCharPrevious
AttributeAppearanceOn(Bold!)
BlockOff




Edit Macro:   Press Switch to Record          Doc 2 Pg 1 Ln 1" Pos 1"
```

Figure 30-5: The macro editing screen.

To insert new codes, press Ctrl-PgUp and then select C (Macro Commands). You'll see a list of commands from which to choose. Other macro commands, called System Variables, can be displayed by selecting 2 (System Variables).

In WordPerfect 5.1, the cursor will now be inside a box, allowing you to edit the codes directly by pressing the appropriate function keys. Pressing Ctrl-F10 enables and disables editing on this screen.

CHAPTER SUMMARY

■ A macro consists of a sequence of codes and text that are executed automatically when you activate the macro.

■ A style consists of formatting codes that are applied when you insert the style.

■ An open style inserts open codes, whereas a paragraph style applies paired codes to a block of text.

■ A style list can be retrieved and used in any document.

■ Alt-key macros are activated by pressing Alt and the letter key. Character macros are activated by pressing Alt-F10 (Macro Play) or selecting *Tools/Macro/Play* and then typing the name.

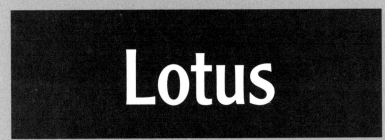

SECTION III

Lotus

Getting Started With Lotus 1-2-3

Learning what's really important in Lotus 1-2-3 can be a challenge because the program has so many features. In its menus, you'll find over 200 commands for organizing and analyzing data. Although the 1-2-3 reference manual explains all the commands, it doesn't point out which ones will be most useful in your day-to-day work.

This section of *Office Companion* doesn't cover every command—the focus here will be on the commands and features that can help increase your productivity. Although you may not be interested in every topic presented, the main objective is to help you develop essential skills that will allow you to get the most from 1-2-3.

ABOUT LOTUS 1-2-3

Lotus 1-2-3 is a versatile and powerful PC program designed to help business people be more productive in three different areas: spreadsheet analysis, record-keeping and graphing.

The program's *spreadsheet* commands let you analyze numbers using formulas and built-in functions. The record-keeping, or *database*, commands make it easy to sort and locate information. And the *graphing* commands let you turn numbers into informative graphs. So 1-2-3 is a program that can help you analyze, organize and present information.

VERSIONS OF 1-2-3

1-2-3 comes in two current versions: Release 2.4 is an improved version of the earlier 2.2 and 2.3 releases, and Release 3.4 is a "three-dimensional" version of the program that lets you work with multiple worksheets.

Because most people won't need the power of a multiple worksheet program, this section of *Office Companion* is written primarily for users of Lotus 1-2-3 releases through 2.4. But if you're using Release 3.4, most of the material here will be useful to you.

> **TIP** If you're using an older version of the program, the basic principles and most of the commands are still the same. But the newest features explained here won't be available to you.

WHAT YOU'LL LEARN

You may already be acquainted with some of these Lotus 1-2-3 techniques. But some of them may be new to you. For example, you can

- Print a worksheet using small type.
- Protect certain cells so their contents can't be erased.
- Get a printout that shows formulas, column widths, number formats and other formatting information.
- Turn a row of data into a column.
- Convert a worksheet into a text file that can be edited in Word-Perfect.
- Use a mouse to select commands and manipulate data (Release 2.3 and higher).

These are just a few examples of the useful techniques available to you in Lotus 1-2-3.

Now here's a quick look at what you'll learn in this section of *Office Companion.*

Chapters 32 through 34 explain what 1-2-3 can do; how to enter data and make corrections; and how to use menus to access commands and features.

Chapters 35 through 37 cover simple math formulas for adding, subtracting, multiplying and dividing; specialized statistical, financial and other functions; and methods for copying and moving data.

Chapter 38 covers various ways to change and improve your worksheet's appearance. Chapter 39 shows you how to make changes that affect the entire worksheet and determine the way your work is displayed.

In Chapters 40 through 42, you'll learn commands for selective formatting; how to use options to create effective printouts; and how to manage your files.

Creating graphs and using 1-2-3's powerful database commands are covered in Chapters 43 and 44.

The last chapter, "Letting 1-2-3 Do the Typing," shows you how to save time and typing by storing frequently used command sequences in special files called macros.

By the time you reach the end of Chapter 45, you'll know the most practical and useful techniques for getting the most from 1-2-3.

CONVENTIONS USED IN THIS SECTION

The format used in this section of *Office Companion* is similar to the ones used in the DOS and WordPerfect sections. Each chapter begins with a brief introduction to a group of related commands. On most pages, the focus is on one particular command. After a quick overview, you get to try a hands-on exercise. Here's an illustration of the format:

HANDS-ON Change the width of the current column to 12.

Select: **/Worksheet Column Set-Width**

Type: **12** Enter

In these exercises, you'll *select* commands, *type* numbers and words, and *press* keys.

A *Select* instruction will usually involve several steps. In the example above, the instruction means to first press the slash (/) key to display the Command menu. (With a mouse, you simply move the cursor to the top of the screen.) Then you would select the Worksheet, Column and Set-Width commands in turn from successive menus. To select a command from a menu, you can type its initial letter or point to it and click the left mouse button. To cancel a command, you can press the Esc (Escape) key or click the right mouse button.

A *Type* instruction will involve typing a number, word or formula. In the example, you would type the number 12. After typing information, you must press either the Enter key or an arrow key, or click the mouse in the Command menu area.

A *Press* instruction will show you a key to press, usually followed by its Lotus 1-2-3 name. For example, you might be instructed to press F1 (Help). All or part of a screen image will usually follow the exercise to show the effect of the command (see Figure 31-1).

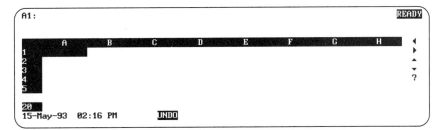

Figure 31-1: Example of a Lotus 1-2-3 screen.

If you're using a 1-2-3 release earlier than 2.4, some of your screens will look slightly different from the ones shown in the following chapters.

CHAPTER SUMMARY

- Release 2.4 is the latest single-worksheet version of Lotus 1-2-3. The latest multiple-worksheet version is 3.4.

- To open the Command menu, press the slash (/) key or move the mouse cursor to the top of the screen.

- Performing an operation will usually involve selecting commands from several menus.

- After typing information, you must press Enter or an arrow key, or click the left mouse button in the Command menu area.

- To cancel an operation, you can press Esc or click the right mouse button.

How Lotus 1-2-3 Works

LOTUS
32

Despite its power, Lotus 1-2-3 is surprisingly easy to use. The key to using the program successfully is understanding how it's designed, how it deals with your data and what it requires from you. In this chapter, you'll learn

- The primary advantages of an electronic worksheet.
- The difference between a spreadsheet and a database.
- How to find your way around 1-2-3's menus.
- How to locate the commands you need.
- How to get help with 1-2-3 commands.

WHAT 1-2-3 CAN DO

Lotus 1-2-3 is one of the most versatile programs for the PC. As you already know, it lets you do three types of work: spreadsheet analysis, record-keeping and graphing. Below, each of these work environments is illustrated.

SPREADSHEET ANALYSIS

The spreadsheet aspect of 1-2-3 lets you make calculations on numbers using math formulas and 1-2-3's own built-in formulas (called functions). For example, you can calculate monthly sales figures, as illustrated in Figure 32-1.

```
Monthly Sales For The First And Second Quarters

                         Regional Office
                    -------------------------------------
Month               Chicago      Atlanta      New York
----------
January             $14,900      $16,599      $15,444
February            $12,050      $13,060      $14,399
March                $9,788      $10,094       $9,967
April                $9,772      $10,209       $8,004
May                  $8,553       $9,477       $7,432
June                 $9,753       $8,950       $4,002
                    -------------------------------------
Total               $64,816      $68,389      $59,248
```

Figure 32-1: Calculating sales figures in a Lotus 1-2-3 spreadsheet.

RECORD-KEEPING

The record-keeping part of 1-2-3 lets you arrange information in a special *database* format. In a database, each row of information (or *record*) is considered a unit. This feature enables you to sort and locate information quickly. A personal phone list is a good example of a database (Figure 32-2).

```
Names and Addresses (updated 05/15/93)

Last      First     Address                      St Zip    Phone
---------------------------------------------------------------------
Anderson  Sam       776 Williams Rd   Tampa      FL 30303  666-303-9909
Brown     Christie  34 Carlton Blvd   Farmville  VA 20101  333-939-3939
Jenkins   Charlie   2322 Elm St       Asheville  NC 27888  555-321-2243
Lawson    Kathleen  333 Breen Circle  Florence   SC 29901  444-345-5432
Smith     Rodney    4419 Pineview Rd  Centerville MO 46991 777-929-4848
West      Judy      555 Park Way      Mayfield   NC 27737  555-339-8293
```

Figure 32-2: You can easily sort and locate information in a database.

GRAPHING

1-2-3's graphing feature lets you turn rows or columns of numbers into a graph. 1-2-3 provides a variety of graph types including pie, line and bar. For example, you could create a bar graph, like the one shown in Figure 32-3, that compares sales for two branch offices.

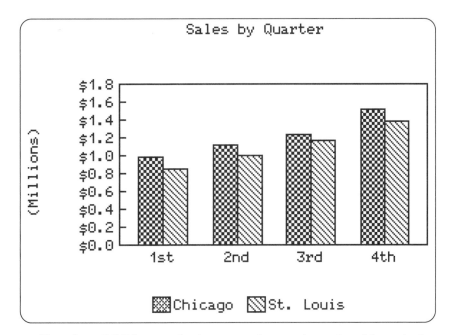

Figure 32-3: Comparing quarterly sales in a bar graph.

How does 1-2-3 know whether a number you've entered is part of a spreadsheet, database or graph? The answer is that it doesn't know until you select a command. If you select a graph command, the number will be treated as a value in a graph. If you then select a spreadsheet command, the number becomes part of a spreadsheet. So the data you enter once can function in various ways, depending on your goals.

ELECTRONIC VS. PAPER WORKSHEETS

1-2-3 doesn't merely let you do what you can already do on paper. The 1-2-3 worksheet is a dynamic environment that lets you make frequent and extensive changes easily and quickly.

> **TIP** Corrections that once involved scissors, tape and correction fluid can be accomplished in 1-2-3 with just a few keystrokes.

GETTING STARTED

If you change to the directory containing the 1-2-3 program (at the DOS prompt) then enter the command **123,** you'll go directly to the 1-2-3 worksheet. But if you enter the command **LOTUS**, you'll be taken to the *Access menu*.

Note: I'll use \123 to represent the directory containing the 1-2-3 program. The actual name of your directory probably indicates the release you're using–for example, \123R24 (for Release 2.4).

THE 1-2-3 ACCESS MENU

The Access menu gives you access to several utility programs that you might occasionally need (see Figure 32-4). You can also go into the 1-2-3 program from here.

HANDS-ON

Bring up the 1-2-3 Access menu.

Type: **LOTUS** [Enter]

Note: If you (or your AUTOEXEC.BAT file) entered a PATH command that contains the name of your 1-2-3 directory, you can start the program from any directory. If typing the command LOTUS had no effect, you need to change to the directory containing your 1-2-3 program files before the command will work. See Chapter 6 in the DOS section of *Office Companion* for more information about the PATH command.

```
Create worksheets, graphs, and databases
1-2-3       PrintGraph      Translate     Install     Exit
```

```
                            Lotus
                       1-2-3 Access Menu
                         Release 2.4

        Copyright 1990, 1991, 1992 Lotus Development Corporation
                       All Rights Reserved.


   To select a program to start, do one of the following:

      *  Use  ←, →, HOME, or END to move the menu pointer
         to the program you want and then press ENTER.

      *  Type the first character of the program's name.

   Press F1 (HELP) for more information
```

Figure 32-4: The 1-2-3 Access menu gives you access to 1-2-3 and several related programs.

COMMAND SUMMARY

At the Access menu, you have the following choices:

1-2-3	Starts the 1-2-3 program.
PrintGraph	Lets you print 1-2-3 graphs (explained in Chapter 43, "Creating Graphs").
Translate	Lets you transfer data between 1-2-3 and certain other programs.
Install	Installs the 1-2-3 program on your PC, or changes selected equipment.
Exit	Exits the Access menu and returns the DOS prompt.

THE 123 COMMAND

Because the menu pointer is on 1-2-3 now, pressing Enter would take you into the 1-2-3 program. However, the Access menu takes up memory. So, if you want to go straight into 1-2-3, don't go through the Access menu.

HANDS-ON Leave the Access menu and start the 1-2-3 program from the DOS prompt.

Select: **Exit**

Type: **123** [Enter]

THE 1-2-3 WORK ENVIRONMENT

When you start 1-2-3, you're presented with a blank *worksheet,* a large work area of 8,192 rows and 256 columns (see Figure 32-5). Only a small portion—initially 20 rows and 8 columns—can be seen onscreen at any time. The columns are labeled with the letters A-Z, then AA-AZ, then BA-BZ, and so on to IV (column 256). The rows are labeled with the numbers 1–8192.

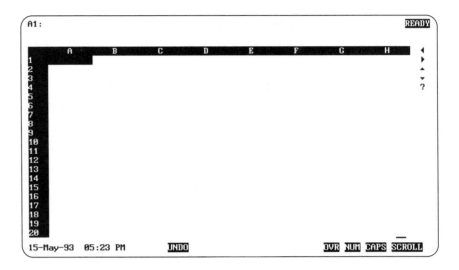

Figure 32-5: A blank 1-2-3 worksheet.

CELLS & CELL ADDRESSES

Each row and column intersection creates a *cell* into which you may enter data. The *cell address* identifies the location of each cell. For example, B3 is the address of the cell at the intersection of column B and row 3.

THE POINTER

The highlighted cell on the worksheet is called the *pointer.* When you enter the program, the pointer will be in cell A1. The pointer shows where information you type will be entered on a worksheet.

THE CONTROL PANEL

Above the cells of the worksheet is the *Control Panel.* It shows the *active cell* (where the pointer is located) and its contents. On the right side of the panel is the *Mode indicator.* It indicates the type of action you may take at any time. Right now, READY means that it's ready for you to enter data. If you were in a menu, the program would be in MENU mode. Other modes are discussed in later chapters.

THE ICON PANEL

Release 2.3 introduced the *Icon Panel,* located to the right of the worksheet. It has four scroll arrows and a symbol (?) for the Help feature. If you're using the mouse, you can scroll through the worksheet by pointing to a scroll arrow and holding down the left mouse button. You can get help with commands by clicking on the ? icon.

SmartIcons

In Release 2.4, you have the option of using the SmartIcons add-in program, which provides many other icons that can simplify your work.

Each SmartIcon performs a useful 1-2-3 operation. For example, there is a SmartIcon for formatting numbers in Currency format with two decimals.

So instead of selecting a series of commands from menus, you simply select the appropriate SmartIcon. Figure 32-6 shows the first of 10 pages of SmartIcons that are available.

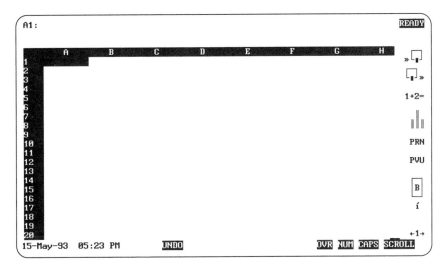

Figure 32-6: The 1-2-3 worksheet with the SmartIcons add-in attached.

See "Add-In Programs" later in this chapter for more information on using SmartIcons and other add-in programs.

OTHER INDICATORS

The bottom of the screen is reserved for several other indicators: Date/Time, Undo, OVR, Num, Caps and Scroll.

The *Date/Time* indicator shows the current date and time (taken from your PC's internal clock). If you'd rather see the current file name here, select /Worksheet Global Default Other Clock Filename, and then /Worksheet Global Default Update.

The *Undo* indicator means that you can press Alt-F4 (Undo) to cancel the changes you just made (available in Release 2.2 and higher). In Release 2.3 and higher, the feature is initially off. To activate it, select /Worksheet Global Default Other Undo Enable. Then to save the change for future work sessions, select Update. (In Release 2.3, select Quit and then Update.)

The *OVR* indicator is turned on and off by pressing the Ins (Insert) key. If it's on, pressing F2 (Edit) will allow you to type over existing data instead of inserting characters within existing data.

The *Num* indicator is turned on and off by pressing the Num Lock key. When it's on, the arrow/number keys on the right side of your keyboard function as numbers. When it's off, those keys function as arrow keys (to move the pointer).

The *Caps* indicator is turned on and off by pressing the Caps Lock key. When it's on, all the letters you type will be uppercase.

The *Scroll* indicator is turned on and off by pressing the Scroll Lock key. When it's on, the pointer will appear stationary on the screen while the worksheet will appear to move.

Some of the less common indicators are covered in later chapters.

MOVING THE POINTER

The pointer's location determines where the data you type will be entered. Some of the common pointer movement techniques, using keyboard and mouse, are listed below.

Keyboard Action	Result
Up arrow and Down arrow	Up and down one cell.
Right arrow and Left arrow	Right and left one cell.
PgUp and PgDn	Up and down one screen.
Ctrl-Right arrow and Ctrl-Left arrow	Right and left one screen.
Home	To cell A1.
End, Home	To the bottom right corner of your data.
Mouse Action	
Point to a cell and click the left button.	Activates the cell.
Point to a scroll arrow and either click or hold down the left button.	Scrolls in the direction chosen.
Click the left button in the upper left corner of the worksheet.	To cell A1.

THE GO TO KEY

The F5 (*Go To*) key lets you move the pointer instantly to any cell.

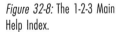 Move the pointer to cell K65.

    Press: **F5 (Go To)**

    Type: **K65** Enter

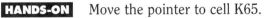

Figure 32-7: The pointer has moved to cell K65.

    Figure 32-7 shows the pointer in cell K65. To return to cell A1, press Home or click the mouse in the upper left corner.

GETTING HELP

    1-2-3's Help feature can provide assistance on almost any topic. When you press F1 (Help) or click on the ? icon, you'll see a menu of topics from which you can choose (see Figure 32-8). To get to the topic you're interested in, you may have to go through several screens.

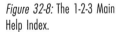 Bring up the Help index.

    Press: **F1** (Help)

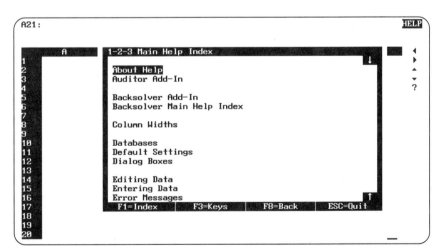

Figure 32-8: The 1-2-3 Main Help Index.

    To get help with a specific topic, move the light bar (using the arrow keys) to it and press Enter. With a mouse, just click on the topic you want.

If the information extends off the screen, you can bring it into view by pressing the Down arrow key or by clicking on the Down scroll arrow.

> **TIP** To exit a Help screen, press Esc or click the right mouse button.

CONTEXT-SENSITIVE HELP

In Release 2.3 and higher, the Help feature is context-sensitive—that is, it takes you to a screen that helps you with your current activity. For example, if you're in the File menu, pressing F1 (Help) will bring up a help screen for File commands. Then you can return to the worksheet by pressing Esc. (Pressing the Esc key or clicking the right mouse button will always take you back one step.)

1-2-3 & DOS

Like WordPerfect (and most other PC software), Lotus 1-2-3 works within the DOS environment. And like WordPerfect, 1-2-3 lets you temporarily go out to the DOS prompt without actually leaving the program.

GOING TO DOS

To temporarily go to DOS, select System from the Command menu.

HANDS-ON Go out to the DOS prompt.

Select: **/System**

```
(Type EXIT and press ENTER to return to 1-2-3)


Microsoft(R) MS-DOS(R) Version 6
             (C)Copyright Microsoft Corp 1981-1993.

C:\123>
```

Figure 32-9: The result of selecting the /System command.

As Figure 32-9 shows, you are now at the DOS prompt, and may use DIR, COPY and other DOS commands. When you're ready to return to the worksheet, type **EXIT** at the DOS prompt and then press Enter.

ADD-IN PROGRAMS

Although the basic 1-2-3 program is powerful, add-ins can make it even better. Add-ins are programs you can use to extend the power of 1-2-3. Release 2.4 comes with seven add-ins:

WYSIWYG: Used for creating presentation-quality printouts and integrating graphs with spreadsheet data.

Auditor: Used for tracking the source of errors in formulas.

Viewer: Used to view the contents of disk files and to create links between worksheets.

Macro Library Manager: Stores macros, formulas and data ranges in a library you can use in any worksheet.

1-2-3 Go!: On-line tutorial for learning to use 1-2-3.

SmartIcons: Allows you to execute command sequences by selecting onscreen icons instead of a series of individual commands from menus.

Backsolver: Performs "what if" analysis by changing the values of one or more variables to achieve a desired result in a formula cell.

Release 2.3 includes all of these add-ins except SmartIcons and Backsolver.

USING ADD-INS

To make an add-in available, you must *attach* it (load it into memory) by selecting /Add-In Attach and then the add-in file name. Then you need to select the way you want to *invoke* the add-in—that is, activate it. You may choose No-Key, meaning that you must select the Invoke command to invoke the add-in; or you may choose either 7, 8, 9 or 10, meaning that you can invoke the add-in by pressing either the F7, F8, F9 or F10 key. If you want to remove an add-in from memory, you must *detach* it by selecting /Add-In Detach and then the add-in file name. Alternatively, you may select /Add-In Clear to clear all add-ins from memory.

> **TIP** To have 1-2-3 attach an add-in automatically when you start the program, use /Worksheet Global Default Other Add-In. Then to save the change, select /Worksheet Global Default Update.

If the add-in program you want is not available, it means that the appropriate files were not transferred to your hard disk during the installation of 1-2-3. So you will have to reinstall 1-2-3 using the Install program.

Some of these add-ins are mentioned briefly in the following chapters, and the basic add-in commands are listed in the Lotus 1-2-3 Quick Reference section of this book. For a complete explanation, refer to your 1-2-3 *User's Guide.*

CHAPTER SUMMARY

- The command 123 takes you directly to a worksheet, while the command LOTUS takes you to the Access menu.
- A cell address identifies the cell's column and row location.
- The pointer shows the cell where the data you type will be entered.
- The Control Panel shows the pointer's address and the current mode.
- When the Undo indicator is displayed, you can press Alt-F4 (Undo) to cancel the last operation.
- To get help, press F1 (Help) or click on the ? icon, and then select a topic.
- To temporarily go to the DOS prompt, select /System. Then to return to 1-2-3, type EXIT and press Enter.
- Pressing Esc or clicking the right mouse button will cancel an operation.
- An add-in program must be attached and invoked before it can be used.

Understanding Menus

LOTUS
33

1-2-3 provides commands for changing a worksheet's appearance, creating graphs, retrieving files and many other operations. These commands are all contained in menus. So in this chapter, you'll learn

- The types of commands available in menus.
- How to preview a menu before opening it.
- The different types of information for which 1-2-3 will prompt you.
- How to exit a menu.
- How to execute command sequences.

You can do a lot with 1-2-3 without opening a menu: entering numbers and labels, writing simple math formulas and using 1-2-3's built-in functions. But 1-2-3's menus contain many other useful features that can help you analyze, organize and display your data.

MENUS

The powerful features of 1-2-3 are found in *menus*. Each menu is a list of related operations. Hidden away in 1-2-3's menus are commands that let you

- Change the width of a column.
- Format numbers so they appear as dollars and cents.
- Erase a range of cells.
- Copy and move ranges of data.
- Save and retrieve files.
- Sort data alphabetically.

And much more.

SELECTING A COMMAND

1-2-3 gives you three ways to select a command from a menu:

■ You can move the pointer to the command (using the Left and Right arrow keys) and then press Enter.

■ You can type the first letter of the command.

■ Using a mouse, you can point to the command and click the left button.

If you're a beginner, the first method is better because it lets you see what you're doing. If you use the second or third method, the change from one menu to the next takes place instantaneously.

THE COMMAND MENU

The first-level menu is the *Command menu* (see Figure 33-1). It's the first stop on your way to 1-2-3's many commands and features.

HANDS-ON   Bring up the Command menu.

Press: / (If you're using a mouse, move the cursor to the Command menu area.)

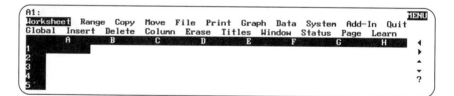

Figure 33-1: The 1-2-3 Command menu.

Each menu, including the Command menu, has two lines. The top line is the actual menu: it shows the commands you may select. The bottom line is the *Preview:* it shows a preview or description of what will happen next if you select the highlighted command. Because the command "Worksheet" is highlighted, the Preview line shows the Worksheet menu. If you move the pointer to the other commands, you'll see the Preview line change.

COMMAND SUMMARY

Here's a summary of the types of work you can accomplish with each command listed on the Command menu.

Worksheet	Controls the appearance of a worksheet and the display of numbers and labels.
Range	Controls the appearance and format of specified portions of a worksheet.
Copy	Copies data, formulas and functions.
Move	Moves data, formulas and functions.
File	Stores and retrieves files.
Print	Prints worksheets (but not graphs).
Graph	Creates graphs.
Data	Sorts, locates and extracts data.
System	Takes you to the DOS prompt without exiting 1-2-3.
Add-In	Lets you use 1-2-3 add-in programs that provide additional capabilities such as publication-quality printing, auditing, enhanced file management and others. (Available in Release 2.2 and higher.)
Quit	Takes you out of the program. The Quit command on all other menus takes you to the previous menu or back to the worksheet.

TIP The most useful commands are usually listed at the beginning of each menu in 1-2-3. For example, in the File menu, the commands Retrieve and Save are listed first.

MENU MODE

When you bring up the Command menu, the Mode indicator changes to MENU. This indicator means you must either select a command or back out and return to READY mode. If you decide not to continue with an operation, you can back out to the previous screen by pressing Esc or clicking the right mouse button.

COMPLETING A COMMAND

When you make a selection from a menu, you have to do one of three things to complete the operation.

■ Select an operation from another menu. For example, if you select the Worksheet command, you'll see the Worksheet menu, as shown in Figure 33-2.

Figure 33-2: A second-level menu.

```
A1:                                                              MENU
Global  Insert  Delete  Column  Erase  Titles  Window  Status  Page  Learn
Format  Label-Prefix  Column-Width  Recalculation  Protection  Default  Zero
```

■ Specify a range of cells. In 1-2-3, a range is any unbroken rectangular array of cells. For example, if you select Copy, you must enter the range of cells you want to copy. Figure 33-3 shows the prompt you'll see.

Figure 33-3: The prompt on-screen where you enter a range of cells.

```
A1:                                                              POINT
Copy what? A1..A5
```

(When you need to specify a range, 1-2-3 shows the pointer's position as the default range. Either press Enter to accept that range, or type another range. To learn more about ranges, see Chapter 36, "Using Functions.")

■ Enter a value or a label. For instance, if you're changing the width of a column, you must enter the width. Figure 33-4 shows the on-screen prompt.

Figure 33-4: The onscreen prompt to enter a value.

```
A1:                                                              POINT
Enter column width (1..240): 9
```

In all of these cases, 1-2-3 prompts you for the information it needs. So, always read the prompts carefully.

TIP If you decide not to continue with an operation, you can press the Esc (Escape) key to back up one step. With a mouse, clicking the right button has the same effect.

Dialog Boxes

Some command sequences will cause 1-2-3 to display a *dialog box*, a window that displays settings for an operation (introduced in Release 2.3). For example, if you select /Data Query, you will see the current database ranges (see Figure 33-5).

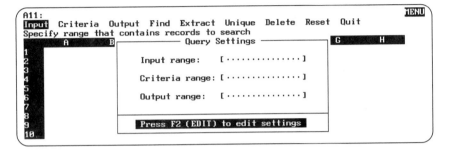

Figure 33-5: A dialog box displays settings.

The settings will be updated as you make changes via the menu commands. In Release 2.3 and higher, you may edit the settings in the box directly by pressing F2 (Edit). If you prefer not to have the box displayed, you can remove it by pressing F6 (Window).

COMMAND SEQUENCES

Some 1-2-3 operations require that you go through as many as four or five levels of menus to get to the command you need. This is an unavoidable consequence of having so many features in one program.

An Illustration

Here's an illustration of the menu structure. If you want all the numbers on a worksheet to appear as dollars and cents to two decimals, you must follow the route shown in Figure 33-6.

Figure 33-6: The menu path to the Currency formatting option.

```
/  →  Worksheet  →  Global   →  Format          →  Fixed
       Range         Insert      Label-Prefix       Sci
       Copy          Delete      Column-Width       Currency  →  2
       . . .         . . .       . . .              . . .
```

At first, so many levels of menus can be overwhelming. But you'll quickly learn how to get to the commands you need. To help you find your way, the "Lotus 1-2-3 Quick Reference" appendix at the end of *Office Companion* summarizes the most frequently used command sequences.

CHAPTER SUMMARY

- To bring up the Command menu, press the slash (/) key or move the mouse cursor to the top of the screen.

- The top line of a menu shows the commands you may select. The bottom line is either a preview of the next menu or a brief description of the command.

- To select a menu option, either move the pointer to it and press Enter or type its initial letter. With a mouse, point to the command and click the left button.

- When 1-2-3 is in MENU mode, you must either complete or exit the operation by pressing the Esc key or clicking the right mouse button.

- When you select a command from a menu, you must either select from another menu, enter a range, or enter a number or label.

- When the SmartIcons add-in is attached, you can perform routine operations by selecting the appropriate icon instead of by selecting a series of commands from menus (Release 2.4 and higher).

Entering Data

Before you can take advantage of 1-2-3's wonderful features, you have to enter some data. You also need to know a few important facts about the way 1-2-3 treats your data. So in this chapter, you'll learn

- Two ways to enter data in a cell.
- What "values" and "labels" are.
- Three ways to position data within a cell.
- How to repeat a character across a cell.
- How to change the content of a cell.
- How to use the Alt-F4 (Undo) feature.

VALUES & LABELS

Every item you enter on a worksheet is either a value or a label. A *value* is a number, or any expression that creates a number (like a formula). A *label* is any item that contains letters or nonnumeric characters (like # or &). So "Expenses," "#7" and "Month-End Accounting" are all labels.

An item is a label if it contains any letters, even if it starts with a number. So, "12 Elm Street" and "4th" are both labels.

When you type a value or label, you have three ways of entering it in the active cell:

- Press Enter, in which case the pointer remains in the active cell.
- Press an arrow key, in which case the item is entered *and* the pointer moves to the next cell.
- If you're using a mouse, click in the Control Panel.

If you're entering a column or row of data, the second method is preferred because it saves you a keystroke each time you enter an item.

Because 1-2-3 treats values and labels differently, let's look at them separately.

ENTERING VALUES

You can enter values using the keys across the top of the standard keyboard or the numeric keypad. To use the numeric keypad, turn on the Number Lock feature by pressing Num Lock.

HANDS-ON   In cell B4, enter the number 375.

Move: Pointer to B4

Type: **375** [Enter]

When you began typing, the Mode indicator changed to VALUE. When you start an entry with a *value*, you may not type alphabetic characters in the same cell.

Figure 34-1: The value 375 entered into cell B4.

Alignment

Notice in Figure 34-1 that the number is on the right side of the cell. You can't change this alignment. In 1-2-3, values are always right-aligned. And because 1-2-3 provides the option of displaying negative numbers in parentheses, an extra space is always included to the right of a value.

ENTERING LABELS

Entering labels is no different from entering values. You simply position the pointer and type the label. But the result of the action is a little different than you might expect. The result is shown in Figure 34-2.

HANDS-ON   Enter the label *Travel Expenses* at the top of the worksheet. Notice that the mode changes to LABEL when you start typing.

Move: Pointer to C1

Type: **Travel Expenses** [Enter]

```
C1: 'Travel Expenses                                        READY

           A        B        C        D        E        F        G        H     ◄
                            Travel Expenses                                     ►
1                                                                               ▲
2                                                                               ▼
3                                                                               ?
4                            375
5
```

Figure 34-2: The label Travel Expenses entered into cell C1.

Although the label appears to occupy two cells, it's really only in C1. If you were to move the pointer to D1, the Control Panel at the top of your screen would show that cell D1 is empty.

Label Prefixes

Now, what *is* in cell C1? Because C1 is the active cell, you can see in the Control Panel that it contains the label 'Travel Expenses. The apostrophe is one of 1-2-3's *label prefixes*. It tells 1-2-3 where to place a label within a cell. If you don't type one yourself, 1-2-3 will type the ' prefix for you to indicate that the label is left-aligned in the cell. 1-2-3's three label prefixes are

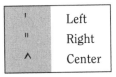

'	Left
"	Right
^	Center

1-2-3 also provides an easy way to position labels *after* you've typed them. This technique is covered in Chapter 40, "Formatting Ranges of Data."

Another Prefix

Another prefix you'll find useful is the backward slash (\). But it's not a *label* prefix—you don't use it to align data. The function of this prefix is to repeat a character across a cell. For example, typing \x would fill the active cell with x's.

HANDS-ON Draw a dashed line under the title of the worksheet.

Move: Pointer to C2

Type: \-

Because the column you filled is only nine characters wide, you're a few dashes short.

Move: Pointer to D2

Type: '- (label prefix plus six dashes)

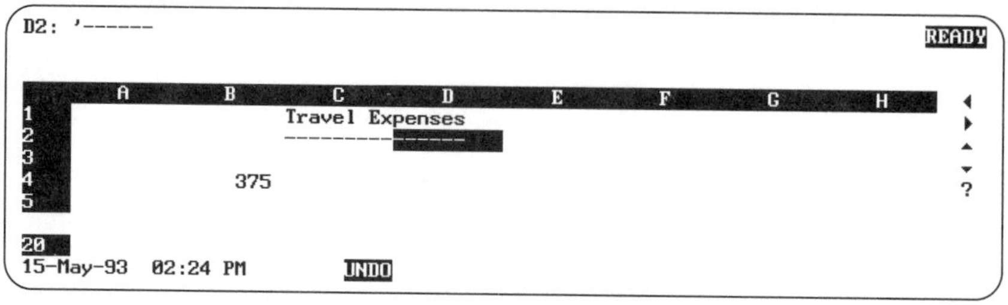

Figure 34-3: Two cells filled with dashes.

The worksheet title is now underlined (Figure 34-3).

If you wanted a line across the entire width of your worksheet, you could fill one cell by typing \- and then copy that cell's contents to other cells. This technique is explained in Chapter 37, "Copying & Moving Data."

MAKING CHANGES

One of the great advantages of usong an electronic worksheet is that you can fix mistakes very easily. 1-2-3 provides several methods for making changes to your data.

THE BACKSPACE KEY

Before you press Enter, you can correct typing mistakes with the Backspace ⬅ key.

TYPING OVER

If you need to change an item you've entered, you can simply enter a new item in the cell. The old item will be erased as the new one takes its place. For a short item, this method is usually quickest.

If you want to erase an item to leave a cell blank, use the /Range Erase command. To erase the contents of just the active cell, press the Del key (Release 2.3 and higher).

> **TIP** If you press the Space bar to blank out a cell, the cell will appear empty but will actually contain a left (') label prefix.

THE EDIT KEY

To make a correction to a long item, you can save some typing by using the F2 (Edit) key. When you go into Edit mode, anything you type will be inserted into the item. If you'd rather type over the item,

press the Ins (Insert) key. The OVR (overstrike) indicator will then be
displayed. When you finish the edit, press Enter or an arrow key, or
click on the left mouse button in the Control Panel.

THE UNDO KEY

The Alt-F4 (Undo) key (available in Release 2.2 and higher) is a feature
that restores a worksheet to its condition prior to your last operation.
Mistakes that used to create great anxiety can now be easily undone.

In Release 2.3 and higher, you must activate the Undo feature with
the command /Worksheet Global Default Other Undo Enable. Then to
save the change, select Update (in Release 2.3, select Quit and then
Update). If you want the change to be saved, select /Worksheet Global
Default Update.

HANDS-ON Cancel the last operation.

Press: **Alt-F4** (Undo)

Figure 34-4: The result of
pressing Alt-F4 (Undo).

In Figure 34-4, you can see that the Undo indicator is still displayed, meaning that you can even undo an Undo operation. Try it.

Press: **Alt-F4** (Undo)

Figure 34-5: The result of
pressing Alt-F4 (Undo) again.

Now the worksheet is back to its original appearance.

A SAMPLE WORKSHEET

The hands-on exercises in the Lotus 1-2-3 section of this book are based on the following sample worksheet. If you type the data exactly as shown below, you'll be able to do all the exercises. If you already have a worksheet to use, you can simply adapt the exercises to fit your data.

Before you create the worksheet shown in Figure 34-6, note the address of each item. For example, *Travel* is in B3, and *15* is in E4. Be sure to put only one item into each cell.

Figure 34-6: A sample worksheet you can use in subsequent hands-on exercises.

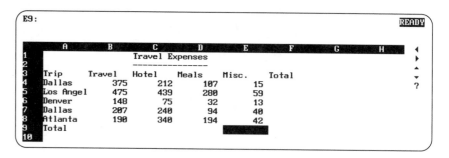

You'll notice that in cell A5, the label Los Angeles will appear to be cut off when you enter the value 475 into cell B5. Later, you'll learn how to widen the column so the label is displayed in its entirety. You'll also learn how to make the headings line up with the numbers.

At this point, don't try to embellish the worksheet. The exercises on the following pages will show you how to improve the worksheet's appearance.

CHAPTER SUMMARY

■ You can enter data with the Enter key or an arrow key.

■ Values are always right-aligned in cells. Labels are left-aligned by default, but they may be positioned right or center.

■ To change a label's alignment as you type it, first type " to right-align it or ^ to center it.

■ The alignment of labels can be changed after you've entered them by using the /Range Label command.

■ To repeat a character across a cell, type \ and the character (for example, \-).

■ To edit the contents of a cell, press F2 (Edit).

■ When the Undo indicator is displayed, it means that you can cancel your last operation by pressing Alt-F4 (Undo).

Doing Math Calculations

LOTUS 35

One of the easiest ways to tap 1-2-3's power is to write math formulas that perform calculations on your numerical data. Whether you need to find a sum or calculate a complex set of formulas, 1-2-3 can quickly provide the answer. So in this chapter, you'll learn

- How to write a simple math formula.
- The difference between the apparent content of a cell and the real content.
- How to determine the order of calculations.
- How to correct errors in your formulas.

CHAPTER OVERVIEW

The advantages of an electronic worksheet are nowhere more apparent than when you begin doing calculations. 1-2-3 can handle complex formulas, interconnected formulas and changes to the data, without any problem. Specifically, the program helps you by recalculating formulas when necessary, identifying errors and allowing you to copy formulas.

FORMULA RECALCULATION

When you make changes to your data, 1-2-3 automatically recalculates formulas that are affected. But if you prefer, you can disable the automatic feature and recalculate formulas at your convenience.

IDENTIFYING ERRORS

On a paper worksheet, you can easily make a mistake without knowing it. But in 1-2-3, many errors are noted immediately, allowing you to make corrections before going ahead. And if you're using Release 2.3 or higher, the Auditor add-in can assist you in tracking down the source of errors.

COPYING FORMULAS

Because of the way 1-2-3 keeps up with cell addresses, you can copy a formula to other cells. And in the process, 1-2-3 adjusts the cell addresses to fit the columns or rows into which the formula is copied. This feature can be a real time-saver when setting up a worksheet.

WRITING FORMULAS

A formula is a math expression you write to perform calculations on your numbers. 1-2-3 lets you use five operators in formulas:

+	Add
–	Subtract
/	Divide
*	Multiply
^	Exponentiate (for example, 3^2 is 3 to the second power, or 9)

WRITING A FORMULA

You can write formulas using both numbers and cell addresses. Here are a few examples of valid formulas:

127/8.3

10*B3

+A6*12

–A6+B4*3

(A3+F9)–12

If a cell address comes first in a formula, it must be preceded by a plus (+), minus (–) or opening parenthesis.

HANDS-ON   On the sample worksheet, add the expenses for the first Dallas trip.

Move: Pointer to F4

Type: **+B4+C4+D4+E4** [Enter]

```
F4: +B4+C4+D4+E4                                              READY

        A         B         C         D         E         F         G         H      ◀
  1                     Travel Expenses                                              ▶
  2                     ─────────────                                                ▲
  3   Trip      Travel    Hotel     Meals     Misc.     Total                        ▼
  4   Dallas       375      212       107        15     709                          ?
  5   Los Angel    475      439       280        59
  6   Denver       148       75        32        13
  7   Dallas       207      240        94        40
  8   Atlanta      190      340       194        42
  9   Total
 10
```

Figure 35-1: The result of entering the formula +B4+C4+D4+E4 into cell F4.

Figure 35-1 shows the expenses and total for the Dallas trip.

You'll want similar formulas to calculate the other trip totals. But instead of typing four more formulas, you can simply copy the formula to the other cells. This technique is explained in Chapter 37, "Copying & Moving Data."

THE REAL CONTENT

Now what does cell F4 really contain? It's not the value 709. Look in the Control Panel and you'll see that the real content of the cell is the formula. This is an important point. It means that when you copy the content of this cell, you'll be copying the formula, not 709.

THE ORDER OF CALCULATIONS

1-2-3 performs calculations in a preset order. For example, multiplication is done before addition. So, in the formula 2*3+4, the result will be 10, not 14. Instead of memorizing the order of calculations, you can simply use sets of parentheses to determine the order. For example, if you wanted to add 3+4 and then multiply by 2, you could write (3+4)*2.

TIP Keep in mind that 1-2-3 will work from the inside out when you use sets of parentheses. For example, if you write (4*(1+2))/3, the program will first add 1+2, then multiply that sum by 4, and finally divide that product by 3.

MAKING CHANGES

What if you change a cell that feeds a formula? 1-2-3 can handle your corrections with ease and automatically recalculate your formula.

HANDS-ON   Change the meals expense for the first Dallas trip.

Move: Pointer to D4

Type: **122** [Enter]

```
D4: 122                                                              READY

         A        B        C        D       E        F        G       H
1                          Travel Expenses
2                          ----------------
3       Trip     Travel   Hotel   Meals    Misc.   Total
4       Dallas     375     212     122       15      724
5       Los Angel  475     439     280       59
6       Denver     148      75      32       13
7       Dallas     207     240      94       40
8       Atlanta    190     340     194       42
9       Total
10
```

Figure 35-2: Worksheet showing that the formula in F4 was recalculated.

Figure 35-2 shows the change in meals expense for the Dallas trip.

The 1-2-3 worksheet is a dynamic worksheet that updates values as needed. As soon as you entered the change, 1-2-3 recalculated the formula in cell F4 to reflect your change.

MANUAL RECALCULATION

On a large worksheet that includes many interconnected formulas, recalculation can take a considerable amount of time. So 1-2-3 gives you the option of turning off the automatic recalculation by selecting /Worksheet Global Recalculation Manual.

As soon as you make a change that necessitates recalculation, the CALC indicator will be displayed. When you've made all of your changes, press F9 (CALC); 1-2-3 will then recalculate all your formulas.

POTENTIAL PROBLEMS

Most of your formulas will probably work fine. But occasionally you may make a fundamental mistake in the way you write a formula. Although 1-2-3 can do a lot, it can't do the impossible. Whenever you write a formula that can't be performed, 1-2-3 will let you know.

THE ERR MESSAGE

The ERR message will be displayed in any cell where you try to do an impossible calculation. For example, if you divide by zero or by a cell containing a label, the ERR message will be displayed.

THE CIRC INDICATOR

The CIRC indicator tells you that you've created a circular reference in your formula. For example, if you type +M1+M2+M3 in cell M3, you've created a circular reference by using the formula's address in the formula. This mistake can lead to incorrect results if you change any of the data. Figure 35-3 gives an example of a circular reference.

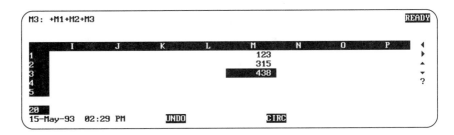

Figure 35-3: Indication of a circular reference in a formula.

Using the Auditor Add-In

If you're using 1-2-3 Release 2.3 or higher, you can use the Auditor add-in program to locate the sources of errors in a spreadsheet. Auditor determines the location of formulas and gives useful information about them. Specifically, the program identifies

■ Cells containing data used by a specified formula (the formula's precedents).

■ Formulas that depend on the data in a specified cell (the cell's dependents).

■ References by a formula to itself (circular references).

See Chapter 32, "How Lotus 1-2-3 Works," for more information on attaching and using Auditor and other add-in programs.

CHAPTER SUMMARY

- The math operators allowed in 1-2-3 are + (add), – (subtract), / (divide), * (multiply) and ^ (exponentiate).

- When a cell address comes first in a formula, it must be preceded by a plus (+), minus (–) or opening parenthesis.

- You can use sets of parentheses to determine the order of the calculations.

- The real content of a formula cell is the formula itself, not the result of the calculation.

- When you change a number that feeds a formula, the formula will be recalculated automatically. But you can turn off the automatic recalculation with the command sequence, /Worksheet Global Recalculation Manual.

- The ERR message means you've probably divided by zero or tried to do an impossible calculation. The CIRC indicator means that you've made a circular reference in your formula.

- The Auditor add-in (Release 2.3 and higher) can help in tracking the sources of errors in formulas.

Using Functions

Sometimes you may want to do a calculation, but you hesitate because it would probably involve too much typing or a level of expertise you don't have. Fortunately, 1-2-3 provides dozens of specialized prewritten formulas called *functions* that can handle the tough calculations. So in this chapter, you'll learn

- How to write a function.
- What a range is.
- How to find sums and averages.
- How to make dates and times understandable to 1-2-3.
- How to calculate payments on a loan.
- How to compare the content of a cell with a specified value or label.

Earlier, you learned how to write a simple formula that added the numbers across several cells. But imagine adding 100 numbers. Do you really want to type a formula with 100 cell addresses to get the answer? Probably not.

1-2-3 FUNCTIONS

To make this type of work easier, 1-2-3 provides built-in formulas called *functions*. They perform repetitive and difficult calculations in a variety of areas including statistics, math and finance.

1-2-3 has dozens of functions. The ones you need to learn will depend on the type of work you do. If you do accounting and investment work, you'll want to look into the financial functions. If you do engineering or scientific work, you'll want to learn some of the statistical and math functions. In this chapter, you'll get a chance to sample a few of the most useful functions.

WRITING A FUNCTION

You write a function by typing @, then the function name, and then, in parentheses, an *argument*. The argument is often a range of cells over which the function will act. For example, if you're adding a set of numbers, you have to tell 1-2-3 where those numbers are. The exercises in this chapter show how to write the argument for a function.

RANGES

Before using functions, it's important to understand exactly what a range is. In 1-2-3, a *range* is any unbroken rectangular array of cells (it doesn't matter whether the cells are empty or full). Most functions require an argument that indicates a range of cells over which the function will act.

> **TIP** Many 1-2-3 operations can take place over a range of cells. For example, you can erase a range or copy a range; you can also format the numbers in a range.

Specifying Ranges

To specify a range, you can type the first (upper left) and last (lower right) cell address, separated by two periods. With a mouse, point to one corner of the range and then drag the range to the size you want. Figure 36-1 shows a few examples of ranges and the way you would write them in a command. Notice that even a single cell can be a range.

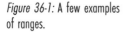

Figure 36-1: A few examples of ranges.

1-2-3 gives you two other ways to specify ranges using the keyboard:

- You can use the arrow keys to "stretch" the pointer to cover the range. This *Point* method is explained later in this chapter.
- If you've named the range using /Range Name Create, you can enter the name of the range. See Chapter 40, "Formatting Ranges of Data," for more on this technique.

USING STATISTICAL FUNCTIONS

Statistical functions are the functions you'll probably use most often. They calculate descriptive statistics, such as sums and averages.

THE @SUM FUNCTION

The @SUM function adds numbers in one or more ranges.

HANDS-ON Add the travel expenses for all of the trips using the @SUM function.

Move: Pointer to B9

Type: **@SUM(B4..B8)** [Enter]

Figure 36-2: The result of the function @SUM(B4..B8) in cell B9.

```
B9: @SUM(B4..B8)                                                    READY

       A         B         C         D         E         F         G         H
1                      Travel Expenses
2                      ---------------
3    Trip      Travel    Hotel     Meals     Misc.     Total
4    Dallas       375       212       122        15       724
5    Los Angel    475       439       280        59
6    Denver       148        75        32        13
7    Dallas       207       240        94        40
8    Atlanta      190       340       194        42
9    Total       1395
10
```

Figure 36-2 shows the combined total expenses for all trips.

This function accomplished the same result as the formula +B4+B5+B6+B7+B8 would have.

THE @AVG FUNCTION

The @AVG function finds the average of numbers in one or more ranges.

Note: Sometimes the pointer will be anchored (allowing you to stretch it), and sometimes it won't. If you need to anchor the pointer, press the period (.) key.

HANDS-ON Find the average hotel bill for the five trips. Use the Point method to specify the range.

Move: Pointer to C11

Type: **@AVG(** [Enter]

Move: Pointer to C4

Press: **.** (a period, to anchor the pointer)

Press: Down arrow four times

Type: **)** [Enter]

```
C11: @AVG(C4..C8)                                          READY

      A         B        C        D        E       F      G      H    ◄
 1                    Travel Expenses                                 ►
 2                   ----------------                                 ▲
 3   Trip      Travel   Hotel    Meals    Misc.   Total              ▼
 4   Dallas      375      212      122       15     724              ?
 5   Los Angel   475      439      280       59
 6   Denver      148       75       32       13
 7   Dallas      207      240       94       40
 8   Atlanta     190      340      194       42
 9   Total      1395
10
11                  ▌  261.2 ▐
12
```

Figure 36-3: The average Hotel expense, shown in cell C11.

The average hotel expense now appears in cell C11 as shown in Figure 36-3. The one big advantage of pointing to a range is that you can see immediately if you're making a mistake.

> **TIP** To keep the sample worksheet uncluttered, you can remove the @AVG function by pressing Alt-F4 (Undo), or by pressing the Del key (Release 2.3 and higher).

VARIATIONS

Another way to write the argument for statistical functions is to include several ranges. For example, you could add three ranges, separating them with commas, like this: @SUM(K1..K5,L2,M2..M4).

Or instead of specifying ranges as the argument, you can type a list of numbers. For example, entering @SUM(4,6,3) will give you the result 13.

USING DATE & TIME FUNCTIONS

Dates and times present a problem to 1-2-3. If you type '14-May-1993 in one cell and '12:30:00 in another, 1-2-3 doesn't understand that you've entered a date and a time. It sees those entries only as labels.

To make dates and times understandable to 1-2-3, you have to convert them to *date numbers* and *time numbers*. That's because 1-2-3 treats January 1, 1900 as Day 1 and 12:00:00 midnight as Time 0. So any date number is the number of days since Day 1, and any time number is the number of seconds since Time 0. Because it deals with dates and times as quantities, 1-2-3 can perform calculations such as finding the number of days between two dates.

THE @DATE FUNCTION

To translate dates into the date-number format, enter each date using the @DATE function, like this: @DATE(year,month,day). For example, to enter the date January 12, 1993, you would type @DATE(93,1,12). The date can be displayed so that you can understand it, but the real content is a date number that 1-2-3 can understand.

HANDS-ON Type "Departed" in G3 and "Returned" in H3. Then enter the dates for each trip in columns G and H, as shown in Figure 36-4. Each date you enter will be displayed as a date number.

Figure 36-4: The way to enter dates on a worksheet.

	G	H
3	Departed	Returned
4	@DATE(93,1,22)	@DATE(93,1,25)
5	@DATE(93,3,15)	@DATE(93,3,21)
6	@DATE(93,7,1)	@DATE(93,7,2)
7	@DATE(93,10,13)	@DATE(93,10,16)
8	@DATE(93,12,11)	@DATE(93,12,13)

The default date format displays the date number, as shown in Figure 36-5.

Figure 36-5: Dates displayed as date numbers.

H9:								READY
	A	B	C	D	E	F	G	H
1			Travel Expenses					
2			----------------					
3	Trip	Travel	Hotel	Meals	Misc.	Total	Departed	Returned
4	Dallas	375	212	122	15	724	33991	33994
5	Los Angel	475	439	280	59		34043	34049
6	Denver	148	75	32	13		34151	34152
7	Dallas	207	240	94	40		34255	34258
8	Atlanta	190	340	194	42		34314	34316
9	Total	1395						
10								

Once a date is expressed as a date number, you can display it in a more conventional format.

HANDS-ON Display the dates on the worksheet in the DD-MMM (day month) format (date option 2).

Select: **/Range Format Date 2**

Type: **G4..H8** [Enter]

```
H9:                                                              READY
       A         B        C        D        E        F        G        H
 1                      Travel Expenses
 2                      ----------------
 3    Trip      Travel   Hotel    Meals    Misc.    Total    Departed Returned
 4    Dallas      375     212      122       15      724     22-Jan   25-Jan
 5    Los Angel   475     439      280       59               15-Mar   21-Mar
 6    Denver      148      75       32       13               01-Jul   02-Jul
 7    Dallas      207     240       94       40               13-Oct   16-Oct
 8    Atlanta     190     340      194       42               11-Dec   13-Dec
 9    Total      1395
10
```

Figure 36-6: Dates displayed in DD-MMM format.

Figure 36-6 shows the result of the formatting operation. To change all general format numbers on the worksheet, use /Worksheet Global Format Date.

THE @TIME FUNCTION

To convert times to time numbers, use the @TIME function. Be sure to write the times in terms of a 24-hour clock, using this format:

@TIME(hours,minutes,seconds). For example, to enter 8:05 PM, you'd type @TIME(20,5,0) because 8:05:00 is 20:05:00 on a 24-hour clock. But 8:05:00 AM would be written @TIME(8,5,0).

If you want to change the way time numbers are displayed, use /Range Format Date Time to change a selected range or use /Worksheet Global Format Date Time to change the entire worksheet.

A SAMPLER OF FUNCTIONS

1-2-3 provides more than 100 functions to help you with calculations in math, finance, statistics and other areas. You've already learned some of the statistical and calendar functions. A few other useful functions are described below.

@SQRT

@SQRT is a *math* function that finds the square root of a number. The format of the function is @SQRT(number or cell address).

So to find the square root of 12, you would enter @SQRT(12). If you wanted the square root of the value in cell B3, you would enter @SQRT(B3).

@PMT

The @PMT function is a *financial* function that calculates payments on a loan. The format of the function is @PMT(principal, interest rate, payments).

The interest rate must be written as a percentage. So 9.5 percent is really 9.5/100, or .095. The rate must also be written in terms of the payment period. So, if the payments are monthly, the interest must be expressed as a monthly amount (by dividing the yearly rate by 12). For convenience, you can do this division in the function. So to calculate the monthly payments on a $100,000 loan at 9.5 percent for 30 years (360 payments), you'd enter @PMT(100000,.095/12,360). The payment would be $840.85.

@IF

The @IF function is a *logical* function that lets you compare the content of a cell to a value or label you specify. If there's a match, 1-2-3 will take one action; if there's not a match, 1-2-3 will take another action. The format of the command is @IF(comparison,action if match,action if no match).

The actions could be to write a label or number, perform a calculation, or some other operation. If an action is to write a label, you must enclose the label in quotes.

For example, let's say your worksheet lists 100 trips and you want to mark with an asterisk the ones that cost more than $600. You could write an @IF function in cell I4 like this: @IF(+F4>600,"*"," "). This function means that if the amount in cell F4 is greater than 600, write an asterisk ("*") in the current cell. If it's not greater than $600, write nothing (" ").

Once you've written the function, you could copy it down column I so that every trip's total would be evaluated. The result would be an asterisk beside each trip that totals over $600.

CHAPTER SUMMARY

A range is any unbroken rectangular array of cells.

You can specify a range by typing its first and last cells separated by two periods, by stretching the pointer or by typing the name of a named range.

Functions are written with @, then the function name, then the argument, like this: @SUM(A1..B4).

To translate a date into a format that 1-2-3 can understand, type it in this form: @DATE(year,month,day)—for example, type in @DATE(93,3,26).

To translate a time into a format that 1-2-3 can use, type it in this form: @TIME(hour,minute,second)—for example, @TIME(3,45,0).

To display date and time numbers in a conventional format, use either /Range Format Date or /Worksheet Global Format Date.

The @PMT function calculates payments on a loan.

The @IF function allows you to compare the content of a cell with a value or label you specify.

Copying & Moving Data

In 1-2-3, you can change your mind as often as you wish about where you want data located on a worksheet. Copying or moving data is quick and easy and involves only a few keystrokes. So in this chapter, you'll learn how to

- Copy formulas, functions and ranges of data.
- Move a range of data.
- Distinguish between relative and absolute cell addresses.
- Copy the results of formulas instead of the formulas themselves.
- Turn a row of data into a column, and vice versa.

The great thing about an electronic worksheet like 1-2-3 is that it lets you rearrange your work with only a few keystrokes. In this chapter, you'll learn several techniques for copying and moving data.

SPECIFYING RANGES

When you move or copy data, you have to specify *two* ranges. The first range identifies the present location of the data. The second range tells 1-2-3 where to place the moved or copied data. Thus you specify a "from" range (containing the data) and a "to" range (the destination). For some reason, this is often a source of confusion among beginners. But 1-2-3 always prompts you for the information it needs, so just read the prompts before typing.

EXAMPLE 1

If you wanted to copy the range A3..B9 to cells A13..B19, you'd specify the ranges shown in Figure 37-1. In this type of copying, 1-2-3 lets you specify just the upper left cell of the "to" range.

```
A20:                                                                   READY

              A       B        C       D       E       F       G       H   ◄
1                         Travel Expenses                                   ►
2            --------------                                                 ▲
3            Trip    Travel  Hotel   Meals   Misc.   Total   Departed Returned ▼
4            Dallas     375    212     122     15      724    22-Jan   25-Jan  ?
5            Los Angel  475    439     280     59             15-Mar   21-Mar
6            Denver     148     75      32     13             01-Jul   02-Jul
7            Dallas     207    240      94     40             13-Oct   16-Oct
8            Atlanta    190    340     194     42             11-Dec   13-Dec
9            Total     1395
10            ↑
11            "FROM" RANGE (A3..B9)
12
13
14            ↑
15            "TO" RANGE (A13..A13)
16
```

Figure 37-1: Example of a "from" range and a "to" range for copying.

EXAMPLE 2

The other way to copy involves copying the content of one cell to several cells. For example, if you wanted to copy the content of B9 (the @SUM function) to cells C9, D9 and E9, you'd specify the ranges shown in Figure 37-2.

```
A20:                                                                   READY

              A       B        C       D       E       F       G       H   ◄
1                         Travel Expenses                                   ►
2            --------------                                                 ▲
3            Trip    Travel  Hotel   Meals   Misc.   Total   Departed Returned ▼
4            Dallas     375    212     122     15      724    22-Jan   25-Jan  ?
5            Los Angel  475    439     280     59             15-Mar   21-Mar
6            Denver     148     75      32     13             01-Jul   02-Jul
7            Dallas     207    240      94     40             13-Oct   16-Oct
8            Atlanta    190    340     194     42             11-Dec   13-Dec
9            Total     1395
10            ↑       ↑
11            "FROM"  "TO" RANGE (C9..E9)
12            RANGE
13            (B9..B9)
```

Figure 37-2: An example of a multicell "to" range for copying.

TIP The multicell copying technique is most useful for copying a formula or function to several cells.

COPYING DATA

The /Copy command copies a specified range of cells to another location. You must specify the "from" range and the "to" range (the prompts will say "Copy what?" and "To where?").

COPYING A FORMULA

HANDS-ON Copy the formula in F4 to rows 5 through 8.

Select: **/Copy**

Type: **F4** (the "from" range) [Enter]

Type: **F5..F8** (the "to" range) [Enter]

```
F4: +B4+C4+D4+E4                                            READY

        A         B        C        D        E        F        G        H      ◀
  1                    Travel Expenses                                          ▶
  2                    ─────────────────                                        ▲
  3   Trip      Travel  Hotel    Meals    Misc.   Total   Departed Returned     ▼
  4   Dallas      375     212      122       15     724    22-Jan   25-Jan      ?
  5   Los Angel   475     439      280       59    1253    15-Mar   21-Mar
  6   Denver      148      75       32       13     268    01-Jul   02-Jul
  7   Dallas      207     240       94       40     581    13-Oct   16-Oct
  8   Atlanta     190     340      194       42     766    11-Dec   13-Dec
  9   Total      1395
 10
```

Figure 37-3: The result of copying the formula in F4 to the range F5..F8.

The formula in F4 has been copied to the range F5..F8, as shown in Figure 37-3.

RELATIVE CELL ADDRESSES

If you move the pointer to cell F5, you'll see +B5+C5+D5+E5 in the Control Panel. This is exactly what you want. But the formula you copied from cell F4 was +B4+C4+D4+E4. What happened? The answer is that 1-2-3 uses *relative* cell addresses unless you specifically tell it not to.

TIP The advantage of a relative address is that it changes to fit the row or column into which it's copied.

COPYING A FUNCTION

HANDS-ON Now copy the @SUM function in cell B9 to columns C through F.

Select: **/Copy**

Type: **B9** (the "from" range) [Enter]

Type: **C9..F9** (the "to" range) [Enter]

```
B9: @SUM(B4..B8)                                                    READY

        A          B          C          D          E          F          G          H      ◀
1                             Travel Expenses                                               ▶
2                        ---------------                                                    ▲
3  Trip       Travel     Hotel      Meals      Misc.      Total      Departed Returned       ▾
4  Dallas        375        212        122         15        724      22-Jan   25-Jan        ?
5  Los Angel     475        439        280         59       1253      15-Mar   21-Mar
6  Denver        148         75         32         13        268      01-Jul   02-Jul
7  Dallas        207        240         94         40        581      13-Oct   16-Oct
8  Atlanta       190        340        194         42        766      11-Dec   13-Dec
9  Total        1395       1306        722        169       3592
10
```

Figure 37-4: The result of copying the function in B9 to the range C9..F9.

As you can see in Figure 37-4, each column of expenses is now totaled. Again, the relative cell addresses changed as the function was copied to other rows.

> **TIP** Caution: The main thing to be careful about here is overwriting data. If the area you copy data to isn't empty, the data that's already there will be erased.

ABSOLUTE CELL ADDRESSES

In the previous section, you learned that 1-2-3 uses relative cell addresses. The alternative is to specify *absolute* cell addresses.

Consider the formulas in the sample spreadsheet: (In Figure 37-5, column F has been formatted with /Range Format Text so the formulas, instead of the values, are displayed.)

```
F4: (T) [W17] +B4+C4+D4+E4                                          READY

        A          B          C          D          E                    F              ◀
1                             Travel Expenses                                           ▶
2                        ---------------                                                ▲
3  Trip       Travel     Hotel      Meals      Misc.              Total                  ▾
4  Dallas        375        212        122         15             +B4+C4+D4+E4           ?
5  Los Angel     475        439        280         59             +B5+C5+D5+E5
6  Denver        148         75         32         13             +B6+C6+D6+E6
7  Dallas        207        240         94         40             +B7+C7+D7+E7
8  Atlanta       190        340        194         42             +B8+C8+D8+E8
9
10
```

Figure 37-5: The actual content of cells F4..F8.

In cell F4, you have the formula +B4+C4+D4+E4. In the last exercise, you copied that formula to rows 5, 6, 7 and 8. The relative cell addresses in the formula changed to fit the new rows into which the formula was copied.

But what if you want an address to remain exactly as it is regardless of where you copy it? To make an address absolute, type a dollar sign ($) in front of both the column and the row part of the address, like this: $A$1. To make just the column or the row part absolute, include $ in front of the appropriate part, like this: $A1 or A$1.

Here's an illustration. Let's say your company decides to reimburse you for $15 of miscellaneous expenses for each trip, regardless of the actual amount. Because "15" is the entry in cell E4, the formula in F4 would need to be written +B4+C4+D4+$E$4. The copies of the formula would then look like they do in Figure 37-6.

```
F4: (I) [W17] +B4+C4+D4+$E$4                                          READY

            A          B          C          D          E                  F        ◀
 1                         Travel Expenses                                           ▶
 2                        ────────────────                                           ▲
 3  Trip        Travel     Hotel      Meals      Misc.              Total            ▼
 4  Dallas         375        212        122         15      +B4+C4+D4+$E$4          ?
 5  Los Angel      475        439        280         59      +B5+C5+D5+$E$4
 6  Denver         148         75         32         13      +B6+C6+D6+$E$4
 7  Dallas         207        240         94         40      +B7+C7+D7+$E$4
 8  Atlanta        190        340        194         42      +B8+C8+D8+$E$4
 9
10
```

Figure 37-6: Examples of formulas using an absolute cell address ($E$4).

So regardless of the miscellaneous amounts for each trip, 15 would be used in each formula because that is what cell E4 contains.

MOVING DATA

The /Move command moves a specified range of cells to another location. It involves the same procedure as copying: you first specify the "from" range and then the "to" range (the prompts will say "Move what?" and "To where?").

HANDS-ON Move the expense totals (row 9) down one row.

Select: **/Move**

Type: **A9..F9** (the "from" range) [Enter]

Type: **A10** (the "to" range) [Enter]

```
A9:                                                                   READY

           A         B         C         D         E         F         G         H   ◀
 1                      Travel Expenses                                              ▶
 2                     ────────────────                                             ▲
 3  Trip        Travel    Hotel     Meals     Misc.     Total    Departed  Returned  ▼
 4  Dallas         375       212       122        15       724    22-Jan    25-Jan   ?
 5  Los Angel      475       439       280        59      1253    15-Mar    21-Mar
 6  Denver         148        75        32        13       268    01-Jul    02-Jul
 7  Dallas         207       240        94        40       581    13-Oct    16-Oct
 8  Atlanta        190       340       194        42       766    11-Dec    13-Dec
 9
10  Total         1395      1306       722       169      3592
```

Figure 37-7: The result of moving A9..F9 down one row.

As you can see in Figure 37-7, the "Total" has been moved down.

> **TIP** Caution: The same caution that applies to copying also applies here. If the area you move data to isn't empty, the data that's already there will be erased.

TWO SPECIAL COPYING COMMANDS

Two of the /Range commands—Value and Trans—are covered here because they're really copying commands.

Value

The /Range Value command copies the displayed values in a range instead of underlying formulas and functions. As with the /Copy command, here you have to specify "from" and "to" ranges. So if you were to use the /Range Value command to copy cell B10, you'd be copying the value 1395, not the function @SUM(B4..B8).

Trans

The /Range Trans command transposes one or more rows into columns, or vice versa. Although it's not a command you'll use often, it's comforting to know that you can completely reorganize your worksheet without retyping everything.

HANDS-ON Transpose the entire data set.

Select: **/Range Trans**

Type: **A3..H10** (the "from" range) [Enter]

Type: **A13** (the "to" range) [Enter]

```
A9:                                                                    READY

      A         B         C         D         E         F         G         H
 1                       Travel Expenses
 2                       ----------------
 3   Trip      Travel    Hotel     Meals     Misc.     Total     Departed  Returned
 4   Dallas       375       212       122        15       724     22-Jan    25-Jan
 5   Los Angel    475       439       280        59      1253     15-Mar    21-Mar
 6   Denver       148        75        32        13       268     01-Jul    02-Jul
 7   Dallas       207       240        94        40       581     13-Oct    16-Oct
 8   Atlanta      190       340       194        42       766     11-Dec    13-Dec
 9
10   Total       1395      1306       722       169      3592
11
12
13   Trip      Dallas    Los AngelDenver    Dallas    Atlanta             Total
14   Travel       375       475       148       207       190               1395
15   Hotel        212       439        75       240       340               1306
16   Meals        122       280        32        94       194                722
17   Misc.         15        59        13        40        42                169
18   Total        724      1253       268       581       766               3592
19   Departed  22-Jan    15-Mar    01-Jul    13-Oct    11-Dec
20   Returned  25-Jan    21-Mar    02-Jul    16-Oct    13-Dec
```

Figure 37-8: The data set shown in its original form and its transposed form.

Now restore the worksheet by pressing Alt-F4 (Undo) or by using /Range Erase over the range A13..H20.

CHAPTER SUMMARY

When you move or copy data, you must specify a "from" range and a "to" range.

Cell addresses are relative unless you specify absolute addresses. To write an absolute cell address, include a dollar sign ($) in front of the column and/or row part of the address.

When a formula or function is copied to another location, relative cell addresses are adjusted; absolute cell addresses are not.

The /Range Value command copies only values and not their underlying formulas or functions.

The /Range Trans command turns one or more rows of data into columns (or vice versa) as it copies.

Changing a Worksheet's Appearance

LOTUS
38

1-2-3 gives you considerable freedom in changing the way a worksheet looks. With this flexibility, you can design each work sheet to meet specific requirements. So in this chapter, you'll learn how to

■ Change the width of one or more columns.

■ Insert blank rows and columns.

■ Keep a row or column in view regardless of the part of the worksheet you're using.

■ Look at two portions of a worksheet on the same screen.

■ Erase the entire worksheet.

1-2-3 lets you make changes that determine the way a worksheet looks and the way your work is displayed. The commands used to adjust a worksheet's appearance are found in the /Worksheet menu.

HANDS-ON   Bring up the /Worksheet menu (see Figure 38-1).

Select: **/Worksheet**

```
A1:                                                                      MENU
Global  Insert  Delete  Column  Erase  Titles  Window  Status  Page  Learn
Format  Label-Prefix  Column-Width  Recalculation  Protection  Default  Zero
        A         B       C         D        E        F        G.        H      ◄
1                       Travel Expenses                                         ►
2                       ───────────────                                         ▲
3   Trip      Travel   Hotel     Meals    Misc.    Total    Departed Returned   ▼
4   Dallas       375     212       122       15      724     22-Jan   25-Jan    ?
5   Los Angel    475     439       280       59     1253     15-Mar   21-Mar
```

Figure 38-1: The /Worksheet menu commands let you adjust the appearance of your worksheets.

COMMAND SUMMARY

Here's a brief description of the commands in the Worksheet menu:

Global	Sets attributes that affect an entire worksheet (covered in detail in Chapter 39, "Making Global Changes").
Insert	Inserts one or more rows or columns.
Delete	Deletes one or more rows or columns.
Column	Sets the width of the current column from 1 to 240 characters.
Erase	Erases an entire worksheet.
Titles	Allows selected rows and columns to remain in view at all times.
Window	Splits the screen into two windows so you can see two different portions of a worksheet onscreen.
Status	Displays the current worksheet settings.
Page	Creates a page break on a worksheet for printing.
Learn	Used in creating macros—special files that automatically type commands for you. (Available in Release 2.2 and higher.)

CHANGING COLUMN WIDTH

You can change the width of any column on a worksheet from the default of 9 to any number between 1 and 240.

HANDS-ON   Change the width of column A to 12.

Move: Pointer to any row in column A

Select: **/Worksheet Column Set-Width**

Type: **12** Enter

Notice in Figure 38-2 that 1-2-3 keeps you informed of the format changes you make. In the Control Panel, the indicator [W12] means you've changed the width of the current column to 12.

Figure 38-2: Column A set to a width of 12.

```
A1: [W12]                                                           READY

            A           B         C         D        E        F         G        ◄
 1                                 Travel Expenses                               ►
 2                               ---------------                                 ▲
 3     Trip        Travel    Hotel     Meals    Misc.    Total    Departed       ▼
 4     Dallas         375       212       122       15      724    22-Jan        ?
 5     Los Angeles    475       439       280       59     1253    15-Mar
 6     Denver         148        75        32       13      268    01-Jul
 7     Dallas         207       240        94       40      581    13-Oct
 8     Atlanta        190       340       194       42      766    11-Dec
 9
10     Total         1395      1306       722      169     3592
```

TIP There's a potential problem that you need to be aware of when changing a column's width: if you make the column too narrow to fully display a number, 1-2-3 will display asterisks (*) in place of that number. To get rid of the asterisks, just widen the column.

CHANGING SEVERAL COLUMNS

The /Worksheet Column Column-Range Set-Width command lets you change several columns to the same width. (Available in Release 2.2 and higher.) When 1-2-3 prompts you to enter the range, you can enter any range that includes the desired columns. For example, entering A1..C1 would specify columns A, B and C.

SETTING THE WIDTH TO ZERO

With the /Worksheet Column Hide command, you can hide columns temporarily onscreen.

HANDS-ON Hide columns B through E.

Select: **/Worksheet Column Hide**

Type: **B1..E1** [Enter]

```
A1: [W12]                                                    READY

       .A        F        G        H        I       J       K      ◄
  1                                                                 ▶
  2                                                                 ▲
  3   Trip       Total   Departed  Returned                         ▼
  4   Dallas      724    22-Jan    25-Jan                           ?
  5   Los Angeles 1253   15-Mar    21-Mar
  6   Denver      268    01-Jul    02-Jul
  7   Dallas      581    13-Oct    16-Oct
  8   Atlanta     766    11-Dec    13-Dec
  9
 10   Total      3592
```

Figure 38-3: Worksheet with columns B through E hidden.

Columns B, C, D and E are now hidden, as shown in Figure 38-3.

When you use a command that requires a range (such as /Range Format), the hidden columns will pop up and be marked with asterisks. So you can't create a range from nonadjacent columns even though that's what you see onscreen.

The exception is when you print the worksheet. The range you set with /Print Printer Range will not include hidden columns. So you can print management reports that leave out the details and show just the essential information.

When you're ready to display the hidden columns again, you can bring them back into view.

HANDS-ON Restore the hidden columns.

> Select: **/Worksheet Column Display**
>
> Type: **B1..E1** [Enter]

Columns B through E are once again displayed.

INSERTING A ROW OR COLUMN

The /Worksheet Insert command inserts rows and columns into a worksheet. All the existing information moves over to accommodate the new rows and columns. When you insert a row, 1-2-3 puts it *above* the pointer; when you insert a column, 1-2-3 puts it to the *left* of the pointer.

Let's say you want to number your business trips. Because there's no room, you'll have to make room.

HANDS-ON Insert a column to the left of your data.

> Move: Pointer to A1 (or any cell in column A)
>
> Select: **/Worksheet Insert Column**
>
> Press: [Enter] (to accept range A1..A1)

Now change the width of Column A to 2 using /Worksheet Column Set-Width. Figure 38-4 shows the result.

```
A1: [W2]                                                      READY

        A      B         C       D        E      F       G        H
                              Travel Expenses
  1
  2
  3        Trip      Travel   Hotel   Meals   Misc.   Total   Departed
  4        Dallas       375     212     122      15     724    22-Jan
  5        Los Angeles  475     439     280      59    1253    15-Mar
  6        Denver       148      75      32      13     268    01-Jul
  7        Dallas       207     240      94      40     581    13-Oct
  8        Atlanta      190     340     194      42     766    11-Dec
  9
 10        Total       1395    1306     722     169    3592
```

Figure 38-4: Result of inserting a column.

The important feature here is that 1-2-3 adjusts all your cell references as needed in formulas and functions. So, for example, the function @SUM(B4..B8) for the travel expenses was changed to @SUM(C4..C8).

INSERTING SEVERAL ROWS OR COLUMNS

If you want to insert more than one row or column, you have two options after selecting /Worksheet Insert Column:

▪ Type a range that includes the columns or rows, like this: A1..C1.
▪ Stretch the pointer with an arrow key to include the desired columns or rows.

DELETING ROWS & COLUMNS

The /Worksheet Delete command lets you delete rows and columns. The worksheet "collapses" to fill the void. This operation is different from erasing data in rows and columns. If you use /Range Erase, the empty cells will still be displayed.

TITLES

Consider this potential problem with the sample worksheet: let's say you add a number of other trips to the worksheet, and find that you have more information than can be displayed on one screen. So when you're working in row 21, you'll no longer see the labels that identify which column is for which expense. Thus, it would be easy to enter a number in the wrong column.

SETTING A TITLES AREA

The /Worksheet Titles command is the solution to this problem. With it, you select certain rows and/or columns near the top or left side of a worksheet that you want to remain onscreen at all times. In the sample worksheet, you would select the rows above row 4 as a Titles area so that the expense category names are always displayed.

HANDS-ON Select the rows above row 4 as a Titles area.

Move: Pointer to row 4

Select: **/Worksheet Titles Horizontal**

Now, move the pointer to row 21 by pressing the PgDn key. Notice in Figure 38-5 that rows 1 through 3 remain in view.

```
A21: [W2]                                              READY

   A      B        C        D       E       F      G        H      ◄
1                          Travel Expenses                         ►
2                          ----------------                        ▲
3      Trip      Travel   Hotel    Meals   Misc.   Total  Departed  ▼
21                                                                  ?
22
23
24
25
26
27
```

Figure 38-5: Creating a Titles area allows selected rows to remain in view.

If you decide you don't want the Titles area any longer, you can remove it with /Worksheet Titles Clear.

The following examples assume the Titles area has been cleared.

WINDOW

The /Worksheet Window command is another way of looking at two different parts of a worksheet on the same screen. Unlike the Titles feature, Window lets you move around the worksheet in each part.

THE WINDOW FEATURE

Although the advantages of Window are more obvious on a larger worksheet, you can use it here to see how it works.

HANDS-ON Split the screen horizontally.

Move: Pointer to row 11

Select: **/Worksheet Window Horizontal**

```
A10: [W2]                                              READY

   A      B        C        D       E       F      G        H      ◄
1                          Travel Expenses                         ►
2                          ----------------                        ▲
3      Trip      Travel   Hotel    Meals   Misc.   Total  Departed  ▼
4      Dallas      375      212     122      15      724   22-Jan   ?
5      Los Angeles 475      439     280      59     1253   15-Mar
6      Denver      148       75      32      13      268   01-Jul
7      Dallas      207      240      94      48      581   13-Oct
8      Atlanta     190      340     194      42      766   11-Dec
9
10     Total      1395     1306     722     169     3592
   A      B        C        D       E       F      G        H
11
12
13
14
15
16
17
18
19
```

Figure 38-6: The worksheet is now divided into two horizontal windows.

To move from one window to the other, press F6 (Window) or click the mouse inside the window. (Remember that you're working with two different windows, not different worksheets.) When you want to return to one window, select /Worksheet Window Clear. The following examples assume that the Windows have been cleared.

SYNCHRONIZED WINDOWS

When you create horizontal windows, both windows will move at the same time when you move the pointer left or right. This is normally the way you would want it to work. But if you don't want them synchronized, select /Worksheet Window Unsync.

OTHER WORKSHEET COMMANDS

The Worksheet menu lists four other commands: Erase, Status, Page and Learn. You'll probably use these commands less often than the ones described earlier.

ERASE

The /Worksheet Erase command erases everything on a worksheet. If you haven't saved the worksheet, Release 2.3 and higher will warn you; earlier releases won't.

STATUS

The /Worksheet Status command gives information about your PC's memory and about circular references in formulas.

PAGE

The /Worksheet Page command inserts a page break (for printing) above the pointer. The break is indicated by two colons (::). This command also inserts a blank row, so make sure you put the break where it won't interfere with your data.

LEARN

The /Worksheet Learn command (available in Release 2.2 and higher) causes 1-2-3 to save a series of keystrokes as a macro. When you type the name of the macro, 1-2-3 will type all the keystrokes in it. (This type of file is covered in Chapter 45, "Letting 1-2-3 Do the Typing.")

THE WYSIWYG ADD-IN

If you really want to enhance the appearance of a worksheet, you'll probably want to learn to use the WYSIWYG add-in program. Introduced in Release 2.3, this spreadsheet publishing program lets you customize the appearance of worksheets onscreen and in printouts. Specifically, WYSIWYG allows you to incorporate graphics into your worksheets, format data using various type sizes and styles, and print presentation-quality documents.

> **TIP** Another option in Release 2.4 lets you print worksheets in landscape mode (that is, horizontally rather than vertically, allowing you to include more columns across the page).

See Chapter 32, "How Lotus 1-2-3 Works," for more information on attaching and using WYSIWYG and other add-in programs.

CHAPTER SUMMARY

- /Worksheet commands change the appearance of the worksheet.
- The /Worksheet Column Set-Width command sets the width of one column. The /Worksheet Column Column-Range Set-Width command sets the width of several columns.
- The /Worksheet Insert command lets you insert one or more rows above the pointer or one or more columns to the left of the pointer.
- The /Worksheet Titles command freezes rows and/or columns so they'll remain on-screen at all times.
- The /Worksheet Window command splits the screen horizontally or vertically to provide two views of the worksheet. /Worksheet Window Clear returns the screen to one window.
- The /Worksheet Erase command erases an entire worksheet.
- The WYSIWYG add-in program, introduced in Release 2.3, allows you to integrate graphics with worksheets, format data and print presentation-quality documents.

Making Global Changes

The /Worksheet Global commands change the appearance of your data, letting you adjust number formats, label alignment and other default settings. So in this chapter, you'll learn how to

■ Change the width of all columns.

■ Change the alignment of all labels.

■ Change the format of all numbers.

■ Change 1-2-3's default formats.

■ Suppress the display of zero values.

In Chapter 38, "Changing a Worksheet's Appearance," you learned how to use Worksheet commands to adjust the way a worksheet looks. In this chapter, you'll learn how to use the /Worksheet Global commands to determine the appearance of your data.

> **TIP** /Worksheet Global commands affect the entire worksheet, except for ranges that you've already formatted. For example, if you've changed the width of column K to 12, changing the global column width to 7 won't have any effect on column K.

HANDS-ON Display the /Worksheet Global menu.

Select: **/Worksheet Global**

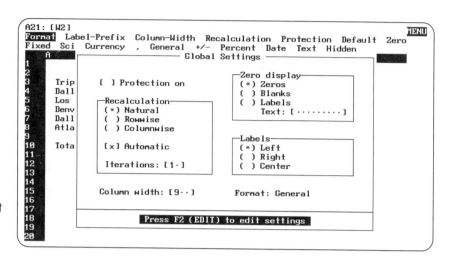

Figure 39-1: The / Worksheet
Global menu and Global
Settings box.

Figure 39-1 shows the / Worksheet Global menu and the global settings. If you prefer to hide the Global Settings box, press F6 (Window).

COMMAND SUMMARY

Here's a brief look at what each command can accomplish:

Format	Determines the way all numbers are displayed.
Label-Prefix	Determines the alignment of all labels.
Column-Width	Sets the width of all columns.
Recalculation	Sets the method of recalculating formulas and functions.
Protection	Protects all cells from being overwritten.
Default	Changes certain default settings.
Zero	Suppresses the display of zero values.

CHANGING COLUMN WIDTHS

The / Worksheet Global Column-Width command changes all columns to a width you specify. The default width is 9. If all or most of your columns need to be a certain width, set them with the global command. Then change individual columns using / Worksheet Column Set-Width.

HANDS-ON Change the global column width to 8.

Select: **/Worksheet Global Column-Width**

Type: **8** [Enter]

```
A1: [W2]                                                          READY

     A      B          C       D        E      F       G       H        I        ◄
 1                           Travel Expenses                                      ►
 2                          ----------------                                      ▲
 3          Trip        Travel  Hotel   Meals  Misc.   Total   DepartedReturned   ▼
 4          Dallas        375    212     122     15      724   22-Jan  25-Jan     ?
 5          Los Angeles   475    439     280     59     1253   15-Mar  21-Mar
 6          Denver        148     75      32     13      268   01-Jul  02-Jul
 7          Dallas        207    240      94     40      581   13-Oct  16-Oct
 8          Atlanta       190    340     194     42      766   11-Dec  13-Dec
 9
10          Total        1395   1306     722    169     3592
```

Figure 39-2: The result of changing the global column width to 8.

Columns A and B, whose widths you changed earlier, were not affected (see Figure 39-2). 1-2-3 respects your changes to individual ranges, rows and columns. It assumes that you made the changes for a reason; therefore it doesn't override them when you make a global change.

Notice the effect of the width change on the dashed line under the worksheet's title. Earlier, you entered \- into cell D2 to fill that cell with dashes. Because the width is now 8 instead of 9, there's one dash too few to underline the title. To correct this problem, type a label prefix and seven dashes in cell E2.

As you can see, columns H and I are a little cramped, so let's widen them a bit.

HANDS-ON Set columns H and I to a width of 10.

Select: **/Worksheet Column Column-Range Set-Width**

Type: **H1..I1** [Enter]

Type: **10** [Enter]

Columns H and I are now wide enough to display the dates.

CHANGING NUMBER FORMATS

The way you display numbers will depend on what type of numbers you use. If your numbers are dollar amounts, you'll want to display them with a dollar sign. If they're very large numbers, you might want to display them in scientific notation. When you change the way the numbers look onscreen, the actual numbers aren't changed.

NUMBER FORMATS

Figure 39-3 gives some examples of the number formats available.

```
How 32.50 is displayed in various formats:

      32.5     General
    32.500     Fixed, 3 decimals
        33     Fixed, 0 decimals
  3.25E+01     Scientific, 2 decimals
    $32.50     Currency, 2 decimals
     3250%     Percent, 0 decimals
```

Figure 39-3: A few examples of number formats.

The default format is General, which means numbers are displayed exactly as you type them but without trailing zeros. If a number is too big to fit the cell, 1-2-3 will convert the display to scientific notation.

TIP To change the global number format, select /Worksheet Global Format. Then select the format you want.

All numbers on the worksheet, except any you've changed using /Range Format, will change to the new global format. Any new number you enter will also be displayed in the new format.

So use /Worksheet Global Format when all or most of the numbers on a worksheet will be of one type. Then use the /Range Format command to change any numbers that need a different format.

SEEING YOUR FORMULAS

Text format causes 1-2-3 to display your formulas and functions instead of the results of those calculations.

HANDS-ON Display all formulas and functions.

Select: /**Worksheet Global Format Text**

```
A1: (T) [W2]                                                    READY

    A.    B          C       D       E      F      G        H         I
1                           Travel Expenses
2            ----------------
3          Trip       Travel  Hotel   Meals  Misc.  Total    Departed  Returned
4          Dallas     375     212     122    15     +C4+D4+  @DATE(93  @DATE(93
5          Los Angeles 475    439     280    59     +C5+D5+  @DATE(93  @DATE(93
6          Denver     148     75      32     13     +C6+D6+  @DATE(93  @DATE(93
7          Dallas     207     240     94     40     +C7+D7+  @DATE(93  @DATE(93
8          Atlanta    190     340     194    42     +C8+D8+  @DATE(93  @DATE(93
9
10         Total      @SUM(C4 @SUM(D4 @SUM(E4 @SUM(F4 @SUM(G4
```

Figure 39-4: The entire worksheet displayed using the text format.

Formulas are usually longer than the numbers they produce (see Figure 39-4). So you'd have to widen the columns to see them fully.

To remove the display of formulas now, press Alt-F4 (Undo) or select /Worksheet Global Format General.

CHANGING THE ALIGNMENT OF LABELS

You learned earlier that you can change the alignment of individual labels by using label prefixes. But you can also change the global alignment of labels. The default is left-aligned.

To change the global alignment of labels, select /Worksheet Global Label-Prefix, and then either Left, Right or Center.

Using this command does *not* affect the individual labels that you've entered using label prefixes or the /Range Label command. Thus, existing labels are treated differently from existing values when you make a global change.

> **TIP** If all or most of your labels will be centered or right-aligned, set the alignment with the Global command. Then use the /Range Label command to change those ranges you want aligned differently.

DEFAULT SETTINGS

The /Worksheet Global Default menu lets you change some of 1-2-3's defaults, including printer settings and the default directory.

HANDS-ON Bring up the Default menu.

Select: **/Worksheet Global Default**

Figure 39-5: The /Worksheet Global Default menu and Default Settings box.

```
A1: [W2]                                                              MENU
Printer  Directory  Status  Update  Other  Autoexec  Quit
Specify printer interface and default settings
                          ──── Default Settings ────
 1
 2     Directory: [C:\123.......................]    ┌Clock────────
 3                                                    │(*) Standard
 4     [x] Auto-execute Macros on                     │( ) International
 5     [ ] Instant access to Help file                │( ) None
 6     [x] Undo on                                     │( ) File name
 7     [ ] Enhanced expanded memory on
 8     [x] Computer Bell on
 9
10    ┌Auto-attach add-ins─────────────────           ┌Add-in Keys──────
11    │ 1: [········]   5: [········]                  │ALT-F7:
12    │ 2: [········]   6: [········]    Invoke:       │ALT-F8:
13    │ 3: [········]   7: [········]                  │ALT-F9:
14    │ 4: [········]   8: [········]                  │ALT-F10:
15
16
17     Configuration file: C:\123\123.CNF
18
19              ┌─Press F2 (EDIT) to edit settings─┐
20
```

Figure 39-5 shows the /Worksheet Global Default menu and the Default Settings box. To hide the Default Settings box, press F6. Any changes you make here will affect the *current* worksheet.

TIP If you want your changes to affect all new worksheets, use the /Worksheet Global Default Update command.

OTHER GLOBAL COMMANDS

The three remaining Global commands are Zero, Recalculation and Protection.

ZERO

The /Worksheet Global Zero command causes any values that are equal to zero to be suppressed (not displayed). The content of those cells is still zero, but the number is not shown onscreen.

RECALCULATION

Normally, 1-2-3 updates the results of all formulas and functions any time you make a change to the data. With average-sized worksheets, automatic recalculation is fast and convenient. But if you create veryllarge worksheets with many interrelated formulas, automatic recalculation can interrupt your work.

The /Worksheet Global Recalculation Manual command turns off automatic recalculation. Now, when you make a change that affects a formula or function, 1-2-3 will show the CALC indicator onscreen. When you're ready to recalculate, press F9 (CALC). If you want to return to automatic recalculation, select /Worksheet Global Recalculation Automatic.

PROTECTION

The /Worksheet Global Protection command protects the worksheet from being overwritten with new information. Because it's used in conjunction with a /Range command, it is covered in Chapter 40, "Formatting Ranges of Data."

CHAPTER SUMMARY

- /Worksheet Global commands change the appearance of the worksheet and your data.

- The /Worksheet Global Column-Width command affects all columns except those adjusted individually.

- The /Worksheet Global Format Command affects all values except those changed with /Range Format.

- The /Worksheet Global Label-Prefix command affects all labels except those typed with particular label prefixes or those changed using /Range Label.

- The /Worksheet Global Default menu lets you change certain global default settings for the current worksheet. To save the change for all new worksheets, select /Worksheet Global Default Update.

- The /Worksheet Global Recalculation command lets you choose between manual and automatic recalculation of formulas and functions.

Formatting Ranges of Data

LOTUS **40**

Not all formatting changes you want to make will affect an entire worksheet. Sometimes you'll want to modify just a selected range of cells. So in this chapter, you'll learn how to

■ Format numbers in a range.

■ Align labels in a range.

■ Hide a range of data.

■ Give a name to a range.

■ Protect a range of cells from being overwritten.

■ Locate a text string in a range.

In the previous two chapters, you learned ways to adjust the appearance of the entire worksheet as well as your numbers and labels. In this chapter, you'll learn how to perform some of these same operations on selected ranges of cells using the /Range commands.

HANDS-ON
Take a look at the /Range menu.

Select: **/Range**

Figure 40-1: The /Range menu displays the commands used to modify ranges.

```
A1: [W2]                                                              MENU
Format Label Erase  Name  Justify  Prot  Unprot  Input  Value  Trans  Search
Fixed  Sci  Currency  ,  General  +/-  Percent  Date  Text  Hidden  Reset
    A       B        C        D         E      F         G         H         I      ◄
1                          Travel Expenses                                         ►
2                       ----------------
3        Trip        Travel  Hotel   Meals  Misc.   Total   Departed  Returned     ▼
4        Dallas        375     212     122     15     724    22-Jan    25-Jan      ▲
5        Los Angeles   475     439     280     59    1253    15-Mar    21-Mar      ?
```

COMMAND SUMMARY

These are the operations available in the /Range menu, as shown in Figure 40-1.

Format	Sets the appearance of numbers in a range.
Label	Sets the alignment of labels in a range.
Erase	Erases the contents of cells (but not the formatting) in a range.
Name	Names a range.
Justify	Formats a line of text into a specified width.
Prot	Reprotects cells you've unprotected with /Range Unprot.
Unprot	Unprotects a range of cells on a protected worksheet.
Input	Allows the pointer to move only to selected cells within an unprotected range.
Value	Copies values instead of their underlying formulas or functions.
Trans	Transposes a row into a column and vice versa.
Search	Finds/replaces a text string in a range. (Available in Release 2.2 and higher.)

Because Value and Trans are really copying commands, they're covered in Chapter 37, "Copying & Moving Data."

CHANGING FORMATS

The /Range Format command changes the format of numbers within a specified range. This command overrides any global format change you've already made or will make later.

TIP When you change number formats, the actual numbers aren't affected— only their onscreen appearance changes.

HANDS-ON Change the dollar amounts to Currency format with no decimals.

Select: **/Range Format Currency**

Type: **0** (zero) Enter

Type: **C4..G10** (the range to format) Enter

```
A1: [W2]                                                          READY

    A       B        C        D        E        F        G        H        I      ◄
1                          Travel Expenses                                        ►
2                          ----------------                                       ▲
3        Trip     Travel   Hotel    Meals    Misc.    Total    Departed Returned  ▼
4        Dallas     $375    $212     $122      $15     $724     22-Jan   25-Jan   ?
5        Los Angeles $475   $439     $280      $59   $1,253     15-Mar   21-Mar
6        Denver     $148     $75      $32      $13     $268     01-Jul   02-Jul
7        Dallas     $207    $240      $94      $40     $581     13-Oct   16-Oct
8        Atlanta    $190    $340     $194      $42     $766     11-Dec   13-Dec
9
10       Total    $1,395  $1,306     $722     $169   $3,592
```

Figure 40-2: Dollar amounts displayed in Currency format with no decimals.

Figure 40-2 shows the range C4..G10 displayed in Currency format with no decimals. If you move the pointer to any cell in the range, the Control Panel will indicate the format with (C0)—Currency format, 0 decimals.

You can also format empty cells. For example, if you format cells J1..J8 with Fixed format (two decimals), the only apparent change now will be the (F2) indicator in the Control Panel when you move the pointer to column J. Later, when you enter numbers into those cells, the numbers will be displayed in Fixed format with two decimals.

CHANGING THE DATE FORMAT

If you enter dates using the @DATE function, 1-2-3 displays the date number for each date. The /Range Format Date command lets you format the date numbers in a selected range so they appear in a more intelligible form. 1-2-3 offers five ways to display date numbers. Below, the date May 9, 1993, is shown in each of the date formats.

1(DD-MMM-YY)	09-May-93
2(DD-MMM)	09-May
3(MMM-YY)	May-93
4(Long Intn'l)	05/09/93
5(Short Intn'l)	05/93

TIP These date options are also available under /Worksheet Global Format Date.

HANDS-ON Format the Departed and Returned dates using the Short International format (option 5).

Select: **/Range Format Date 5**

Type: **H4..I8** [Enter]

```
H4: (D5) [W9] @DATE(91,1,22)                                    READY
```

	A	B	C	D	E	F	G	H	I
1				Travel Expenses					
2				------------------					
3		Trip	Travel	Hotel	Meals	Misc.	Total	Departed	Returned
4		Dallas	$375	$212	$122	$15	$724	01/22	01/25
5		Los Angeles	$475	$439	$280	$59	$1,253	03/15	03/21
6		Denver	$148	$75	$32	$13	$268	07/01	07/02
7		Dallas	$207	$240	$94	$40	$581	10/13	10/16
8		Atlanta	$190	$340	$194	$42	$766	12/11	12/13
9									
10		Total	$1,395	$1,306	$722	$169	$3,592		

Figure 40-3: Dates displayed in Short International format.

The dates are now displayed in the Short International format (Figure 40-3).

Formatting choices for times you enter using the @TIME function are available under /Range Format Date Time.

HIDING DATA

1-2-3's /Range Format Hidden command lets you suppress the display of data in selected ranges. When the pointer is in a hidden cell, the Control Panel will show the (H) indicator along with the cell's actual content. The /Range Format Reset command brings the hidden cells back into view.

CHANGING THE ALIGNMENT OF LABELS

The /Range Label command lets you position a range of labels on the left, right or center of their cells. This command overrides any global alignment command that you've already made or will make later.

HANDS-ON   Right-align the expense category titles.

Select: **/Range Label Right**

Type: **C3..G3** [Enter]

```
C3: "Travel                                                     READY
```

	A	B	C	D	E	F	G	H	I
1				Travel Expenses					
2				------------------					
3		Trip	Travel	Hotel	Meals	Misc.	Total	Departed	Returned
4		Dallas	$375	$212	$122	$15	$724	01/22	01/25
5		Los Angeles	$475	$439	$280	$59	$1,253	03/15	03/21
6		Denver	$148	$75	$32	$13	$268	07/01	07/02
7		Dallas	$207	$240	$94	$40	$581	10/13	10/16
8		Atlanta	$190	$340	$194	$42	$766	12/11	12/13
9									
10		Total	$1,395	$1,306	$722	$169	$3,592		

Figure 40-4: Right-aligned column headings (range C3..G3).

Every label in the range C3..G3 now has the Right label prefix (")
to indicate right alignment (but you'll see this only in the Control
Panel). Figure 40-4 shows that cell C3 contains the Right label prefix.

NAMING A RANGE

You've seen that you can specify a range either by typing its first and
last cells or by stretching the pointer to cover the range. The third,
and final, way to specify a range is to enter its name.

THE ADVANTAGE

The main advantage of naming a range is that names are descriptive
and easier to remember than cell addresses.

HANDS-ON   Give the name HOTEL to the range D4..D8.

Select: **/Range Name Create**

Type: **HOTEL** `Enter`

Type: **D4..D8** `Enter`

When you name a range that has already been referenced in a
formula or function, 1-2-3 substitutes the name for that range. So the
function you wrote in D10 as @SUM(D4..D8) is now @SUM(HOTEL).

JOGGING YOUR MEMORY

What if you forget which ranges belong to which names? Don't worry—
1-2-3 will list range names and their ranges. Just move to a blank area
of the worksheet, select /Range Name Table and then enter a one-cell
range. 1-2-3 will list the range names beginning in that cell.

JUSTIFYING TEXT

Although 1-2-3 is not a word processor, it allows you to perform some
modest text formatting.

> **TIP** Using the /Range Justify command, you can convert a long label into
> a paragraph format. It's useful for adding notes to a worksheet.

HANDS-ON Type a note to the right of your data and format it to fit within columns K and L.

Move: Pointer to cell K1.

Type: **This spreadsheet is designed to calculate monthly travel expenses.** Enter

Select: **/Range Justify**

Type: **K1..L1** Enter

Figure 40-5: The contents of K1 formatted using /Range Justify.

	E	F	G	H	I	J	K	L	
	K7:								READY
1	xpenses						This		◄
2							spreadsheet is		►
3	────						designed to		▲
	Meals	Misc.	Total	Departed	Returned		calculate		▼
4	$122	$15	$724	01/22	01/25		monthly travel		?
5	$280	$59	$1,253	03/15	03/21		expenses.		
6	$32	$13	$268	07/01	07/02				
7	$94	$40	$581	10/13	10/16				
8	$194	$42	$766	12/11	12/13				
9									
10	$722	$169	$3,592						

The entire label is now contained in columns K and L, as shown in Figure 40-5.

> **TIP** If you attach the WYSIWYG add-in program, you'll have more flexibility in formatting text.

PROTECTING & UNPROTECTING CELLS

On some of your worksheets you're likely to have some very important data you'd really hate to lose. For example, you may have written a long formula or entered some complex numbers and labels. Fortunately, 1-2-3 lets you protect cells that contain important information.

This technique is a bit strange. First, you must protect the entire worksheet. Then you unprotect cells in which you want to be able to enter data.

HANDS-ON Protect all cells except the range C4 to F8.

Select: **/Worksheet Global Protection Enable**

Select: **/Range Unprot**

Type: **C4..F8** Enter

```
A1: PR [W2]                                                       READY

    A      B         C         D         E       F       G       H       I     ◄
1                         Travel Expenses                                      ►
2                         ----------------                                     ▲
3         Trip      Travel    Hotel     Meals   Misc.   Total Departed Returned ▼
4         Dallas    $375      $212      $122    $15     $724   01/22   01/25    ?
5         Los Angeles $475    $439      $280    $59   $1,253   03/15   03/21
6         Denver    $148      $75       $32     $13     $268   07/01   07/02
7         Dallas    $207      $240      $94     $40     $581   10/13   10/16
8         Atlanta   $190      $340      $194    $42     $766   12/11   12/13
9
10        Total   $1,395   $1,306      $722    $169  $3,592
```

Figure 40-6: Worksheet incorporating the Protection feature.

Items in the unprotected cells (range C4..F8) are shown in green (or bold on a monochrome monitor). In the Control Panel, protection is indicated with the PR indicator. Unprotected cells are identified with the U indicator (see Figure 40-6).

REMOVING PROTECTION

If you want to remove the protection from an entire worksheet, first reprotect any unprotected ranges (C4..F8 in the previous example), using /Range Prot. Select /Worksheet Global Protection Disable. The following examples assume that protection has been disabled.

SEARCHING & REPLACING

The /Range Search command lets you locate a text string in a range. The string can be an entire word or part of a word or formula. You have the option of replacing the string with another string.

HANDS-ON   Replace all occurrences of Total with TOTAL.

Select: **/Range Search**

Type: **A1..I10** [Enter]

Type: **Total** (the string to search for) [Enter]

Select: **Labels Replace**

Type: **TOTAL** (the replacement string) [Enter]

Select: **All**

```
G3:  "TOTAL                                                                      READY

     A       B          C       D       E       F        G       H         I        ◄
 1                          Travel Expenses                                          ►
 2                       ────────────────                                            ▲
 3        Trip          Travel  Hotel   Meals   Misc.   TOTAL Departed  Returned      ▼
 4        Dallas         $375   $212    $122    $15     $724  01/22     01/25         ?
 5        Los Angeles    $475   $439    $280    $59   $1,253  03/15     03/21
 6        Denver         $148    $75     $32    $13     $268  07/01     07/02
 7        Dallas         $207   $240     $94    $40     $581  10/13     10/16
 8        Atlanta        $190   $340    $194    $42     $766  12/11     12/13
 9
10        TOTAL        $1,395 $1,306    $722   $169   $3,592
```

Figure 40-7: The result of replacing "total" with "TOTAL."

Figure 40-7 shows the result of the search and replace operation. To broaden the search, you can use the wildcard characters ? and * in the search string. For example, D* would find all labels beginning with the letter D.

CHAPTER SUMMARY

◼ Erasing a range removes the cells' contents, but not their formats.

◼ A range can be specified by typing its first and last cells, by stretching the pointer or by entering the name of a named range.

◼ The /Range Format command formats a range of values using Fixed, Scientific, Percent or other formats.

◼ The /Range Justify command formats a line of text into a specified width.

◼ /Worksheet Global Protection Enable protects all cells on a worksheet.

◼ The /Range Unprot command unprotects a range of cells on a protected worksheet.

◼ The /Range Search command lets you locate a text string and, optionally, replace it with another string.

Printing
Your Work

LOTUS
41

1-2-3 makes it easy to print a worksheet. A basic printout requires only two steps. But the program also provides a number of options that enable you to improve the way your printouts look. So in this chapter, you'll learn how to

■ Print a worksheet.

■ Tell 1-2-3 where the top of the paper is in your printer.

■ Use print options to improve the appearance of a worksheet.

■ Locate errors in a worksheet.

■ Save a worksheet so it can be edited in WordPerfect.

The 1-2-3 /Print commands let you print worksheets and control certain printer features.

HANDS-ON Display the /Print menu.

Select: **/Print**

Figure 41-1: The /Print menu displays the commands used to print worksheets and control printer features.

```
G3: "TOTAL                                                         MENU
Printer  File  Encoded  Background
Send print output directly to a printer
    A        B         C        D       E       F       G        H        I      ◄
1                            Travel Expenses                                     ►
2                         --------------                                         ▲
3   Trip            Travel     Hotel   Meals   Misc.   TOTAL Departed Returned   ▼
4   Dallas          $375       $212    $122    $15     $724    01/22    01/25    ?
5   Los Angeles     $475       $439    $288    $59   $1,253    03/15    03/21
```

The /Print menu contains the following four options as shown in Figure 41-1.

Printer	Allows you to print the current worksheet.
File	Saves the current worksheet as an unformatted ASCII text file.
Encoded	Saves the worksheet as an encoded file, which includes both data and printer codes. Encoded files may be printed later at the DOS prompt (Release 2.3 and higher).
Background	Prints the worksheet while allowing you to continue with your work or quit the 1-2-3 program (Release 2.3 and higher).

Selecting Printer brings up the next print menu. In Figure 41-2, 1-2-3 shows you the current settings. To hide the Print Settings box, press F6 (Window).

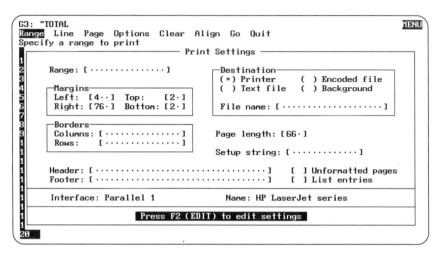

Figure 41-2: The /Print Printer menu and Print Settings box.

COMMAND SUMMARY

Here are the commands available on this second-level menu:

Range	Specifies the range of cells to be printed.
Line	Advances the page one line.
Page	Advances the top of the next page to the printer head.
Options	Lets you improve and enhance your printout.
Clear	Clears all print settings.
Align	Tells 1-2-3 that the top of a page is at the printer head.
Go	Starts the printing.

THE PAGE LENGTH

1-2-3's default page length is 66 lines; but your printer's maximum page length may be different. For example, your printer might allow only 60 lines per page. (This information is given in your printer's user manual.) If you need to change the default page length, select /Worksheet Global Default Printer Pg-Length and then type the new length. Then select Quit and Update to save the change.

ALIGNING THE PAPER

Before printing with a dot matrix printer, you should align the paper so that the top of a sheet is at the printer head. If you have a laser printer, the paper is already in position. But if you have a dot-matrix printer, you'll have to align the paper manually. Then you want to tell 1-2-3 what you've done by selecting /Print Printer Align.

There's a good reason for going through this step. When you print, you might print only a small portion of a page. If you aligned the paper as described above, you can select /Print Printer Page and 1-2-3 will advance the paper to the top of the next sheet. The alternative is to position the paper yourself after each printout.

HANDS-ON Notify 1-2-3 that you've aligned the paper in your printer. Make sure the printer is online.

Select: **/Print Printer Align**

1-2-3 now knows that the printer head is at the top of a page.

BASIC PRINTING

The quickest and easiest way to print is to use 1-2-3's default print settings.

HANDS-ON Print the worksheet (make sure your printer is online).

Select: **/Print Printer Range**

Type: **A1..I10** Enter

Select: **Go**

```
                        Travel Expenses
                        ---------------
   Trip          Travel      Hotel      Meals       Misc.      TOTAL  Departed   Returned
   Dallas         $375       $212       $122         $15       $724    01/22      01/25
   Los Angeles    $475       $439       $280         $59     $1,253    03/15      03/21
   Denver         $148        $75        $32         $13       $268    07/01      07/02
   Dallas         $207       $240        $94         $40       $581    10/13      10/16
   Atlanta        $190       $340       $194         $42       $766    12/11      12/13
   TOTAL        $1,395     $1,306       $722        $169     $3,592
```

Figure 41-3: A printout of the worksheet.

If your printer is connected to a network, you might need to select Quit now to complete the Print command.

HANDS-ON Advance the paper in the printer to the top of the next sheet.

Select: **/Print Printer Page**

TIP /Print Printer Page doesn't reset the page number to 1. But if you follow the command with /Print Printer Align, the next printout will be page 1. This point is important only if you include page numbers on your printouts.

PRINT OPTIONS

1-2-3's printing options give you a variety of ways to improve a printed worksheet.

HANDS-ON Bring up the Options menu.

Select: /**Print Printer Options**

Figure 41-4: The /Print Printer Options menu displays the commands used to improve the printout of a worksheet.

```
A1: [W2]                                                             MENU
Header  Footer  Margins  Borders  Setup  Pg-Length  Other  Quit
Create a header
                              ──────── Print Settings ────────
1
```

COMMAND SUMMARY

Here's a brief look at the print options, shown in Figure 41-4:

Header	Adds a header line to every page.
Footer	Adds a footer line to every page.
Margins	Adjusts the page margins.
Borders	Designates certain rows and/or columns to be printed on every page (the printed equivalent of the /Worksheet Titles command).
Setup	Changes the printed characters to small, bold, italic and other attributes.
Pg-Length	Changes the default page length for the current worksheet.
Other	Prints either the worksheet data or the underlying formulas, functions and formatting.

The commands you'll probably use most often are the Header, Footer and Margins commands.

ADDING HEADERS & FOOTERS

Headers and *footers* are text lines that print at the top and bottom of every page of your printout. They can include the title of the work and often some additions, such as the page number or today's date.

POSITIONING HEADERS & FOOTERS

Vertical bars (|) are used to tell 1-2-3 where to place text in headers and footers. The first bar you include tells 1-2-3 to center the text, and the second one tells it to right-align the text. Without a bar, the text is automatically left-aligned.

HANDS-ON   Add a centered header to the printout.

Select: **/Print Printer Options Header**

Type: **|Travel Expenses for 1993**

Now print the worksheet by selecting /Print Printer Go. Because you've already specified the range, you don't have to enter it again. Figure 41-5 shows how the printout looks with a header.

```
                        Travel Expenses for 1993

                   Travel Expenses
                   ---------------
     Trip            Travel      Hotel    Meals     Misc.     TOTAL  Departed   Returned
     Dallas           $375       $212     $122       $15      $724    01/22     01/25
     Los Angeles      $475       $439     $280       $59    $1,253    03/15     03/21
     Denver           $148        $75      $32       $13      $268    07/01     07/02
     Dallas           $207       $240      $94       $40      $581    10/13     10/16
     Atlanta          $190       $340     $194       $42      $766    12/11     12/13
     TOTAL          $1,395     $1,306     $722      $169    $3,592
```

Figure 41-5: A printout featuring a header.

Now advance the paper with /Print Printer Page and then reset the page number to 1 by selecting /Print Printer Align.

ENHANCING HEADERS & FOOTERS

Two very useful additions to a header (or footer) are page numbers and the current date. To include the page number, type #, and to include today's date, type @.

For example, the header @ **|Travel Expenses for 1993 |Page #** would print today's date on the left, the worksheet title in the center, and the page number on the right (preceded by the word "Page").

DEBUGGING A WORKSHEET

One problem with worksheets is that they don't always behave as you want them to; you expect one thing but get another. It happens all the time. The only way to find the problem is to determine exactly what's in each cell. 1-2-3 provides the option of printing the actual contents of cells, including formatting information, instead of the displayed contents.

HANDS-ON Print the real contents of each cell.

Select: **/Print Printer Options Other Cell-Formulas**

```
                        Travel Expenses for 1993

    D1: 'Travel Expenses
    D2: \-
    E2: '-------
    B3: [W12] 'Trip
    C3: "Travel
    D3: "Hotel
    E3: "Meals
    F3: "Misc.
    G3: "TOTAL
    H3: [W9] 'Departed
    I3: [W9] 'Departed
    B4: [W12] 'Dallas
    C4: (C0) 375
    D4: (C0) 212
    E4: (C0) 122
    F4: (C0) 15
    G4: (C0) +C4+D4+E4+F4
    H4: (D5) [W9] @DATE(93,1,22)
    I4: (D5) [W9] @DATE(93,1,25)
    B5: [W12] 'Los Angeles
    C5: (C0) 475
    D5: (C0) 439
    E5: (C0) 280
    F5: (C0) 59
    G5: (C0) +C5+D5+E5+F5
```

Figure 41-6: Printout showing the actual content of each cell.

Now print the worksheet. As you can see in Figure 41-6, the Cell-Formulas option creates a printout that shows your data, formulas and functions, formatting, and cell widths. If you want to return to the normal printout, select /Print Printer Options Other As-Displayed.

After printing, advance the paper with /Print Printer Page.

USING SETUP CODES

Some printers have special print capabilities such as printing enlarged or condensed type. By entering a *setup code,* you can change the size and style of the characters used in a 1-2-3 printout.

USING CONDENSED PRINT

The most commonly used setup code prints your worksheet in condensed type.

HANDS-ON Using a dot-matrix printer, print the worksheet in condensed print.

Select: **/Print Printer Options Setup**

Type: **\015** [Enter]   (Notice that \ is a backward slash and that 0 is a zero.)

When you print the worksheet, it will be in condensed type.
To return to normal print, go back into /Print Printer Options Setup and delete the setup code.

ADJUSTING THE MARGINS

Because condensed printing allows more characters per line, you'll want to widen the right margin if your worksheet is wider than 72 characters. To adjust the margin, select /Print Printer Options Margins Right. Then enter the maximum number of characters.

"PRINTING" TO A FILE

1-2-3 lets you save a worksheet as an unformatted ASCII text file using the /Print File command. In this form, the worksheet can be used in word processing programs, such as WordPerfect.

CREATING A PRINT FILE

HANDS-ON Save the current version of the worksheet as an ASCII text file.

Select: **/Print File**

Type: **TEXTTEST** [Enter]

Select: **Range**

Type: **A1..I10** [Enter]

Select: **Align Go**

1-2-3 adds a .PRN extension to identify it as a print file.

> **TIP** If your worksheet has headers, footers and page breaks, you can exclude them from the text file by selecting Options Other Unformatted before selecting Go.

EDITING A PRINT FILE

If you want to import an ASCII print file into WordPerfect for editing, see Chapter 18, "Learning the Basics," in the WordPerfect section of *Office Companion*.

BACKGROUND PRINTING

In Release 2.3 and higher, you can print the worksheet and then immediately continue working or quit the program. To use background printing, you must use the /Quit command (not the /System command) to return to the DOS prompt, and type BPRINT.

When you return to the programs and select /Print Printer Background, 1-2-3 creates an encoded file (with the extension .ENC), and then prints it. You can also print the file later at the DOS prompt by entering BPRINT and the appropriate file name (for example, BPRINT EXPENSES.ENC).

CHAPTER SUMMARY

■ The /Print Printer Align command informs 1-2-3 that you've positioned the top of a page at the printer head. It also resets the page number to 1.

■ The /Print Printer Page command advances the paper after you finish printing.

■ In a header or footer, including @ causes the date to be printed; and including # causes the page number to be printed.

■ The basic requirements for printing are that you specify a range and then select the Go command.

■ The Setup string \015 causes the worksheet to be printed in condensed type on most dot-matrix printers.

■ The /Print Printer Options Other Cell-Formulas command prints the real content of each cell along with formatting information.

■ /Print File saves the present version of the worksheet as an unformatted ASCII file that can be edited in a word processing program.

■ /Print Printer Background prints while you continue with your work. You have to first run the BPRINT program from the DOS prompt.

Managing Your Files

ile management is an essential part of using 1-2-3 or any other PC program effectively. Some of the operations that you know how to do at the DOS prompt, like listing and erasing files, can also be done in 1-2-3. The program also provides some special file management techniques. So in this chapter, you'll learn how to

- Save and retrieve files.
- Protect a worksheet with a password.
- Erase files.
- Change the default directory.
- Combine part of the current worksheet into a file on a disk.
- Bring part of a disk file into the current worksheet.

1-2-3's /File commands let you perform routine file management operations like saving, retrieving, listing and erasing files.

TYPES OF FILES

When you create and save a file, 1-2-3 adds an extension to the file name to indicate the file type. The file types you're most likely to use are

- Worksheet file (.WK1 extension), created with /File Save.
- Picture (graph) file (.PIC extension), created with /Graph Save.

Other types of files are

- Print file, an unformatted text file version of the worksheet (.PRN extension), created with /Print File.
- Encoded file, another type of unformatted file that can be printed at the DOS prompt (.ENC extension), created with /Print Encoded.

THE FILE MENU

HANDS-ON Bring up the /File menu.

Select: **/File**

```
A1: [W2]                                                              MENU
Retrieve  Save  Combine  Xtract  Erase  List  Import  Directory  Admin
Erase the current worksheet from memory and display the selected worksheet
     A       B        C        D        E        F       G        H        I    ◄
1                           Travel Expenses                                     ►
2                          ----------------                                     ▲
3    Trip          Travel   Hotel    Meals    Misc.    TOTAL Departed Returned   ▼
4    Dallas        $375     $212     $122     $15      $724  01/22    01/25     ?
```

Figure 42-1: The /File menu displays the commands used to work with files.

COMMAND SUMMARY

Here's a quick look at 1-2-3's /File commands, shown in Figure 42-1:

Retrieve	Retrieves a worksheet file from a disk.
Save	Saves the current worksheet to a disk.
Combine	Brings all or part of a file into the current worksheet.
Xtract	Saves a specified part of the current worksheet to a file.
Erase	Erases a file from a disk.
List	Lists the 1-2-3 files on a disk.
Import	Imports non-1-2-3 data into a worksheet.
Directory	Displays and/or changes the current directory.
Admin	Brings up specialized miscellaneous file commands. (Available in Release 2.2 and higher.)
View	Locates and displays hard disk files; simplifies many data management tasks. This option appears only if you have attached the Viewer add-in.

SAVING FILES

The /File Save command is used to save the current worksheet to a disk. 1-2-3 displays the default drive and directory, allowing you to enter the file name. (Later in this chapter, you'll learn how to change the default directory.)

HANDS-ON Save the current worksheet with the name EXPENSES.

Select: **/File Save**

Type: **EXPENSES** Enter

1-2-3 adds the extension .WK1 to indicate that this is a worksheet file, so the file is really named EXPENSES.WK1.

UPDATING A FILE

The next time you select /File Save, 1-2-3 will show the current file name. If you press Enter, you'll be prompted to select Cancel, Replace or Backup. To update the file with the newer version, select Replace.

> **TIP** The /File Save command can also serve as a copy command. Simply save the file. Then select /File Save again, but this time type a new name. You will then have two files that are exactly alike.

ADDING A PASSWORD

You can protect a worksheet file from being opened by unauthorized users by giving it a password when you save it. The same cautions apply here as in WordPerfect: if you forget the password, there's no way to get into the file.

To add the password, select /File Save and then type the file name, a space, and P (or just add the space and P to the file name if you've already saved the file). 1-2-3 will prompt you to type the password. Then it will ask you to type it again to verify.

HANDS-ON Add the password TEST1 to the current worksheet.

Select: **/File Save**

Type: **EXPENSES P** [Enter]

Type: **TEST1** [Enter]

Type: **TEST1** [Enter] (to verify the password)

Select: **Replace**

> **TIP** To remove a password, select /File Save and delete the PASSWORD PROTECTED indicator. Then press Enter and select Replace.

Caution

Be aware that the password feature knows the difference between uppercase and lowercase letters. So, if your password is "TEST1," 1-2-3 won't let you open the file with the password "test1."

RETRIEVING FILES

The /File Retrieve command retrieves worksheet files from your disk. When you select the command, you'll see a list of your worksheet files, as in Figure 42-2.

```
List    ◄   ►   ▲   ▼   ?   ..   A:  B:  C:                              FILES
Name of file to retrieve: C:\123\MISC\*.wk?
ADDRESS.WK1      EXPENSES.WK1      FORGRAPH.WK1      MSALES.WK1      SALESAPR.WK1
    A        B          C          D          E        F        G         H         I
1                               Travel Expenses
2                            ─────────────────
3        Trip          Travel    Hotel     Meals     Misc.    TOTAL  Departed  Returned
4        Dallas        $375      $212      $122      $15      $724   01/22     01/25
5        Los Angeles   $475      $439      $280      $59      $1,253 03/15     03/21
```

Figure 42-2: The result of selecting /File Retrieve.

If you have lots of files, the list of files will extend off the screen to the right.

At this point, you can type the name of the file you want to retrieve (you don't have to type the .WK1 extension). Or if you prefer, you can move the menu pointer to the file you want and then press Enter. With a mouse, just click on the file name.

CAUTION

If you have a worksheet onscreen, retrieving another file will erase the first. If you haven't saved the current worksheet, Release 2.3 and higher will prompt you before executing the Retrieve command; earlier releases will not.

LISTING FILES

The /File List command is like the DIR command in DOS because it lists your 1-2-3 files. And just as you do with the DIR command, you can specify subgroups of files to list. For a review of file names, see Chapter 8, "Creating & Erasing Files," in the DOS section of *Office Companion.*

TIP The /File List command lets you list Worksheet files, Print files or Graph files. To see all three types, select the Other option.

HANDS-ON List all worksheet files in the default directory (here, it's C:\123\MISC).

Select: **/File List Worksheet**

Figure 42-3: A list of all worksheet files in the default directory.

As you can see in Figure 42-3, 1-2-3 shows you all worksheet files (*.WK1) in the default directory.

Now to return to the worksheet, press Enter.

LISTING SELECTED FILES

By using wildcard characters (* and ?), you can specify subgroups of files to list.

HANDS-ON List just the worksheet files whose names begin with SALES.

Select: /**File List Worksheet**

Press: **Esc**

Type: **SALES*** Enter

Figure 42-4: A list of all the file names beginning with "SALES."

CHANGING THE DEFAULT DIRECTORY

The /File List command shows you the files in the default directory. If you've organized your files into subdirectories, you may want to change the default directory to make it easier to get to certain groups of files. The /File Directory command lets you change the default directory for the current 1-2-3 session.

> **TIP** You might also want to change the default directory for future 1-2-3 sessions. Just select /Worksheet Global Default Directory, type the new directory name and press Enter, then select Update (in Release 2.3, select Quit Update).

OTHER FILE COMMANDS

Other File commands you'll find useful are Combine, Xtract and Erase.

COMBINE

The /File Combine command lets you bring part of a file into the current worksheet. The Copy option copies a range of cells into a blank area of the current worksheet. The Add and Subtract options add and subtract values from a file and the current worksheet. These two options can be useful if you have two worksheets that contain related information. For example, let's say you have two worksheets that are set up identically. One (on disk) has first-quarter sales figures; the other (the current worksheet) has second-quarter sales figures. To get a year-to-date total, you can add the figures together using /File Combine Add.

XTRACT

The /File Xtract command is really a type of Save command. It lets you select part of the current worksheet and save it to a separate file (either a new one or an existing one). You have the choice of saving either the displayed values or their underlying formulas and functions.

ERASE

The /File Erase command lets you erase 1-2-3 files from the disk. It works just like the ERASE command you've used at the DOS prompt. *You can't undo this operation, so be careful.*

CHAPTER SUMMARY

- 1-2-3 uses different extensions for different types of files: .WK1 for worksheet files, .PIC for graph files, .PRN for print files, and .ENC for encoded files.

- You can create a copy of the current worksheet by selecting /File Save and then typing a different file name.

- To add a password to a file, select /File Save and type the file name, a space and P. Then type the password twice (the second time is to verify).

- The /File List command can be used to list selected files or all files.

- The /File Directory command changes the default directory for the current session. The /Worksheet Global Default Directory command changes the default directory for future sessions.

- The /File Combine command copies parts of a file into the current worksheet. The /File Xtract command does the opposite: it saves part of the current worksheet to a file.

Creating Graphs

LOTUS
43

Although a page of numbers can present facts, it can't give an immediate understanding of what the data are really saying. But graphs can. So in this chapter, you'll learn how to

- Create line, bar and pie graphs.
- Use options to improve the appearance and effectiveness of your graphs.
- Create several graphs on one worksheet.
- Print a graph.

> **TIP** 1-2-3 isn't a sophisticated graphing program. But it can present data clearly and dramatically in a way that words and numbers can't.

1-2-3 GRAPHS

1-2-3 lets you create seven types of graphs: line, bar, stacked bar, pie, XY, high-low-closing-opening (HLCO) and mixed (lines plus bars). The last two are available in Release 2.3 and higher.

Line, bar and stacked bar graphs all compare different categories along one variable. Figure 43-1 shows a line graph.

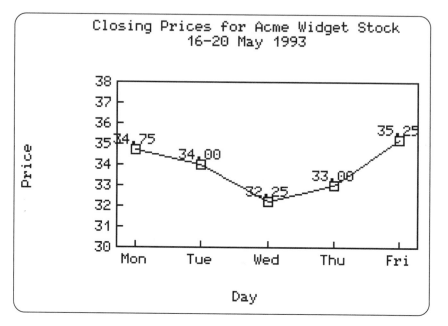

Figure 43-1: This line graph compares closing stock prices over a five-day period.

A mixed graph is a combination line and bar graph. It allows up to three line ranges and three bar ranges.

A pie graph shows the relative sizes of the parts that make up only one category, as shown in Figure 43-2.

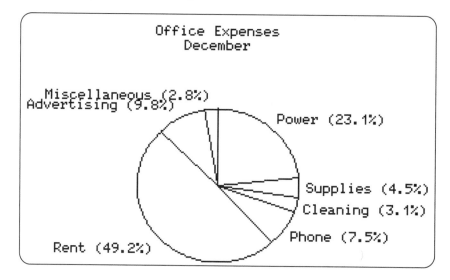

Figure 43-2: A pie graph comparing percentages of office expense categories.

An XY graph, illustrated in Figure 43-3, shows the relationship between two variables. Notice the difference between this graph and the line graph. The XY graph's X-axis represents a variable, not several independent categories.

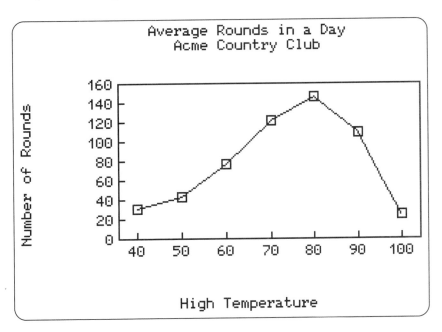

Figure 43-3: An XY graph showing the number of rounds of golf played in relation to the temperature.

An HLCO graph shows the high, low, closing and opening prices for a stock. Figure 43-4 gives an example.

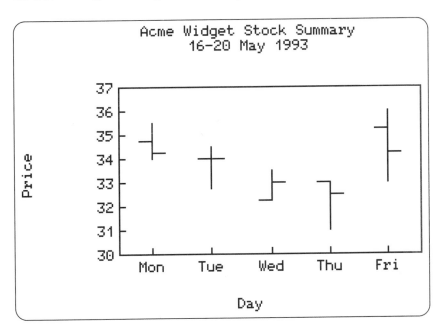

Figure 43-4: An HLCO graph comparing sales figures over a five-day period.

GRAPH TERMINOLOGY

Before you start, you need to know some basic terminology that 1-2-3 uses when making a graph:

X axis: The horizontal axis of the graph.
Y axis: The vertical axis of the graph.
Data range: A set of numbers used in the graph. Lotus 1-2-3 graphs allow from one to six data ranges, depending on the graph type. The data ranges are labeled A-F, but these names do not refer to columns A-F–the ranges can be anywhere on the worksheet.
X range: The labels or values for the X axis, or the labels for pie graph slices.

The following chart tells you how to designate the required ranges for each type of graph.

Graph	Range	Description
Line, Bar, Stacked Bar	X	X-axis labels.
	A–F	Data ranges.
Pie	X	Labels for pie slices.
	A	Values for pie slices.
	B	Values for controlling hatch patterns or colors.
XY	X	X-axis values.
	A–F	Data ranges.
HLCO	X	X-axis labels.
	A	High value.
	B	Low value.
	C	Closing value.
	D	Opening value.
Mixed	X	X-axis labels.
	A–C	Data ranges for bars.
	D–F	Data ranges for lines.

THE GRAPH MENU

The /Graph menu lists commands that allow you to create, view and save graphs.

 Bring up the /Graph menu.

Select: **/Graph**

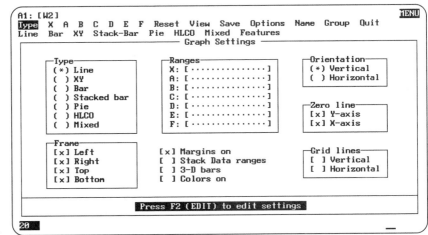

Figure 43-5: The /Graph
menu and Graph Settings box.

In Figure 43-5, you see the /Graph menu and the Graph Settings box. To hide the Graph Settings box, press F6 (Window).

COMMAND SUMMARY

Type	Lets you choose the type of graph. Also lets you choose features for enhancing a graph (Release 2.3 and higher).
X	Sets the range containing the X-axis labels or values.
A F	Sets data ranges A through F.
Reset	Resets all graph settings to the defaults.
View	Displays the graph.
Save	Saves the current graph for printing.
Options	Enhances the graph.
Name	Names a graph and its settings. Enables you to create more than one graph on a worksheet.
Group	Sets all ranges for a graph at one time. (Available in Release 2.2 and higher.)

CREATING GRAPHS

To create a graph in 1-2-3, you first must have a worksheet. On it, you have to specify two pieces of information: the type of graph you want and the ranges of numbers you want to use in the graph.

HANDS-ON Create a bar graph that compares the major expenses for the two Dallas trips.

Select: **/Graph Type Bar X**

Type: **C3..E3** (X-axis labels) [Enter]

Select: **A**

Type: **C4..E4** (first data range) [Enter]

Select: **B**

Type: **C7..E7** (second data range) [Enter]

That's all there is to it. You now have a simple bar graph with two data ranges.

VIEWING A GRAPH

You can take a look at the graphs you create by selecting /Graph View. You will be successful if your monitor can display graphics and you installed the program correctly. To return to the worksheet after viewing, press Enter or Esc.

SETTING ALL RANGES AT ONCE

The /Graph Group command lets you set the X-axis range and up to six data ranges at one time. (Available in Release 2.2 and higher.) But to use this time-saving command, your ranges must be arranged in columns or rows in the order shown in Figure 43-6.

```
E19:                                                                    READY

           A          B          C          D          E      F
1   Monthly Sales For The First And Second Quarters
2
3                          Regional Office
4          -----------------------------------------------
5   Month          Chicago      Atlanta      New York
6   ----------
7   January       $14,900      $16,599      $15,444
8   February      $12,050      $13,060      $14,399
9   March          $9,788      $10,094       $9,967
10  April          $9,772      $10,209       $8,004
11  May            $8,553       $9,477       $7,432
12  June           $9,753       $8,950       $4,002
13
14       ↑            ↑            ↑            ↑
15    X RANGE      A RANGE      B RANGE      C RANGE      ETC.
```

Figure 43-6: Proper arrangement of data for using the /Graph Group command.

> **TIP** To use this method, select /Graph Group and specify the range that includes all your data ranges (here, it would be A7..D12). Then select either Columnwise or Rowwise to divide the large range into the graph ranges.

NAMING & SAVING GRAPHS

Naming a graph and saving a graph are two entirely different operations that are sometimes confused.

NAMING A GRAPH

If you want to create more than one graph on a worksheet, you have to name each graph after you create it with /Graph Name Create.

HANDS-ON Name the bar graph BAR1.

Select: **/Graph Name Create**

Type: **BAR1** [Enter]

Before creating another graph, you can use /Graph Reset to reset some or all the previous settings. This command has no effect on your first graph. Then, when you've created another graph, name it with /Graph Name Create.

> **TIP** If you create and name more than one graph on a worksheet, you can make any one of them the current graph with /Graph Name Use.

SAVING A GRAPH

If you want to print a graph, you must save it with the /Graph Save command. Saving the worksheet (with / File Save) will save the graph *settings* in the worksheet, but not the graph image.

HANDS-ON Save the current graph for printing.

Select: **/Graph Save**

Type: **BAR1** [Enter]

1-2-3 adds the extension .PIC to the name to identify this file as a picture (graph) file.

USING GRAPH OPTIONS

A basic graph usually leaves much to be desired. So 1-2-3 provides a number of ways of improving your graph to make it look better and convey information more effectively.

HANDS-ON Bring up the Options menu.

Select: **/Graph Options**

Figure 43-7: The /Graph Options menu displays the commands used to improve a graph's appearance and effectiveness.

```
A1: [W2]                                                              MENU
Legend  Format  Titles  Grid  Scale  Color  B&W  Data-Labels  Quit
Create legends for data ranges
───────────────────────────── Graph Settings ─────────────────────────
```

The /Graph options, shown in Figure 43-7, are explained below.

Legend	Identifies each data range.
Format	Lets you choose to display lines, points, both or neither for each data range.
Titles	Lets you add titles and axis labels to the graph.
Grid	Draws a horizontal and/or vertical grid on the graph.
Scale	Lets you set the X- and Y-axis scales yourself.
Color	If you have a color monitor, lets you see the graph in color.
B&W	Displays the graph in black and white.
Data-Labels	Writes the actual value of each point on the graph.

ADDING A LEGEND

A legend identifies the data ranges on a graph.

HANDS-ON Add a legend to the bar graph.

Select: **/Graph Options Legend A**

Type: **First Trip** [Enter]

Select: **Legend B**

Type: **Second Trip** [Enter]

ADDING TITLES

The Titles option lets you create a title for the graph, as well as labels for the X-axis and Y-axis.

HANDS-ON   Add a main title and axis labels to the graph.

> Select: **/Graph Options Titles First**
>
> Type: **Two Trips to Dallas** Enter
>
> Select: **Titles X-axis**
>
> Type: **Expense** Enter
>
> Select: **Titles Y-axis**
>
> Type: **Amount** Enter

If you view the graph, you'll see your changes.

Now save this updated version of the graph using the same name (BAR1).

ADDING A 3-D EFFECT

Another graphing option that you might like—presenting graphs with a 3-D effect—isn't located on the /Graph Options menu. If you want to add a 3-D effect to a graph, you have to select /Graph Type Features 3D-Effect Yes. This option is available in Release 2.3 and higher.

PRINTING A GRAPH

If you want to print your graph, you can't do it from the /Graph menu. In fact, you can't even do it in the 1-2-3 program. To print a graph, you have to quit 1-2-3 and go into the PrintGraph program. If you think this is an awkward way to do things, you're right.

> **TIP** Remember that you must save a graph with /Graph Save in order to print it. And be sure to save the worksheet with /File Save.

HANDS-ON   Quit 1-2-3. Then start the PrintGraph program.

> Select: **/Quit Yes**

The PrintGraph program is listed on the Access menu. If you entered the 1-2-3 program through the Access menu, that's where you are now. You can simply select PrintGraph from the menu. But if you're at the DOS prompt, you can type PGRAPH to enter the program.

```
Copyright 1986, 1991, 1992 Lotus Development Corp.  All Rights Reserved.    MENU

Select graphs to print or preview
Image-Select  Settings  Go  Align  Page  Exit

    GRAPHS     IMAGE SETTINGS                          HARDWARE SETTINGS
    TO PRINT   Size              Range colors          Graphs directory
               Top        .395   X                       C:\123
               Left       .750   A                     Fonts directory
               Width     6.500   B                       C:\123
               Height    4.691   C                     Interface
               Rotation   .000   D                       Parallel 1
                                 E                     Printer
               Font              F                       HP LJ +/II/high
               1  BLOCK1                                Paper size
               2  BLOCK1                                  Width      8.500
                                                          Length    11.000

                                                      ACTION SETTINGS
                                                      Pause  No   Eject  No
```

Figure 43-8: The PrintGraph menu displays the commands used to change image and hardware settings.

The PrintGraph screen (see Figure 43-8) shows the current settings for the way the image will print and the way your hardware is set up. The menu gives you the following choices:

Image-Select	Lets you select the graphs you want to print.
Settings	Lets you change the image, hardware and action default settings.
Go	Prints the graphs you've selected.
Align	Informs 1-2-3 that you've aligned the top of the paper at the printer head.
Page	Advances the printer paper to the top of the next sheet (if you've aligned the paper using the Align command).
Exit	Exits the PrintGraph program.

For an explanation of the Align and Page commands, see "Aligning the Paper" in Chapter 41, "Printing Your Work."

BASIC PRINTING

TIP Before printing a graph, check the Hardware Settings. In particular, make sure that the correct printer is specified and that the Graphs directory tells 1-2-3 where your .PIC files are located. If the settings are correct, then the only requirements for printing are that you select a graph and then select Go.

HANDS-ON Print the graph you saved as BAR1.

Select: **Image-Select**

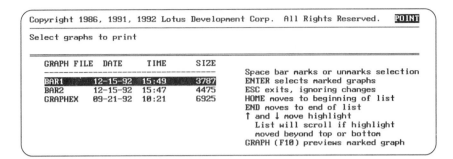

Figure 43-9: The result of selecting Image-Select.

In Figure 43-9, note the instructions on the right side of the screen.

Move: The highlight bar to the graph BAR1

Press: **Spacebar** (to mark it)

Press: ⌷Enter⌷ (to select it)

Select: **Go**

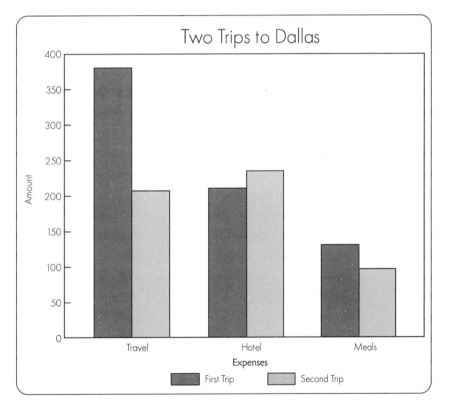

Figure 43-10: Printout of a bar graph.

Figure 43-10 shows a printout of the graph.

To improve the appearance of a graph, you can specify different fonts by selecting Settings Image Font. 1-2-3 lets you choose two fonts: the first affects only the main title; the second affects all other titles and labels. You can also adjust the size and proportions of the graph by selecting Settings Image Size.

To leave the PrintGraph program, select Exit and then Yes from the menu.

CHAPTER SUMMARY

- Only three pieces of information are needed to create a simple bar or line graph: the graph type, the X-axis labels and at least one data range.

- In Release 2.3 and higher, /Graph Type Features gives you access to special formatting features that include a 3-D effect.

- The /Graph View command displays a graph.

- To create more than one graph on a worksheet, you must name each one using /Graph Name Create. After naming a graph, you can reset all or some of the graph settings with /Graph Reset.

- You can print a graph only if you saved it with /Graph Save (but use /File Save to save the worksheet).

- To print a graph, you have to leave the 1-2-3 program and enter the PrintGraph program.

Using Databases

LOTUS
44

One of the most useful features of 1-2-3 is its ability to sort, locate and copy the information you need from your worksheet. But to take advantage of this power, you have to understand what databases are all about. So in this chapter, you'll learn

- What a database is.
- How to fill a range with numbers.
- How to sort data.
- How to find and extract data.
- How to perform calculations on data that meet specific criteria.

> **TIP** 1-2-3's /Data commands let you rearrange data and locate and copy data that meet specific criteria.

HANDS-ON Bring up the /Data menu.

Select: **/Data**

Figure 44-1: The /Data menu displays the commands used to rearrange, locate and copy data.

```
A1: [W2]                                                              MENU
Fill  Table  Sort  Query  Distribution  Matrix  Regression  Parse
Fill a range with a sequence of values
     A      B         C        D       E      F        G        H        I     ◄
1                          Travel Expenses                                    ►
2                     -----------------                                       ▲
3        Trip       Travel    Hotel   Meals  Misc.   TOTAL Departed Returned  ▼
4        Dallas     $375      $212    $122    $15    $724    01/22   01/25    ?
5        Los Angeles $475     $439    $280    $59   $1,253   03/15   03/21
```

Here's a brief description of the /Data commands that are shown in Figure 44-1:

Fill	Fills a range with a sequence of numbers.
Table	Creates tables that show the effects on your data of systematically changing one or two key variables.
Sort	Sorts data alphabetically or numerically.
Query	Locates information that meets your criteria.
Distribution	Counts the number of values that fall within the categories you specify.
Matrix	Inverts a matrix or multiplies one matrix by another.
Regression	Performs regression analyses that help you determine trends in your data.
Parse	Converts a long label into a range of data.

> **TIP** The most commonly used /Data menu features are the commands Fill, Sort and Query.

UNDERSTANDING DATABASES

To use the /Data commands, you have to organize your data in a special *database* format. A database is an arrangement of data that makes it easy to find specific pieces of information.

A phone book is a good example of a database (see Figure 44-2). Each row in the book consists of three categories of information: name, address and phone number. In database language, each row is a *record* and each category is a *field*. A phone book has three fields and thousands of records.

```
Hodges William  910 Edwards.........477-9393
Hodges John  310 Petty Rd...........382-1182
Hodgin P G  418 Clarendon Circle....478-4290
Hodgins Ruth S  2707 Winton Rd......382-0129
Hodgson Judith  4770 N Gregg........477-3225
Hodnett Harvey H  112 Maple.........382-7757
Hodson Phillip W  422 Green.........477-3382
```

Figure 44-2: A portion of a phone book, a familiar database.

Unlike the phone book, a 1-2-3 database isn't limited to one fixed arrangement. 1-2-3 lets you rearrange information to suit your needs. Nor do you have to work with the entire database. You can select just the records you need.

RULES FOR DATABASES

In order for you to use 1-2-3's /Data commands, your data must meet these requirements:

■ The first row of the database must contain the field names.

■ You may not have empty rows or columns within the database.

■ Entries in a particular field must be all numbers or all labels.

The sample worksheet was designed in the database format: notice that it meets all the requirements.

FILLING CELLS WITH NUMBERS

The easiest /Data command to use really has nothing to do with databases. The /Data Fill command simply fills a range with sequential numbers.

To use Fill, you specify a beginning number, a step value (the difference between each number), and an ending number.

HANDS-ON Number the trips on the worksheet. First, add the column label # in cell A3 (be sure to include a label prefix).

Select: **/Data Fill**

Type: **A4..A8** Enter

Type: **1** (the Start value) Enter

Type: **1** (the Step value) Enter

Type: **5** (the Stop value) Enter

Figure 44-3: The result of using /Data Fill in the range A4..A8.

```
A4: [W2] 1                                                        READY

     A        B          C        D       E       F       G       H        I
 1                              Travel Expenses
 2
 3   # Trip            Travel   Hotel   Meals  Misc.   TOTAL Departed Returned
 4   1 Dallas          $375    $212    $122    $15    $724   01/22   01/25
 5   2 Los Angeles     $475    $439    $280    $59  $1,253   03/15   03/21
 6   3 Denver          $148     $75     $32    $13    $268   07/01   07/02
 7   4 Dallas          $207    $240     $94    $40    $581   10/13   10/16
 8   5 Atlanta         $190    $340    $194    $42    $766   12/11   12/13
 9
10     TOTAL         $1,395  $1,306    $722   $169  $3,592
```

If you're filling a range of cells, the Stop number you specify can be any number that's larger than the last number needed. So, in this exercise, you could have entered 2000 as the Stop number and gotten the same results.

SORTING RECORDS

1-2-3's /Data Sort command lets you rearrange your records in a chosen order. For example, you could arrange records alphabetically by trip name, in chronological order, or in order of total expense. The sort may be either ascending (A,B,C...) or descending (Z,Y,X...).

REQUIREMENTS

To sort records, you must specify two ranges:

The *Data Range*: The range that includes all the records you want to sort.

The *Primary Key*: The single cell that contains the name of the field that will determine the sort order.

> **TIP** It's important not to include the field names in the Data Range. If you do, they'll be sorted along with your records!

SORTING ALPHABETICALLY

HANDS-ON Sort the trip records alphabetically. You'll need to specify the ranges shown in Figure 44-4 (B3 is the Primary Key, and A4..I8 is the Data Range).

Figure 44-4: Worksheet showing the Primary Key and Data Range for a sort.

Select: **/Data Sort Data-Range**

Type: **A4..I8** [Enter]

Select: **Primary-Key**

Type: **B3** [Enter]

Select: **A (ascending order)**

Select: **Go**

```
A11: [W2]                                                          READY

    A     B          C        D         E        F        G        H        I      ◄
1                            Travel Expenses                                       ►
2                            ----------------                                      ▲
3       # Trip        Travel   Hotel    Meals    Misc.    TOTAL Departed Returned   ▼
4       5 Atlanta      $190    $340     $194      $42      $766   12/11   12/13     ?
5       4 Dallas       $207    $240      $94      $40      $581   10/13   10/16
6       1 Dallas       $375    $212     $122      $15      $724   01/22   01/25
7       3 Denver       $148     $75      $32      $13      $268   07/01   07/02
8       2 Los Angeles  $475    $439     $280      $59    $1,253   03/15   03/21
9
10        TOTAL      $1,395  $1,306     $722     $169    $3,592
```

Figure 44-5: The trip records sorted alphabetically.

As you can see in Figure 44-5, the records are now displayed alphabetically by trip name.

THE SECONDARY KEY

The optional Secondary Key command can be used to determine the order of records that have the same data in the Primary Key field. For example, on the sample worksheet, the label "Dallas" occurs in two records. If you were to specify the TOTAL field (cell G3) as the Secondary Key, you could specify whether the Dallas trip with the lower or higher total should come first when you sort on trip names.

UNDERSTANDING THE QUERY COMMAND

Besides Sort, the command that makes databases so useful is Query. With it, you can instruct 1-2-3 to locate records that meet the specific criteria you set. For example, in an address database, you could locate just the people who live in Virginia. Or in an inventory database, you could locate only items purchased after December 31, 1992.

1-2-3 gives you two ways to use the Query command:

With the *Find* option, 1-2-3 highlights the first record that meets your criteria. Then to find other records, you must press the Down arrow key.

With the *Extract* option, 1-2-3 copies the records that meet your criteria to an Output range that you designate.

To use the Find or Extract commands, you must specify two ranges:

An *Input* range that includes all the records you want to involve in the query. The field names *must* be included in this range.

A *Criteria* range where you've written the conditions that must be met during the query. The Criteria range must include two rows: the top row must contain at least one field name; the bottom row must contain the actual criteria.

To use Extract, you must also specify a third range: the *Output* range. 1-2-3 will copy the records that meet your criteria into this range. The top row of this range must include at least one field name.

For convenience, you may specify just this top row as the Output range.

> **TIP** The /Data Query menu lists the Input, Criteria and Output commands that let you set these ranges.

SETTING THE RANGES

The field names in the Criteria and Output ranges must be spelled exactly as they are in the Input range. So to avoid errors, you can copy the row of field names to the Criteria and Output ranges. Use the /Copy command, specifying A3..I3 as the "from" range. The "to" range will be A12 for the Criteria range and A15 for the Output range.

```
A3: [W2] '#                                                       READY

      A     B        C        D       E       F       G       H        I     ◄
1                          Travel Expenses                                   ►
2                          ---------------                                   ▲
3     #  Trip       Travel   Hotel   Meals   Misc.   TOTAL Departed Returned ▼
4     5  Atlanta     $190    $340    $194     $42     $766   12/11   12/13   ?
5     4  Dallas      $207    $240     $94     $40     $581   10/13   10/16
6     1  Dallas      $375    $212    $122     $15     $724   01/22   01/25
7     3  Denver      $148     $75     $32     $13     $268   07/01   07/02
8     2  Los Angeles $475    $439    $200     $59   $1,253   03/15   03/21
9
10       TOTAL     $1,395  $1,306    $722    $169   $3,592
11
12    #  Trip       Travel   Hotel   Meals   Misc.   TOTAL Departed Returned
13
14
15    #  Trip       Travel   Hotel   Meals   Misc.   TOTAL Departed Returned
16
17
18
19
20
```

Figure 44-6: Field names copied from row 3 to rows 12 and 15.

Figure 44-6 shows the field names of the database in the Input, Criteria and Output ranges. Now you need to tell 1-2-3 where those ranges are located.

HANDS-ON Set the Input, Criteria and Output ranges.

Select: **/Data Query Input**

Type: **A3..I8** [Enter]

Select: **Criteria**

Type: **A12..I13** [Enter]

Select: **Output**

Type: **A15..I15** [Enter]

Now you're ready to find and extract records from the database.

WRITING CRITERIA

The criteria you set for a Find or Extract operation can be labels, values or both.

LABEL CRITERIA

To set a label criterion, simply write the chosen label in the Criteria range beneath the appropriate field name. For example, the criterion shown in Figure 44-7 would find all records labeled "Dallas" in the Trip field.

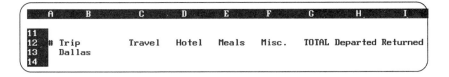

Figure 44-7: Example of a label criterion.

VALUE CRITERIA

To set a value criterion, write the value in the Criteria range beneath the appropriate field name, preceded by one of these *logical operators:*

=	(equal)
< >	(not equal)
>	(greater than)
<	(less than)
<=	(less than or equal)
>=	(greater than or equal)

So to find all records with a TOTAL expense amount greater than $600, you would enter >600 as the criterion (see Figure 44-8).

Figure 44-8: Example of a value criterion.

If you're using a release of 1-2-3 that's earlier than 2.3, the method is a little different. You must include the address of the first cell below the field name in the Input range. Using a 1-2-3 release earlier than 2.3, the criterion shown in Figure 44-8 would have to be written +G4>600 (note the + in front of the cell address).

MULTIPLE CRITERIA

To be even more selective, you can include more than one criterion in the Criteria range. For example, you could find just the trips to Dallas that began after June 30, 1991, by using the criteria that are shown in Figure 44-9.

Figure 44-9: Multiple criteria in the Criteria range.

```
       A         B          C       D       E        F       G         H
  11
  12   #  Trip         Travel   Hotel   Meals   Misc.   TOTAL  Departed
  13      Dallas                                               >@DATE(91,6,30)
```

USING WILDCARDS

1-2-3 also lets you use wildcard characters in your criteria. The asterisk (*) represents any number of characters, and the question mark (?) represents one character—as in DOS commands. The tilde(~) character means "not." For example, the criterion ~Dallas would find all records that don't have Dallas in the Trip field.

A COMMON PROBLEM

A problem can occur when you change your criteria. If you press the Space bar to erase an entry, the cell won't be empty; it will contain a left (') label prefix. So you should use /Range Erase to remove an entry in a Criteria range.

FINDING RECORDS

The /Data Query Find command finds each record that meets your criteria.

HANDS-ON Find all trips to Dallas.

　　Move: Pointer to cell B13

　　Type: '**Dallas** [Enter]

Figure 44-10: Criterion specifying that the Trip field must contain "Dallas."

```
       A         B          C       D       E        F       G         H          I
  11
  12   #  Trip         Travel   Hotel   Meals   Misc.   TOTAL  Departed  Returned
  13      Dallas
  14
```

　　Select: /**Data Query Find**

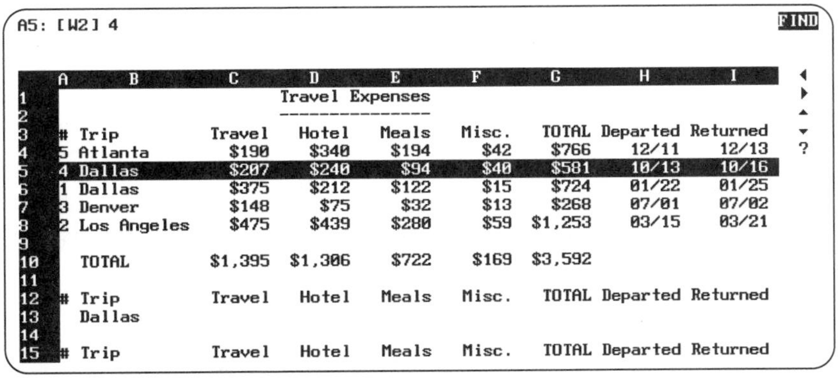

Figure 44-11: Result of the /Data Query Find command.

The /Data Query Find command causes a highlight bar to move to the first record that meets the criterion, as you can see in Figure 44-11.

To find the next record that meets the criterion, press the Down arrow key or click the right mouse button. After finding all the records, press Esc to return to the menu.

EXTRACTING RECORDS

Extracting records involves the same procedure as finding: you have to set an Input range and a Criteria range. But here, you must also set an Output range where 1-2-3 can copy the extracted records.

HANDS-ON Extract the trips to Dallas. Use the same Input and Criteria ranges as in the last exercise.

Select: /**Data Query Extract**

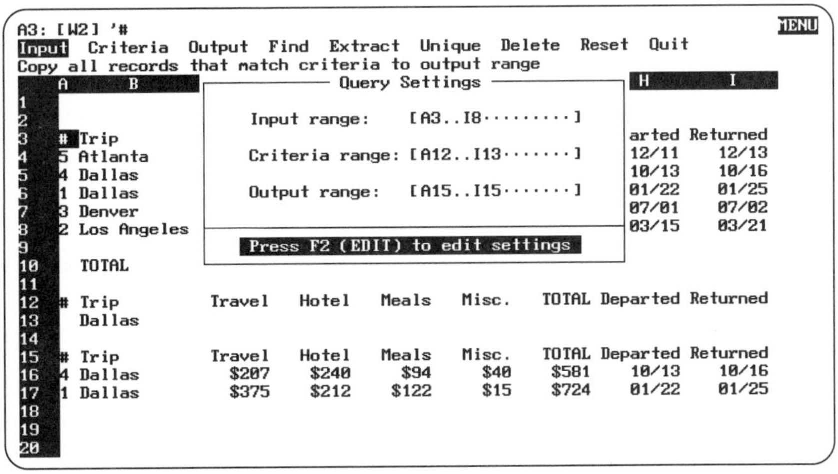

Figure 44-12: The result of the /Data Query Extract command.

You can hide the Query Settings box by pressing F6 (Windows).

USING DATABASE FUNCTIONS

In Chapter 35, "Doing Math Calculations," you learned how to use statistical functions like @SUM and @AVG to perform calculations on ranges of numbers. In a database, you can use special versions of these functions that let you perform calculations on just those records that meet your criteria. Database functions begin with @D. So, the sum function is @DSUM, the average function is @DAVG, and so on.

THE @DAVG FUNCTION

The @DAVG function finds the average of numbers in a specified field. But it uses only the records that meet your criteria. The format of the command is @DAVG(Input range,Field,Criteria range).

TIP The field is a number that tells 1-2-3 which field in the Input range contains the numbers you want to average. The leftmost field in your database is 0 (zero), the next one to the right is 1, and so on.

HANDS-ON Find the average total cost for all trips to Dallas. The Input range is A3..I8; the TOTAL Field is field 6; and the Criteria range is A12..I13.

Move: Pointer to G20

Type: **@DAVG(A3..I8,6,A12..I13)**

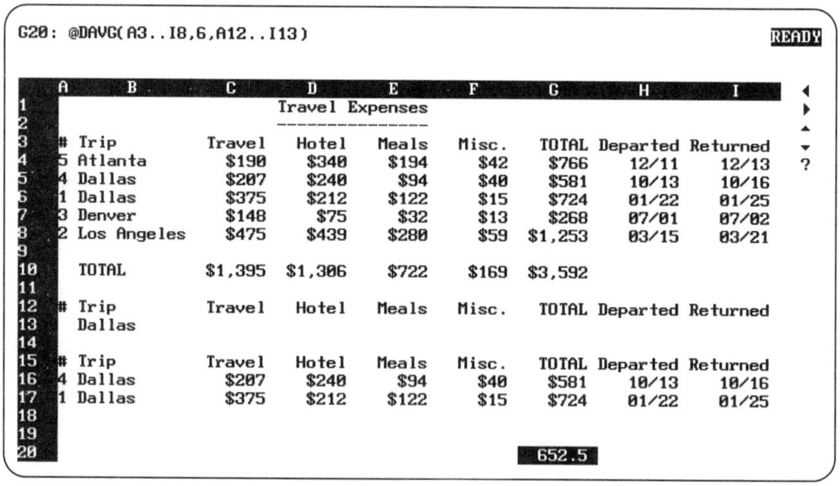

G20: @DAVG(A3..I8,6,A12..I13) READY

	A	B	C	D	E	F	G	H	I
1				Travel Expenses					
2				---------------					
3	#	Trip	Travel	Hotel	Meals	Misc.	TOTAL	Departed	Returned
4	5	Atlanta	$190	$340	$194	$42	$766	12/11	12/13
5	4	Dallas	$207	$240	$94	$40	$581	10/13	10/16
6	1	Dallas	$375	$212	$122	$15	$724	01/22	01/25
7	3	Denver	$148	$75	$32	$13	$268	07/01	07/02
8	2	Los Angeles	$475	$439	$280	$59	$1,253	03/15	03/21
9									
10		TOTAL	$1,395	$1,306	$722	$169	$3,592		
11									
12	#	Trip	Travel	Hotel	Meals	Misc.	TOTAL	Departed	Returned
13		Dallas							
14									
15	#	Trip	Travel	Hotel	Meals	Misc.	TOTAL	Departed	Returned
16	4	Dallas	$207	$240	$94	$40	$581	10/13	10/16
17	1	Dallas	$375	$212	$122	$15	$724	01/22	01/25
18									
19									
20							652.5		

Figure 44-13: The result of the @DAVG function in cell G20.

As you can see in Figure 44-13, 1-2-3 found the records that met the criterion, and then averaged their TOTAL amounts (581 and 724).

OTHER DATA COMMANDS

Here's a brief look at the remaining /Data commands.

DISTRIBUTION

The /Data Distribution command counts the number of values in a range that fall into the numerical intervals you specify. For example, in an employee database, you could find out how many employees have used vacation days in particular intervals: 1–2 days, 3–4 days, 5–6 days, and so on.

MATRIX

The /Data Matrix command performs special calculations on matrices that help solve simultaneous equations.

PARSE

If you import a text file into 1-2-3 using /File Import Text, the data will be placed in just one column. The /Data Parse command lets you break up the data into a range of individual cells.

REGRESSION

The /Data Regression command lets you perform a regression analysis on your data. The analysis can help spot trends and make predictions based on the data.

TABLE

The /Data Table command lets you perform "what if" analyses on your data by systematically varying key factors.

CHAPTER SUMMARY

- Each row in a database is a record, and each record contains fields.

- To fill a range with numbers using /Data Fill, you must specify the start number, step value and end number.

- To sort records using /Data Sort, you must specify the Data Range (excluding field names) and a Primary Key field.

- To find records using /Data Query Find, you must specify an Input range (including field names) and a Criteria range. To extract records using /Data Query Extract, you must also specify an Output range.

- A label criterion is written as a label. A value criterion is written as a value preceded by a logical operator (in releases earlier than 2.3, the operator must be preceded by the address of the first cell below the field name).

- Database statistical functions (such as @DAVG) perform calculations on specific data fields in records that meet your criteria.

Letting 1-2-3 Do the Typing

LOTUS 45

Like DOS and WordPerfect, 1-2-3 provides a way to save commands in a file. In 1-2-3, it's called a macro. When you're ready to execute those commands, you simply type the name of the macro. So in this chapter, you'll learn

- When a macro would be worthwhile.
- How to write a macro.
- How to edit a macro.
- How to find errors in a macro.

A *macro* is a series of keystrokes such as commands, labels and pointer movement instructions. When you type the name of the macro, 1-2-3 executes all the commands in the macro. Almost any task you can perform in 1-2-3 can be saved as a macro.

> **TIP** The value of a macro is that you have to type the commands only once. After you've made the macro, you can activate it at any time by pressing just two keys.

In Release 2.3 and higher, you can attach the Macro Library Manager add-in to manage your macros. It allows you to create libraries of macros and to use them in any worksheet.

TYPICAL USES

Macros can be real time-savers when it comes to doing repetitive or tedious operations. Here are two examples of cases where a simple macro can save you some typing.

Setting a pattern for data entry. For example, you might need to enter data in columns A, D, E and G, and then do the same on the next row. A macro would let you press Enter after each entry to get to the correct cell.

Setting the format of a range. For example, you might need to use the Percent format on a number of individual, nonadjacent cells. A macro would let you do this by pressing only two keys (a saving of four keystrokes each time).

> **TIP** Considering how easy macros are to create, you'll probably want to use them for many routine keystroke sequences.

COMMANDS

You can create a macro to automate any series of keystrokes. A macro may contain five types of statements:

■ Pointer movement instructions. For example, {right} moves the pointer right one cell.

■ Menu command sequences. For example, '/WCS15~ executes the sequence /Worksheet Column Set-Width and sets the width to 15.

■ Labels. For example, Enter Your Name writes the label "Enter Your Name" in the specified cell.

■ Formulas and functions. For example, {@SUM(A1..B5)} calculates the sum of the numbers in cells A1 through B5.

■ Advanced commands for working with files, manipulating data and controlling program flow.

MACRO INSTRUCTIONS

Some of the more common macro instructions are explained in the following list. You may use uppercase or lowercase letters in writing them.

Instruction	Result
~ (tilde)	The Enter key.
/ (slash)	Brings up the Command menu.
{end}	The End key.
{?}	Waits for you to type a response and press Enter.
{right}	Right one cell.
{left}	Left one cell.
{up}	Up one cell.
{down}	Down one cell.
{pgup}	Up one screen.
{pgdn}	Down one screen.
{bigright}	Right one screen.
{bigleft}	Left one screen.
{home}	To cell A1.
{goto}cell~	To the cell indicated (for example, {goto}K12~).

You can also move the pointer several cells at one time. For example, {right 3} would move the pointer three cells to the right.

WRITING A MACRO

You may write a macro anywhere on a worksheet. But to make things easy, pick an out-of-the-way spot where you'll always put your macros (for example, cell M1).

RULES

1-2-3 has very strict requirements for macros:

■ Every instruction in a macro must be a label. To simplify matters and avoid mistakes, you may want to type the left (') label prefix in front of every macro instruction.

■ Labels and command sequences must not be enclosed in brackets, but all other instructions must be.

■ The cell below the last macro instruction must be empty.

SUGGESTIONS

You may write a macro as one long series of commands, like the example in Figure 45-1.

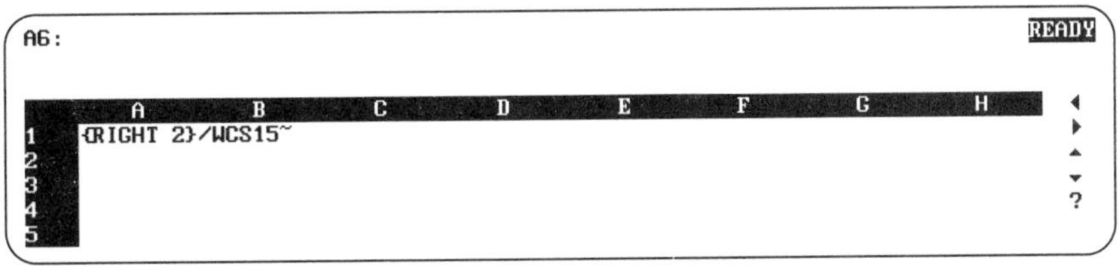

Figure 45-1: One way to write a macro.

But a better way is to put each part of the macro on a separate line, as shown in Figure 45-2.

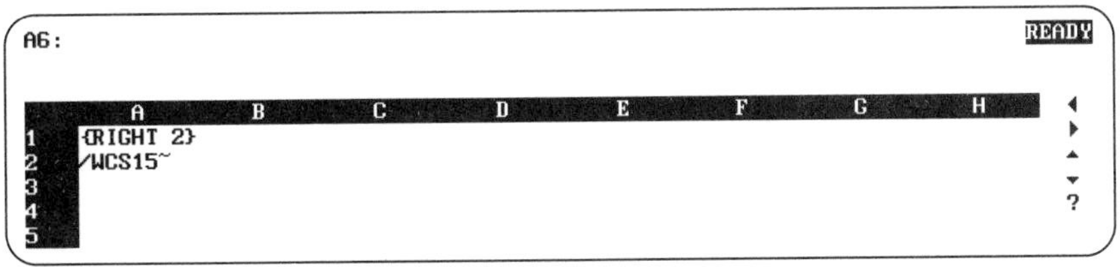

Figure 45-2: A better way to write a macro.

TIP Having each instruction of a macro on a separate line makes it easier to find mistakes and make corrections.

DOCUMENTING

Because of their cryptic appearance, macros become more challenging to understand as time goes by. So it's important to document the macro in plain English. The most practical way to do this is to write an explanation of each command in an adjacent column. Figure 45-3 gives an example.

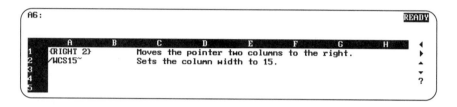

Figure 45-3: A macro with documentation.

NAMING A MACRO

To name a macro, move the pointer to the first cell of the macro, and select /Range Name Create. Then use one of these two methods: type \ followed by a single letter (for example, \B); or type a name containing up to 15 characters (for example, MONTHLY_EXP). The way you name a macro determines the way you activate it.

ACTIVATING A MACRO

Once you've written and named a macro, you're ready to use it. First, move the pointer to the place where you want the macro to be executed. Then, to activate a single-letter macro, press Alt and the single-letter name you gave the macro. For example, to activate a macro named \B, you would press Alt-B. To activate a multiple-letter macro, press Alt-F3 (RUN), type the macro's name, and press Enter.

INTERRUPTING A MACRO

You can interrupt a macro and return to READY mode by pressing Ctrl-Break twice or Ctrl-Esc.

EXERCISES

The following exercises will show you how to create and use macros. To start on a fresh worksheet, save your present worksheet and then erase the worksheet using /Worksheet Erase Yes.

FORMATTING A RANGE

HANDS-ON Create a macro that formats the current cell using the /Range Format command and specifies Fixed format with one decimal place. Name the macro \F.

> Move: Pointer to M1
>
> Type: '/**RFF1**~~ [Enter]
>
> Select: /**Range Name Create**
>
> Type: **F** [Enter]
>
> Press: [Enter] (to accept range M1..M1)

Now to use the macro, move the pointer to any cell and press Alt-F. Unless there's a number in the cell, the only change you'll see is the (F1) indicator in the Control Panel.

FORMATTING DATES

HANDS-ON Create a macro that saves time and typing when entering a column of dates. Specifically, this macro will

■ Type '**@DATE(93**, and wait for you to type the month and day and press Enter.

■ Format the date number using /Range Format Date and specifying option 4 (Long Intn'l).

■ Move the pointer down to the next cell.

■ Activate the macro again by branching to \D (the name that you'll give the macro).

Type the instructions exactly as shown in cells A1 through A4 *using a label prefix in front of each.* Then add the documentation in cells C1 through C7, as shown in Figure 45-4.

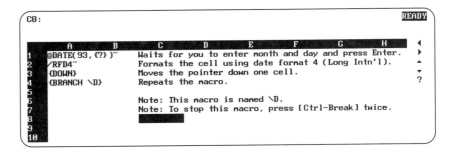

Figure 45-4: A macro for formatting dates using the Long International option.

Now name the macro.

Move: Pointer to A1

Select: **/Range Name Create**

Type: **\D** [Enter]

Press: [Enter] (to accept range A1..A1)

To use the macro, move to any cell and press Alt-D. When the macro pauses, type a month and day like this: 5,30. Then press Enter and the macro will continue.

Because this macro will keep repeating, press Ctrl-Break twice or Ctrl-Esc when you're ready to stop it.

EDITING & DEBUGGING

Editing a macro is easy. Just move the pointer to the instruction and either retype it or press the F2 (Edit) key to edit it.

TIP If you add a new line to the macro, you don't need to rename it. As long as the last instruction is followed by a blank cell, 1-2-3 will know what you've done.

DEBUGGING A MACRO

Macros don't always work correctly at first. The slightest mistake will create a result that you hadn't expected. To help you find where the problem is, 1-2-3 lets you go through the macro step by step.

HANDS-ON Go through the \D macro, step by step.

Press: **Alt-F2** (STEP)

Press: **Alt-D**

Then press Enter to move through each step.

To exit the Step feature after executing a macro, press Alt-F2 (STEP). To exit during execution, press Ctrl-Break and then Alt-F2.

COMMON ERRORS

If a macro doesn't work correctly, answer these questions:

- Does the ~ symbol appear everywhere the Enter key should be pressed?
- Are all entries labels?
- Are all command sequences complete?
- Are all formulas, functions and pointer movement instructions enclosed in brackets?

Other problems may occur if you move the macro or insert rows or columns in your data.

CHAPTER SUMMARY

- Each entry in a macro must be a label.
- The cell below the last instruction in a macro must be blank.
- After writing a macro, you can use /Range Name Create to name the macro. The name may be either \ followed by a letter, or a name with up to 15 characters.
- You activate a macro by pressing Alt and the macro's single-letter name, or by pressing Alt-F3 (RUN) and then entering the multiple-letter name.
- To turn on the single-step mode, press Alt-F2 (STEP) and then activate the macro. Press Enter to move through each step. Then press Alt-F2 (STEP) and then Ctrl-Break to turn off the step mode.
- Pressing Ctrl-Break twice or Ctrl-Esc will interrupt a macro.

APPENDIX A

DOS QUICK REFERENCE (3.1 THROUGH 6)

Items shown in uppercase letters must be typed exactly as spelled (using either uppercase or lowercase letters). Lowercase letters are used to describe items that you must supply. Italics are used to represent optional parts of the commands. **The plus sign indicates that the version number listed and all subsequent versions apply.**

Remember that *directories* are one level below the *Root;* and *subdirectories* are one level below their parent directories. The commands below assume that the files being manipulated are in the current directory.

Note: Some commands have only one correct format, so no example is given for those commands.

FORMATTING DISKETTES

ACTION	FORMAT	EXAMPLE
Format a diskette.	FORMAT target-drive	FORMAT A:
Format a diskette with a volume label.	FORMAT target-drive /V:label	FORMAT A: / V:REPORTS
Add a label to a formatted diskette.	LABEL target-drive:label	LABEL A:WP FILES
Reformat a formatted diskette quickly (DOS 5+).	FORMAT target-drive /Q	FORMAT A: /Q

WORKING WITH DIRECTORIES

ACTION	FORMAT	EXAMPLE
Make a directory. (Root is current.)	MD directory	MD SAMPLE
Change to a directory. (Root is current.)	CD directory	CD 123
Change to a subdirectory within the current directory.	CD subdirectory	CD REPORTS
Change from one directory to another.	CD ..\directory	CD ..\WP
Change to the parent directory.	CD ..	
Change to the Root.	CD \	
Remove an empty directory. (Root is current.)	RD directory	RD SAMPLE
Remove a directory and the files it contains (DOS 6).	DELTREE directory	DELTREE \123\REPORTS

ERASING & RECOVERING FILES

ACTION	FORMAT	EXAMPLE
Erase a file.	ERASE filename	ERASE WEEKLY.RPT
Restore an erased file (DOS 5+).	UNDELETE filename	UNDELETE WEEKLY.RPT

LISTING FILES

ACTION	FORMAT	EXAMPLE
List all files.	DIR	
List all files compactly.	DIR /W	
List all files, one screen at a time.	DIR /P	
List files sorted alphabetically.	DIR |SORT DIR /O:N (DOS 5+)	
List files sorted in date order.	DIR |SORT /+24 DIR/O:D (DOS 5+)	
List sorted files, one screen at a time.	DIR |SORT |MORE DIR /O:N /P (DOS 5+)	
Save a DIR list in a file.	DIR > filename	DIR > NOV92.DIR
Print a DIR list.	DIR > PRN	
List files in a directory and its subdirectories (DOS 5+).	DIR /S	
List directories only (DOS 5+).	DIR /A:D	
List files only (DOS 5+).	DIR /A:-D	

COPYING & MOVING FILES

ACTION	FORMAT	EXAMPLE
Copy a file within a directory.	COPY filename copy-filename	COPY 1Q.RPT 1QCOPY.RPT
Copy a file to another directory using the same name.	COPY filename target	COPY 1Q.RPT A:
Copy files from a directory and its subdirectories.	XCOPY filename target /S	XCOPY *.LET A: /S
Copy files created or modified on or after a date.	XCOPY filename target /D:date	XCOPY *.LET A: /D:2-15-92
Copy one diskette to another.	DISKCOPY source-drive target-drive	DISKCOPY A: A:
Copy hard disk files to diskettes in a space-saving format (before DOS 6).	BACKUP source-drive \directory target-drive	BACKUP C:\WP A:
Restore backup files from diskettes to the hard disk (before DOS 6).	RESTORE backup-drive target-drive\directory	RESTORE A: C:\123\REPORTS
Copy hard disk files to diskettes in a space-saving format (DOS 6).	MSBACKUP	MSBACKUP
Restore backup files from diskettes to the hard disk (DOS 6).	MSBACKUP	
Move a file (DOS 6) to another directory.	MOVE filename target	MOVE APRIL.RPT \123\REPORTS

MANIPULATING GROUPS OF FILES

ACTION	FORMAT	EXAMPLE
Manipulate files with a common name.	Command filename.*	ERASE WEEKLY.*
Manipulate files with a common extension.	Command *.extension	DIR *.RPT
Manipulate all files.	Command *.*	COPY *.* A:

MISCELLANEOUS

ACTION	FORMAT	EXAMPLE
Change the DOS prompt.	PROMPT *qualifiers*	PROMPT PG
Set alternative search paths for executable files.	PATH *paths*	PATH \ ;\DOS;\WP
Rename a file.	REN filename new-filename	REN 1Q.RPT 1QUARTER.RPT
Display the disk structure, one screen at a time.	TREE |MORE	
Display the disk structure, including files, one at a time.	TREE /F |MORE	
Display a text file.	TYPE filename	TYPE PICNIC.MEM
Substitute a drive name for a path.	SUBST drive path	SUBST E:\WP\REPORTS
Get help with a command (DOS 5+).	HELP command	HELP COPY
Make a file read-only (DOS 5+).	ATTRIB +R filename	ATTRIB +R EXPENSES.93
Remove read-only status (DOS 5+).	ATTRIB –R filename	ATTRIB –R EXPENSES.93

WORDPERFECT 5.1 & 6.0 QUICK REFERENCE

The command sequences below show the keys to press and the commands to select to initiate the actions described.

FORMATTING TEXT

ACTION	COMMAND SEQUENCE 5.1	COMMAND SEQUENCE 6.0
Change initial font for all new documents.	Shift-F1, 4, 5, Ctrl-F8, 4	Shift-F8, 4, 3, 1, 4
Change initial font for the current document.	Shift-F8, 3, 3	Shift-F8, 5, 3, 1
Change the base font.	Ctrl-F8, 4	Ctrl-F8, 1
Turn the block feature on or off.	Alt-F4	Alt-F4
Repeat the last block.	Alt-F4, Ctrl-Home, Ctrl-Home	Not available
Change the size of blocked text.	Ctrl-F8, 1	Ctrl-F8, 2
Change the appearance of blocked text.	Ctrl-F8, 2	Ctrl-F8, 3
Change word and letter spacing.	Shift-F8, 4, 6, 3	Shift-F8, 7, 9, 6

FORMATTING LINES & PARAGRAPHS

ACTION	COMMAND SEQUENCE 5.1	COMMAND SEQUENCE 6.0
Change line spacing.	Shift-F8, 1, 6	Shift-F8, 1, 3
Change the alignment of text.	Shift-F8, 1, 3	Shift-F8, 1, 2
Set tabs.	Shift-F8, 1, 8	Shift-F8, 1, 1
Turn on automatic hyphenation.	Shift-F8, 1, 1, Y	Shift-F8, 1, 6
Position text on the page.	Shift-F8, 4, 1	Shift-F8, 7, 6

FORMATTING PAGES

ACTION	COMMAND SEQUENCE 5.1	COMMAND SEQUENCE 6.0
Change left /right margins.	Shift-F8, 1, 7	Shift-F8, 2, 1/2
Change top/bottom margins.	Shift-F8, 2, 5	Shift-F8, 2, 3/4
Center a page top to bottom.	Shift-F8, 2, 1, Y	Shift-F8, 3, 2
Add a header/footer.	Shift-F8, 2, 3/4	Shift-F8, 5, 1/2, 1/2, C
Edit a header/footer.	Shift-F8, 2, 3/4, 1/2, 5	Shift-F8, 5, 1/2, 1/2, E
Set the page number.	Shift-F8, 2, 6, 1	Shift-F8, 3, 1, 2

MAKING CHANGES

ACTION	COMMAND SEQUENCE 5.1	COMMAND SEQUENCE 6.0
Bring back deleted text.	F1, 1	Esc, 1
Search for text.	F2, text, F2	F2, text, Enter, F2
Replace text with other text.	Alt-F2, Y/N, text, F2, text, F2	Alt-F2, text, Enter, text, Enter, F2
Extend search or replace to headers/footers.	Press Home before searching or replacing.	Press Home before searching or replacing.
Move blocked text.	Ctrl-F4, 1, 1	Ctrl-F4, 1
Copy blocked text.	Ctrl-F4, 1, 2	Ctrl-F4, 2
Repeat the last move or copy.	Shift-F10, Enter	Shift-F10, Enter
Check spelling.	Ctrl-F2	Ctrl-F2
Find alternatives for a word.	Alt-F1	Alt-F1, 2

MANAGING YOUR FILES

ACTION	COMMAND SEQUENCE 5.1	COMMAND SEQUENCE 6.0
Save the current document.	F10	F10
Retrieve a document.	Shift-F10	Shift-F10
Add a password to a document.	Ctrl-F5, 2, 1	F10, F8
Retrieve an ASCII file.	Ctrl-F5, 1, 2	Shift-F10
Save a document as an ASCII file.	Ctrl-F5, 1, 1	F10
List files in the default directory.	F5, Enter	F5, Enter
Change the default directory.	F5, =	F5, =

PRINTING

ACTION	COMMAND SEQUENCE 5.1	COMMAND SEQUENCE 6.0
Print the current document.	Shift-F7, 1	Shift-F7, 1
Print the current page.	Shift-F7, 2	Shift-F7, 2
Print selected pages.	Shift-F7, 5	Shift-F7, 4
Change the number of copies.	Shift-F7, N	Shift-F7, N
Include the current date in a printout.	Shift-F5, 2	Shift-F5, 2
Download fonts that you've marked for downloading.	Shift-F7, 7, Y	Shift-F7, 8

USING COLUMNS

ACTION	COMMAND SEQUENCE 5.1	COMMAND SEQUENCE 6.0
Define columns.	Alt-F7, 1, 3	Alt-F7, 1, 1
Turn columns on/off.	Alt-F7, 1/2	Alt-F7, 1, OK/OFF
Move the cursor between columns.	Ctrl-Home, Right/Left arrow	Ctrl-Home, Right/Left arrow

WORKING WITH MULTIPLE DOCUMENTS

ACTION	COMMAND SEQUENCE 5.1	COMMAND SEQUENCE 6.0
Split the screen into two windows.	Ctrl-F3, 1	Ctrl-F3, 1, 4,
Move the cursor between Doc 1 and Doc 2.	Shift-F3	Shift-F3
Insert a subdocument in a master document.	Alt-F5, 2	Alt-F5, 3, 3
Expand a master document.	Alt-F5, 6, 3	Alt-F5, 3, 1
Condense a master document.	Alt-F5, 6, 4	Alt-F5, 3, 2

WORKING WITH ACCESS AIDS

ACTION	COMMAND SEQUENCE 5.1	COMMAND SEQUENCE 6.0
Define a table, list, index or cross-reference.	Alt-F5, 5	Alt-F5, 2
Generate a table, list, index or cross-reference.	Alt-F5, 6, 5, Y	Alt-F5, 4
Mark blocked text for a table, list or index.	Alt-F5	Alt-F5

USING GRAPHICS

ACTION	COMMAND SEQUENCE 5.1	COMMAND SEQUENCE 6.0
Draw a line.	Alt-F9, 5	Alt-F9, 2, 1
Create a graphics box.	Alt-F9, box-type, 1	Alt-F9, 1, 1
Edit a graphics box.	Alt-F9, box-type, 2, box-number	Alt-F9, 1, 2
Edit a graphic image.	Alt-F9, box-type, 2, box-number, 9	Alt-F9, 1, 2, E, 3

MERGING DOCUMENTS

ACTION	COMMAND SEQUENCE 5.1	COMMAND SEQUENCE 6.0
Insert the ENDFIELD code in a data (secondary) file.	F9	F9
Insert other codes in a data (secondary) file.	Shift-F9, 6	Shift-F9, M
Insert a field code in a form (primary) file.	Shift-F9, 1	Shift-F9, 1
Change merge file type.	N/A	Shift-F9, T
Merge a data (secondary) and form (primary) file.	Ctrl-F9, 1	Ctrl-F9, 1

USING STYLES & MACROS

ACTION	COMMAND SEQUENCE 5.1	COMMAND SEQUENCE 6.0
Create a style.	Alt-F8, 3	Alt-F8, 2
Save a list of styles.	Alt-F8, 6	Alt-F8, 7
Retrieve a style list.	Alt-F8, 7	Alt-F8, 8
Record a macro.	Ctrl-F10	Ctrl-F10
Play a macro.	Alt-F10	Alt-F10

WORDPERFECT FUNCTION KEYS

KEY	SHIFT-KEY	ALT-KEY	CTRL-KEY
F1	Help	Setup	Writing Tools	Shell
F2	>Search	<Search	Replace	Spell
F3	Switch To	Switch	Reveal Codes	Screen
F4	>Indent	>Indent<	Block	Move
F5	File Manager	Date/Outline	Mark Text	Undo
F6	Bold	Center	Flush Right	Tab Align
F7	Exit	Print	Columns/Tables	Footnote
F8	Underline	Format	Style	Font
F9	End Field	Merge Codes	Graphics	Merge/Sort
F10	Save As	Retrieve	Macro Play	Macro Record

Note: In version 5.1: F1 is Cancel; F3 is Help; Ctrl-F5 is Text In/Out; Alt-F1 is Thesaurus.

LOTUS 1-2-3 QUICK REFERENCE (2.2 through 2.4)

The sequences below show the commands you must select to initiate the actions described. Items shown in uppercase letters must be typed exactly as spelled, using either uppercase or lowercase letters. Lowercase letters are used to describe items that you must supply.

CHANGING THE WORKSHEET'S APPEARANCE

ACTION	COMMAND SEQUENCE
Change the width of the current column.	/Worksheet Column Set-Width
Change the width of several columns.	/Worksheet Column Column-Range Set-Width
Hide columns.	/Worksheet Column Hide
Display hidden columns.	/Worksheet Column Display
Insert a column (row).	/Worksheet Insert Column (Row)
Delete a column (row).	/Worksheet Delete Column (Row)
Set a horizontal (vertical) titles area.	/Worksheet Titles Horizontal (Vertical)
Split the screen into two (vertical) windows.	/Worksheet Window Horizontal (Vertical)
Erase the entire worksheet.	/Worksheet Erase Yes
Insert a page break for printing.	/Worksheet Page

MAKING GLOBAL CHANGES

ACTION	COMMAND SEQUENCE
Change the width of all columns.	/Worksheet Global Column-Width
Change the format of all values.	/Worksheet Global Format
Change the alignment of all labels.	/Worksheet Global Label-Prefix
Suppress the display of zero values.	/Worksheet Global Zero
Turn global protection on (off).	/Worksheet Global Protection Enable (Disable)
Change the default directory.	/Worksheet Global Default Directory
Save a global default change.	/Worksheet Global Default Update

CHANGING SELECTED RANGES

ACTION	COMMAND SEQUENCE
Format the values in a range.	/Range Format
Suppress the display of data in a range.	/Range Format Hidden
Format a range to display formulas and functions.	/Range Format Text
Align the labels in a range.	/Range Label
Name a range.	/Range Name Create
Unprotect a range on a protected worksheet.	/Range Unprot
Erase a range of cells.	/Range Erase
Erase the active cell.	Press Del (Release 2.3+)

WORKING WITH DATES & TIMES

ACTION	COMMAND SEQUENCE
Enter a date.	@DATE (year,month,day) Example: @DATE(93,4,30)
Enter a time.	@TIME (hours,minutes,seconds) Example: @TIME(15,30,00)
Format date numbers in a range.	/Range Format Date
Apply a date format to all cells.	/Worksheet Global Format Date
Format time numbers in a range.	/Range Format Date Time
Apply a time format to all cells.	/Worksheet Global Format Date Time

PRINTING

ACTION	COMMAND SEQUENCE
Set a print range.	/Print Printer Range
Start a print job.	/Print Printer Go
Reset to top of page and reset page number to 1.	/Print Printer Align
Advance the paper after printing.	/Print Printer Page
Add a header (footer).	/Print Printer Options Header (Footer)

MANAGING FILES

ACTION	COMMAND SEQUENCE
Save the current worksheet.	/File Save
Retrieve a file.	/File Retrieve
List 1-2-3 files.	/File List
Change the default directory for the current session.	/File Directory
Erase a file from the disk.	/File Erase

WORKING WITH GRAPHS

ACTION	COMMAND SEQUENCE
View the current graph.	/Graph View
Set all data ranges at one time.	/Graph Group
Name the current graph.	/Graph Name Create
Use a named graph.	/Graph Name Use
Save a graph for printing.	/Graph Save
Add a legend to a graph.	/Graph Options Legend
Add a main title to a graph.	/Graph Options Titles First
Start the PrintGraph program.	From the Access Menu: Select PrintGraph From the DOS prompt: Type PGRAPH and press Enter.
Select a graph for printing.	Image Select Then move the light bar to the file, press Space bar and press Enter.
Print a selected graph.	Go

USING DATABASES

ACTION	COMMAND SEQUENCE
Fill a range with sequential numbers.	/Data Fill
Note: The following assume the correct Input, Criteria and Output ranges have been set.	
Sort a database.	/Data Sort Go
Find records that meet criteria.	/Data Query Find
Extract records that meet criteria.	/Data Query Extract

USING MACROS

ACTION	COMMAND SEQUENCE
Activate a single-letter-name macro.	Press Alt and the macro's letter name.
Activate a multiple-letter-name macro.	Press Alt-F3 (Run), type the name, and press Enter.
Interrupt a macro.	Press Ctrl-Esc.
Go through a macro step by step.	Press Alt-F2 (STEP) and then activate the macro. Press Enter to execute each step.

USING ADD-INS

ACTION	COMMAND SEQUENCE
Attach an add-in.	/Add-In Attach add-in No-Key
Activate an attached add-in from the menu.	/Add-In Invoke add-in
Attach an add-in and assign it to an Alt key.	/Add-In Attach add-in Alt-key
Activate an attached add-in with a key.	Alt-F7, Alt-F8, Alt-F9 or Alt-F10
Detach an add-in.	/Add-In Detach add-in
Clear all add-ins from memory.	/Add-In Clear

LOTUS 1-2-3 FUNCTION KEYS

F1	Help
F2	Edit Cell Contents
F3	List Named Ranges
F4	Create Absolute Cell Reference
F5	Go To Cell
F6	Window
F7	Query a Database
F8	Repeat /Data Table Operation
F9	Recalculate Formulas
F10	Display Current Graph
Alt-F4	Undo
/	Opens the Command Menu
Esc	Backs up one step

DOS INDEX

Colophon

This book was produced using Aldus PageMaker 4.0 on a 486/50 PC clone and proofed on a LaserWriter IIg. Final output was on film using a Linotronic 330.

Screen captures were made using SNAP Display Utility, Version 3.2.

The body copy is in Digital Typeface Corporation's ITC Clearface; heads, titles and most display copy are set in DTC Clearface Gothic.

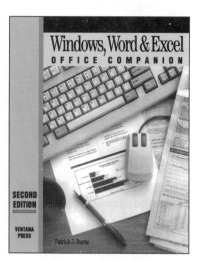

Ventana Companions

Windows, Word & Excel Office Companion, Second Edition
$21.95
544 pages, illustrated
ISBN: 1-56604-083-3
Your Microsoft business bible. This three-in-one reference is organized as a quick course in each program. Chapters contain valuable information on basic commands and features, plus helpful tutorials, tips and shortcuts.

Voodoo DOS, Second Edition
$21.95
325 pages, illustrated
ISBN: 1-56604-046-9
Increase your productivity with the "magic" of *Voodoo DOS*! Packed with tricks for all versions of DOS through 6.0, this book is designed for all users and offers a variety of time-saving techniques—customizing, using the DOS editor, drive management and more.

Desktop Publishing With WordPerfect 6
$24.95
370 pages, illustrated
ISBN: 1-56604-049-3
The new graphics capabilities of WordPerfect 6.0 can save you thousands of dollars in design and typesetting costs. Includes invaluable design advice and annotated examples.

To order any Ventana Press title, use the form in the back of this book or contact your local bookstore or computer store.

For Creative Computing!

Voodoo NetWare

$27.95
217 pages, illustrated
ISBN: 1-56604-077-9
Advice for troubleshooting, streamlining and maximizing networks for network managers and end users of the world's most widely used network operating system—NetWare 4.0. Includes tips, tricks and shortcuts to overcome network woes.

Voodoo Windows

$19.95
282 pages, illustrated
ISBN: 1-56604-005-1
A unique resource, *Voodoo Windows* bypasses the technical information found in many Windows books to bring you an abundance of never-before-published tips, tricks and shortcuts for maximum Windows productivity. A one-of-a-kind reference for beginners and experienced users alike.

Desktop Publishing With WordPerfect 6 for Windows

$24.95
261 pages, illustrated
ISBN: 1-56604-086-8
A Windows bestseller, WordPerfect 6.0's vastly improved graphics tools and features can save you thousands of dollars in design and typesetting costs. Includes invaluable design advice and annotated examples.

Immediate shipment guaranteed!
Full money-back guarantee!

Advertising From the Desktop
$24.95
427 pages, illustrated
ISBN: 1-56604-064-7
Advertising From the Desktop offers unmatched design advice and helpful how-to instructions for creating persuasive ads. With tips on how to choose fonts, select illustrations, apply special effects and more, this book is an idea-packed resource for improving the looks and effects of your ads.

The Presentation Design Book, Second Edition
$24.95
320 pages, illustrated
ISBN: 1-56604-014-0
The Presentation Design Book is filled with thoughtful advice and instructive examples for creating business presentation visuals, including charts, overheads, type, etc., that help you communicate and persuade. The *Second Edition* adds advice on the use of multimedia. For use with any software or hardware.

The Gray Book, Second Edition
$24.95
262 pages, illustrated
ISBN: 1-56604-073-6
This "idea gallery" for desktop publishers offers a lavish variety of the most interesting black, white and gray graphic effects that can be achieved with laser printers, scanners and high-resolution output devices. The *Second Edition* features new illustrations, synopses and steps, added tips and an updated appendix.

Looking Good in Print, Third Edition
$24.95
412 pages, illustrated
ISBN: 1-56604-047-7
For use with any software or hardware, this desktop design bible has become the standard among novice and experienced desktop publishers alike. With over 200,000 copies in print, *Looking Good in Print* is even better, with new sections on photography and scanning.

Looking Good With CorelDRAW!, Second Edition
$27.95
361 pages, 230 illustrations
ISBN: 0-56604-061-2
Contains a wealth of professional tips, techniques, ideas and all-new, start-to-finish, step-by-step examples for intermediate to advanced users. Fully updated for all the newest tools and features in versions 3 and 4 of CorelDRAW! 24 color pages.

Newsletters From the Desktop
$23.95
306 pages, illustrated
ISBN: 0-940087-40-5
Now the millions of desktop publishers who produce newsletters can learn how to improve the design of their publications. Filled with helpful design tips and illustrations.

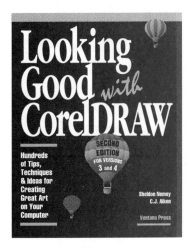

Ordering?   Call toll-free!
800/743-5369 (U.S. only)

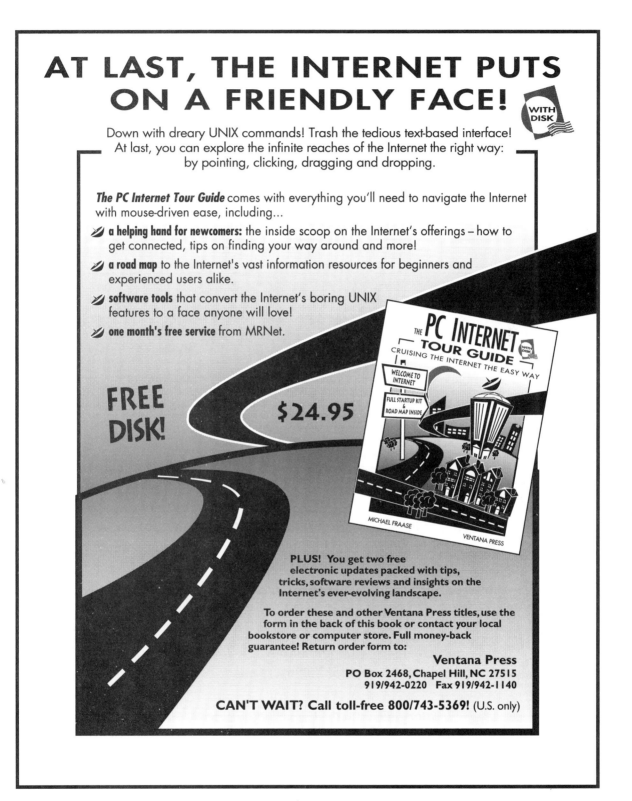

To order any Ventana Press title, fill out this order form and mail it to us with payment for quick shipment.

	Quantity		Price		Total
Advertising From the Desktop	_____	x	$24.95	=	$ _____
The Official America Online for PC Membership Kit & Tour Guide	_____	x	34.95	=	$ _____
Desktop Publishing With WordPerfect 6	_____	x	$24.95	=	$ _____
Desktop Publishing With WordPerfect 6 for Windows	_____	x	$24.95	=	$ _____
The Gray Book, 2nd Edition	_____	x	$24.95	=	$ _____
Looking Good in Print, 3rd Edition	_____	x	$24.95	=	$ _____
Looking Good With CorelDRAW!, 2nd Edition	_____	x	$27.95	=	$ _____
The Makeover Book	_____	x	$17.95	=	$ _____
Newsletters From the Desktop	_____	x	$24.95	=	$ _____
PC Internet Tour Guide	_____	x	$24.95	=	$ _____
The Presentation Design Book, 2nd Edition	_____	x	$24.95	=	$ _____
Voodoo DOS	_____	x	$21.95	=	$ _____
Voodoo NetWare	_____	x	$27.95	=	$ _____
Voodoo Windows	_____	x	$19.95	=	$ _____
Windows, Word & Excel Office Companion, 2nd Edition	_____	x	$21.95	=	$ _____
			Subtotal	=	$ _____

SHIPPING:

For all regular orders, please <u>add</u> $4.50/first book, $1.35/each additional.		=	$ _____
For "two-day air," <u>add</u> $8.25/first book, $2.25/each additional.		=	$ _____
For orders to Canada, <u>add</u> $6.50/book.		=	$ _____
For orders sent C.O.D., <u>add</u> $4.50 to your shipping rate.		=	$ _____
North Carolina residents must <u>add</u> 6% sales tax.		=	$ _____
		TOTAL =	$ _____

Name_____ Company_____
Address (No PO Box)_____
City_____ State_____ Zip _____
Daytime Telephone _____
___ Payment enclosed ___VISA ___MC Acc't #_____
Expiration Date_____ Interbank # _____
Signature _____

Mail or fax to: Ventana Press, PO Box 2468, Chapel Hill, NC 27515   ☎ 919/942-0220   Fax 919/942-1140

CAN'T WAIT? CALL TOLL-FREE ☎ 800/743-5369! (U.S. only)